Pauline Theology

Volume IV

SOCIETY OF BIBLICAL LITERATURE

SBL

SYMPOSIUM SERIES

Gail R. O'Day, Editor

Number 4

PAULINE THEOLOGY

VOLUME IV

Looking Back, Pressing On

edited by
E. Elizabeth Johnson
David M. Hay

E. Elizabeth Johnson
David M. Hay
editors

Pauline Theology
Volume IV

Looking Back, Pressing On

Society of Biblical Literature
Symposium Series

Scholars Press
Atlanta, Georgia

Pauline Theology
Volume IV
Looking Back, Pressing On

edited by
E. Elizabeth Johnson
David M. Hay

The cover art is from *The Chester Beatty Biblical Papyri* by Frederic G. Kenyon, reproduced by kind permission of the Trustees of the Chester Beatty Library, Dublin.

Cover design courtesy of Fortress Press, Minneapolis, Ned Skubic, designer

Library of Congress Cataloging in Publication Data
Pauline theology.

Vol. IV edited by David M. Hay and E. Elizabeth Johnson.
p. cm.
Includes index.
ISBN 0-8006-2929-9 (v. 1 : alk. paper)
ISBN 0-7885-0306-5 (pbk. : alk. paper)
1. Bible. N.T. —Theology. I. Hay, David M., and Johnson, E. Elizabeth.
BS2651.P284 1991
227'.06—dc20 91-17665
CIP

08 07 06 05 04 03 02 5 4 3 2

Printed in the United States of America
on acid-free paper

Contents

Preface

E. Elizabeth Johnson

THE SEARCH FOR Paul's theology is nearly as old as his letters themselves. Within a generation or so of the apostle's death, Christians of widely differing stripes struggled to establish themselves as his rightful theological heirs and authentic interpreters. The writers of Luke-Acts, Ephesians, Colossians, the Pastoral Epistles, and the Acts of Paul appropriated Paul's name and reputation as "Apostle to the Gentiles" in varying ways based on what they considered most central to his thought and necessary to their own ecclesiastical situations.[1] By the second century, Paul's popularity among diverse Christian groups was so great Tertullian lamented that he was becoming "the apostle of the heretics."[2] In the late second and early third centuries, as nascent orthodoxy sifted through the remarkable profusion of Christian literature in search of what would eventually become its canon of scripture, it found already competing "collections" of Paul's letters, each shaped by convictions about what was most true about his theology.[3] The great syntheses of late antiquity and medieval Christianity accorded Paul the role of chief theologian, interpreting his letters in the context of the reigning confessional and philosophical presuppositions, convinced that he spoke with the same theological voice to be heard throughout the rest of the New Testament.

1 For discussions of the various appropriations of Paul in the early church, see Martinus C. de Boer, "Images of Paul in the Post-Apostolic Period," *CBQ* 42 (1980) 359–380; Dennis R. MacDonald, *The Legend and the Apostle: The Battle for Paul in Story and Canon* (Philadelphia: Westminster, 1983); J. Christiaan Beker, *Heirs of Paul: Paul's Legacy in the New Testament and in the Church Today* (Minneapolis: Fortress, 1991). In the Epilogue to the present volume, David Hay poses the question how the quest for Paul's theology can inform the search for the theology of those New Testament letters that bear his name but whose authorship is disputed ("Pauline Theology After Paul").

2 *Against Marcion* 3.5.4.

3 Nils A. Dahl, "The Particularity of the Pauline Epistles as a Problem in the Ancient Church" in *Neotestamentica et Patristica: Eine Freundesgabe an Herrn Prof. Dr. O. Cullmann zu seinem 60. Geburtstag* (NovTSupp 6; Leiden: Brill, 1962) 261–271.

The Reformation produced yet another quest for Paul's theology, one that placed him at the center of Christian orthodoxy and made of his letters the touchstone of Christian confession and even the rest of scripture. The undeniable differences between Galatians and James, for example, caused Martin Luther to judge the latter notably lacking in evangelical proclamation,[4] and Philip Melanchthon dubbed Romans "a summary of all Christian doctrine."[5] The theme of "justification by faith" that the Reformers heard so prominently in Romans and Galatians stood at the center of their own theological programs and would, for nearly the next four centuries, serve for interpreters as the heart of Paul's theology.

The rise of modernity, embodied among biblical theologians in the person of Johan Philip Gabler, self-consciously took into account the historical distance between Paul's letters and his contemporary readers, but nevertheless continued to construe the center of Paul's theology to be the doctrine of justification. It was no longer sufficient to begin with classical doctrinal categories and then arrange the pieces of Paul's letters under those categories; historical criticism required an interpreter to account for the origin and shape of Paul's own thought.[6] Gabler urged that "true biblical theology" seek out the particularity and historical contingency of Paul's letters, and distill from that culturally conditioned language the abiding core of his thought, what Gabler considered "pure biblical theology." Contemporary theologians should then, he said, reappropriate Paul's theology afresh for the needs of contemporary Christians. In large measure, Paul's theological core continued for another 100 years to be the Protestant notion of "justification by faith" until Albert Schweitzer relegated that theme to the status of "subsidiary crater" within what he called Paul's Christ mysticism.[7]

In this century, Rudolf Bultmann's magisterial *Theology of the New Testament*[8] again located Paul's theology, along with that of the Fourth Evangelist, at the center of New Testament theology, and perceived the core of Paul's thought to be his understanding of human beings in their existential encounter with God in Christ. "Paul's theology," said Bultmann, "is, at the same time, anthro-

4 "Preface to the Epistles of St. James and St. Jude" in *Martin Luther: Selections From His Writings*, ed. John Dillenberger (Garden City: Doubleday, 1961) 35–37.

5 *Dispositio orationis in ep. ad Rom.* 15.445, cited in Joseph A. Fitzmyer, *Romans* (AB33; New York: Doubleday, 1992) 74.

6 See Ben C. Ollenburger, "Old Testament Theology: A Discourse on Method" in *Biblical Theology: Problems and Perspectives In Honor of J. Christiaan Beker*, ed. S. J. Kraftchick, C. D. Myers, and B. C. Ollenburger (Nashville: Abingdon, 1995). 81–103.

7 *The Mysticism of the Apostle Paul* (New York: Holt, 1931).

8 New York: Charles Scribner's Sons, 1951–1955; original 1948–1953.

pology. . . . Paul's christology is simultaneously soteriology."[9] Other theologians either responded to Bultmann or proposed alternative construals of the center of Paul's thought,[10] but they all shared his traditional assumptions that a core exists and that it can be described with historical and theological integrity.

A pronounced shift in the search for the center of Pauline theology has taken place during the last twenty years, though, as a heightened consciousness of the diversity within the New Testament and among Paul's letters has moved interpreters to question even the possibility of locating coherence. Heikki Räisänen and E. P. Sanders,[11] for example, maintain that Paul's theology is so full of tensions and contradictions that it resists any systematic ordering at all. J. Christiaan Beker's *Paul the Apostle: The Triumph of God in Life and Thought*[12] makes a virtue of the historical contingency of the individual letters by calling it one of the identifying marks of Paul's interpretation of the gospel for his churches. For Beker, there remains within the apostle himself a coherent conviction of the gospel that, although by no means a systematic theology as that is classically understood, prevents his contingent interpretations of it in individual churches from being merely opportunistic or capricious. "Paul's hermeneutic is shaped by the complex interaction of coherence and contingency; moreover, the coherent theme of Paul's theology is an apocalyptic theme that centers on the coming triumph of God."[13]

In the context of this debate about whether or not one can properly speak at all about Paul's theology, the members of the Pauline Theology Group met annually between 1986 and 1995 to pursue the question. Hans Dieter Betz summarizes the most stubborn of the questions that lay on the table initially:

> Did [Paul] work with a fixed theological "system" in the back of his mind? Or did he develop his arguments *ad hoc*, based only on a limited set of assumptions? Did Paul have a consistent theology throughout his apostolic career, or did his theology gradually evolve in the context of mission and controversy in which he was constantly involved? If he worked from a fixed theological system, was that system pre-Christian (Pharisaic, rabbinic, or apocalyptic) with his Christian convictions simply overlaid or appended? Or was his theology something altogether new that grew out of his vision of Christ and his

9 Ibid., 1.191.

10 E.g., W. G. Kümmel, *The Theology of the New Testament* (Nashville: Abingdon, 1973); Leonhard Goppelt, *Theology of the New Testament* (2 vols.; Grand Rapids: Eerdmans, 1982; original 1976).

11 Heikki Räisänen, *Paul and the Law* (Philadelphia: Fortress, 1983); E. P. Sanders, *Paul and Palestinian Judaism* (Philadelphia: Fortress, 1977).

12 Philadelphia: Fortress, 1980.

13 "Preface to the First Paperback Edition" of *Paul the Apostle* (Philadelphia: Fortress, 1984) xiii.

> commission to take the gospel to the gentiles? In short, how creative and dynamic a theologian was the apostle Paul?[14]

The Pauline Theology Group decided to investigate the letters one by one rather than as a corpus, and to listen to the shortest letters first in isolation from the larger and historically more influential letters to learn what that procedure might uncover about the character of Paul's theology. They thus responded directly to the challenge posed by the diversity and historical contingency of the letters, while still seeking some discernibly coherent theology that could legitimately be called Pauline. The quest was early on beset by still more problems of definition—both of the nature of the Group's quarry (just what *is* theology?) and of the best means to locate it. Jouette Bassler summarized the problem at a preliminary stage in the debate this way:

> Thus far two things are clear. First, Paul was *not* a systematic theologian. Thus, we are not looking for a theological or doctrinal system to emerge from his letters, nor are we seeking to impose such a system on them. Yet the deconstructive analyses of recent years that deny all coherence to Paul's thought seem to go too far in the opposite direction. If Paul was not a systematic theologian, there seems nevertheless to be a pattern, a center, a commitment, a conviction, a vision, a underlying structure, a core communication, a set of beliefs, a narrative, a coherence—something—in Paul's thoughts or behind them that dispels any abiding sense of mere opportunism or intellectual chaos on the part of the apostle. Yet nowhere, it seems, does this core, center, vision, etc. come to expression in a noncontingent way.[15]

Three previous volumes of essays have gathered components of the discussion in roughly chronological order.[16] This final volume in the series contains three distinct but related conversations that were separate parts of the debate. The first exchange, between Paul Achtemeier and Leander Keck, considers what was gained—or not—by the two-year-long discussion of Romans. Achtemeier begins by challenging some widespread assumptions about the letter's occasion. The evidence is really quite scant, he says, for the theory that the alleged return to Rome of Jews previously exiled from the city by the Emperor Claudius created ethnic tensions within the congregation. The letter is shaped much more by Paul's own theology than it is by the situation in Rome.

14 "Paul" in *ABD* (1992) 5.192.

15 "Paul's Theology: Whence and Whither?" in *Pauline Theology II: 1 and 2 Corinthians,* ed. D. M. Hay (Minneapolis: Fortress, 1993), 6.

16 *Pauline Theology, Volume I: Thessalonians, Philippians, Galatians and Philemon*, ed. J. M. Bassler (Minneapolis: Fortress, 1991); *Pauline Theology, Volume II* (see above, note 15) and *Pauline Theology, Volume III: Romans,* ed. D. M. Hay and E. E. Johnson (Minneapolis: Fortress, 1995).

The primary influence on the letter's substance Achtemeier calls "the economy of salvation that informs Paul's understanding of God's redemption of sinful humanity enacted in Christ" (p. 9). The theme of justification is not itself the letter's center but the means by which Paul makes clear how the gospel of God's universal mercy is accessible to Jew and Gentile alike. The eschatological work of God, by which Achtemeier means the faithfulness of the crucified Christ, makes possible a faithful human response to God, because God's way of dealing with the world is precisely God's way of dealing with Christ.

In response, Leander Keck agrees that Paul's own situation weighs more heavily on the shape of Romans than does the situation of the Roman house churches,[17] but he pushes Achtemeier to account more fully for his proposed "economy of salvation." Why, Keck asks, does Paul neglect so many issues in Romans that he addresses in other letters, issues that Achtemeier himself includes in his summary of the "economy"? Jesus' parousia, for example, is barely alluded to in Romans, although it figures prominently in Achtemeier's "economy of salvation," and there is no mention at all in Romans of the Lord's Supper or the church. Keck cautions against too quick an adoption of a particular pattern of thought as the measure of Paul's theology when that pattern itself does not appear in the letters.

The second set of essays actually preceded the first by four years. At an earlier moment in the Pauline Theology Group's deliberations, while reaching for a preliminary synthesis of the insights gained from the letters other than Romans, the discussion took a deliberate detour to attend to a recurring question of both exegesis and theology. At several points, notably in Romans and Galatians, Paul uses a phrase that can be translated either "the faith of Jesus Christ," "the faithfulness of Jesus Christ," or "faith in Jesus Christ" (Rom 3:22, 26; Gal 2:16, 20; 3:22; Phil 3:9). Grammatical and syntactical considerations alone cannot settle the question, and interpreters have long debated the matter. The three essays by Hays, Dunn, and Achtemier that appear here are perhaps the clearest summaries available of the various positions and the most cogent discussions of what is at stake theologically in each. No consensus exists, although it is fair to say that Achtemeier stands more on Hays's side of the divide than on Dunn's.

The final set of essays comes from the last stage of the Group's conversation about Pauline theology and evaluates the results of the entire project. James Dunn questions the basic premise of the Group's work, that moving from the smaller letters to the larger and listening to each in isolation from the others was a fruitful procedure. Dunn argues instead that the church's early impulse to view the corpus as a whole—notably with Romans at its head—was correct all

17 See his own "What Makes Romans Tick?" in *Pauline Theology III,* 3–29.

along. He proposes as the model for making sense of Paul's theology "our own theologizing," which begins with inherited convictions that are shaped by transforming experiences and brought into interpretive conversation with contemporary life (pp. 101–102). The place we have best access to Paul's basic convictions, says Dunn, is Romans, since that is the least explicitly contingent letter and, because of its unknown addressees, the one in which Paul makes the fewest assumptions about what convictions his hearers might share with him. To begin a Pauline theology with Romans, according to Dunn, results in a five-part outline: Paul's theology of God, the framework of Israel's story, the "Christ focus" of Paul's theology, faith as the human response to divine grace, and Paul's attitude toward the law.

Steven Kraftchick's response to Dunn takes issue with Dunn's understanding of the theological task in general and his way of using Romans to approach Paul's theology in particular. It is not at all clear to Kraftchick that contemporary theologizing begins, as Dunn claims, with inherited or shared convictions, even on the most fundamental level of language about God. Furthermore, the widely divergent views of the occasion of Romans call into question Dunn's assumption that it is relatively untouched by the ecclesiastical situation it addresses.

Paul Meyer evaluates the Pauline Theology experiment far more positively than does Dunn. As the subtitle of his essay suggests ("A Proposal for a Pause in Its Pursuit"), Meyer notes that, although significant progress has been made, the task remains unfinished. He nevertheless finds compelling the growing consensus that Paul's theology stands not behind his letters but within them, that "theology is something one 'does' or produces rather than 'has,' and that Paul's theology in particular is not the *father* of his 'theologizing' but its *child*" (p. 152). What stands behind Paul's theological activity is the event of God's raising the crucified Messiah rather than the apostle's theological convictions about it.

Victor Furnish shares Meyer's sense that Paul's theology is to be found not in the premises from which he argues but in the conclusions he reaches in his contingent interpretations of the gospel. Furnish cautions, though, against too facile an appropriation of Meyer's "end product" language to describe Pauline theology. With too concrete a description of theology-as-result, the expectation could be falsely raised that the individual conclusions of discrete arguments might be construed as the building blocks of yet another static view of Paul's theology. Furnish presses Meyer to make room in his portrayal of the "bedrock" on which Paul stands for the existential dimension of faith as well as God's vindication of the crucified Messiah. The for-our-sake-ness of Paul's gospel surely requires that an understanding of his theology attend seriously to what he says about the gospel's power to shape congregations in the knowledge of God.

David Hay's epilogue to this volume asks what can be gained from the Pauline Theology Group's work for the discussion of theology in Ephesians, Colossians, the Pastoral Epistles, and (perhaps) 2 Thessalonians. He notes the methodological advantage of attending to a single document at a time rather than grouping the letters of disputed authorship together; he suggests ways the definitions of "theology" gained by the Pauline Theology conversation might inform discussion of the disputed letters; and he ponders the implications for theological reflection of the perennial difficulty of locating the historical situations of the Disputed Letters. Hay then applies questions about the interplay among doubts, warrants, and convictions he earlier used to trace the shape of theology in 2 Corinthians[18] to the Disputed Letters. He finally traces the presence in the Disputed Letters of guiding convictions—about God, Christ, and the moral life, in particular—that raise significant questions about their relationship to *Pauline* theology, but that nevertheless attempt to engage in *Christian* theology.

As in the previous three volumes of the Pauline Theology series, the abbreviations used in this book are taken from the *American Academy of Religion and Society of Biblical Literature Membership Directory and Handbook 1993*, 391–400. Unless otherwise noted, biblical translations are from the New Revised Standard Version (NRSV).

18 "The Shaping of Theology in 2 Corinthians," *Pauline Theology II*, 135–155.

Contributors

Paul J. Achtemeier
Herbert Worth and Annie H. Jackson Professor of Biblical Interpretation
Union Theological Seminary in Virginia

James D. G. Dunn
Professor of Divinity
University of Durham

Victor Paul Furnish
University Distinguished Professor of New Testament
Perkins School of Theology
Southern Methodist University

David M. Hay
Joseph E. McCabe Professor of Religion
Coe College

Richard B. Hays
Professor of New Testament
The Divinity School
Duke University

E. Elizabeth Johnson
Associate Professor of New Testament
New Brunswick Theological Seminary

Leander E. Keck
Winkley Professor of Biblical Theology
Yale University Divinity School

Steven J. Kraftchick
Assistant Professor of New Testament Studies
Candler School of Theology
Emory University

Paul W. Meyer
Helen H. P. Manson Professor of New Testament Literature and Exegesis, *Emeritus*
Princeton Theological Seminary

Part I

Looking Back on Romans

1 UNSEARCHABLE JUDGMENTS AND INSCRUTABLE WAYS

Reflections on the Discussion of Romans[1]

Paul J. Achtemeier
Union Theological Seminary in Virginia

A PHRASE OFTEN USED by biblical students is "Endzeit gleicht Urzeit" ("the end is as the beginning"), and that applies in this case as well. Our discussion of Romans began with two papers, one by Leander Keck, the other by N. Thomas Wright, that looked at Romans as a theological whole, and it is now to end with a paper on Romans that again looks at it as a theological whole, this time written in light of our intervening discussions of the individual components of that letter. This paper will therefore not be a research report on what other scholars have said in print on various issues; rather it is composed in light of the discussions we have had so far. Nor will the paper take the form of a review and critique of each of the papers that have been presented.[2] Responders and our discussions have taken care of that. Rather what I have to say is shaped in the light of my re-reading all the papers and discussions on Romans that have occupied us here for the past several years, and is composed with the intention of furthering the discussion thus begun.

I want to begin with a quick review of the occasion of the letter, and a discussion of its purpose. This latter is thickly entwined with some theories about

1 This is a modified version of the paper originally presented to the SBL Group on Pauline Theology, printed in the Seminar Papers of 1995. Prof. Keck and I agreed that I should modify the paper in those places where misunderstanding was the result of careless formulation or poor choice of vocabulary on my part, and that he would then respond to the paper so modified. For that reason his response is also different from the one he presented to the Pauline Group at its meeting in November of 1995.

2 Those places where I discuss themes that have been treated in earlier papers and responses will be evident to those who wrote and gave them, and perhaps to others as well; let me simply acknowledge here the validity of their recognition, as well as my debt to them for many of the insights contained in these pages. They can of course not be held responsible for the use I have made of them.

the situation of the Roman house churches, theories that are based in some instances on shaky historical evidence. I want then to discuss briefly some issues pertinent to Paul's argument in Romans: first, the economy of salvation that I take to underlie the entire discussion in the letter, and then in light of that argument, some further theological points that have been current in our discussions, i.e., the theme of the letter, the apocalyptic framework that Paul has adopted and adapted as the form within which to present his gospel, the significance of God's impartiality, and finally, some remarks on the nature of faith and on the law/works vocabulary.

I

A constellation of events seems to have occasioned this letter, not least of which is Paul's hope finally to undertake a long-desired visit to the Christians in Rome (1:10, 11, 13; cf. 15:22). Paul seems to think this time it may come to fruition since he has evangelized the area from Jerusalem in the east all the way to Illyricum in the west, and now finds that he has completed his mission in "these regions," if "completed" is the correct interpretation of μηκέτι τόπον ἔχων ("having no longer a place").[3] His proposed mission to Spain awaits only the successful completion of his visit to Jerusalem with the offering for the poor Christians there, if again this is the correct translation of τοὺς πτωχοὺς τῶν ἁγίων.[4]

One purpose of the letter, therefore, is to apprise his readers of his planned visit, a visit during which, Paul hopes, he may impart some spiritual gift to strengthen them and to experience a mutual encouragement with them in the faith (1:11–12), and to enjoy their company (15:24, 32).[5] Two further stated purposes may be found, the one, that Paul wrote them by way of "reminding them" (15:15), apparently of aspects of Christian doctrine of which they are

3 In another place I have suggested this may mean his opponents have carried the day, as indicated in Acts 15:28–29, probably reflected in Gal 2:11–13, where there is no indication that his rebuke to Peter was effective. That he lost the support even of Barnabas is further indication that he did not prevail.

4 The genitive may be understood either as partitive, in which case the reference is to the poor *among* the saints in Jerusalem, implying some are not poor, or the genitive may be epexegetic, in which case it refers to the self-designation of the Jewish Christians, namely, "the poor," and means simply a general offering for the entire Jerusalem church.

5 Paul seems to be careful not to give the impression that he intends to "preach the gospel" to them, since that would go counter to his commission which is to preach the gospel where Christ is unknown (15:20–21). For that reason, he stresses the mutual nature of their Christian encouragement, and his desire to be refreshed by them, rather than the other way around.

already aware,[6] and the other, to ask them to pray for the success of his visit to Jerusalem (15:30–32).

A purpose that is not stated is to heal a breach between Christians of Jewish and Gentile backgrounds. Because that purpose has become such an important supposition in many of the papers written by members of this group, and has colored the interpretation of much of what Paul has to say throughout this letter, it is necessary to investigate the data and the assumptions that underlie it in some detail.

That purpose may be outlined in the following way: Paul's letter was written at some point after the Jews, expelled by Claudius in 49, returned to Rome subsequent to Claudius' death in 54, only to find that the church in Rome had now become thoroughly gentile in its leadership and outlook. An attitude of superiority over the Jewish Christians whose race, after all, had by and large rejected Christ, a rejection occasioned by God specifically to make room for gentile believers (11:19), provided a less than hearty welcome to the returning Jewish Christians, who, prior to their expulsion, may have occupied leadership roles within the Roman Christian community. Reciprocally, the Jewish Christians called into question the legitimacy of a Christianity that so totally ignored the Jewish law and denied them a role in determining the faith and conduct of the Roman Christian community. Thus, the situation threatened to split that Christian community.

In light of that situation, the purpose of Paul's letter was to address both the (weak) Jewish and (strong) gentile Christians in such a way that they heal their divisions (chaps. 14–15). To accomplish that, Paul was obliged to overcome gentile Christian arrogance, and perhaps Jewish Christian suspicions of the shape of Paul's own faith, by, among other things, discussing the place of Israel in God's salvific plan whose culmination is a Christ more widely accepted by gentiles than by Jews (chaps. 3:1–8; 4; 9–11).

That is the situation widely assumed to underlie and call forth Paul's letter to the Roman Christians, and it is a situation that needs re-examination.

First, the assumption that Claudius expelled all Jews from Rome in the year 49. That Claudius expelled Jews from Rome is attested in Acts 18:2, in Suetonius,[7] and in Orosius.[8] Acts maintains all Jews were expelled, Suetonius simply mentions "Jews," and Orosius is unsure whether Claudius expelled only Jews or

6 That there is no hint here of deficiency in their faith is indicated by the language of 15:14: they are full of goodness, filled with knowledge, and able to take care of one another. This is not the language of one who sees in those churches a faith-threatening division among Jewish and Gentile Christians, on which more below.

7 *de Vita Claudii* 25.4

8 *Historiarum adversum paganos libri septem,* 7.6.15–16.

also Christians. The only one who indicates when it occurred is Orosius, a Christian epitomist writing in the early fifth century (ca. 414–417), who says it was in the ninth year of Claudius' reign (that is, 49), and who gives Josephus as the source of that information.[9] Unfortunately, such a reference in Josephus cannot be located. Such an expulsion by Claudius is explicitly denied by Cassius Dio,[10] however, who says Claudius did not drive them out because their large numbers would have caused too great a tumult. Rather, Claudius forbade them to meet together, although allowing them to continue their traditional mode of life. The data for an expulsion of the Jews from Rome by Claudius is therefore not without its questions, and a date in 49 is based on the suggestion of a late author citing an unknown source.

In order to gain an impression of the extent and kind of data thus available for an expulsion of Jews from Rome under Claudius, it is instructive to compare such scanty and to some extent self-contradictory data with that which attests a similar action by Tiberius some years earlier. In the latter instance, ancient sources are more extensive, and they are unanimous. The expulsion of Jews from Rome by Tiberius is attested in Josephus,[11] Suetonius,[12] Dio Cassius,[13] and Tacitus,[14] with all but Josephus agreeing that the reason had to do with their religion.[15] It would perhaps be too much to say that had Claudius actually expelled Jews from Rome, one would have expected the same kind of evidence one has for their expulsion under Tiberius, yet the kind of evidence available for Tiberius' expulsion does call attention to the relative paucity and unreliability of the evidence for a similar expulsion under Claudius.

The date normally assumed for the expulsion under Claudius, 49, is, as indicated, based solely on a fifth-century writer who cites an apparently non-existent

9 7.6.15: Anno eiusdem nono expulsos per Claudium urbe Iudaeos Iosephus refert. Orosius also cites Suetonius, in this instance verbatim, but of course Suetonius gives no indication of when the expulsion occurred. Orosius may have confused the expulsion of the Jews under Tiberius, which Josephus does report, with the expulsion under Claudius. On the expulsion under Tiberius, see below.

10 *Historiae Romanae* 60.6.

11 *Ant.* 18.83: "the whole Jewish community" (πᾶν τὸ Ἰουδαϊκόν).

12 *de Vita Tiberii* 36: he expelled Jews and Egyptians, with those of military age assigned to provinces of unhealthy climate; others of the same race or similar beliefs were banished from Rome.

13 *Hist. Rom.* 57.18.5a: he cast out "the majority" for proselytizing.

14 *Ann.* 2.85: he abolished foreign cults, especially Egyptian and Jewish. 4000 he sent to Sardinia, while the rest had to leave Italy unless they renounced their cultic beliefs with "profane rituals."

15 Josephus' generally apologetic intent with respect to official Roman toleration of the Jewish religion may be enough to explain his omission of that point in this context.

source. Again, a comparison of that evidence with data concerning trouble with the Jews earlier in Claudius' reign yields a result similar to the comparison between the expulsion under Tiberius, and the one under Claudius. As in the former case, we have firmer evidence that Claudius was confronted with a problem concerning Jews in Alexandria at the beginning of his reign (41), a hold-over from the excesses of his predecessor Gaius Caligula. Here Claudius, depending on whom one reads, either reaffirmed Jewish citizenship[16] or restored former Jewish rights but denied any claims to citizenship.[17] It is thus possible, if not indeed probable, that the difficulty with the Jews in Rome may well have occurred at about this same time, i.e., 41.

That all Jews were expelled and therefore left the city, as is also often assumed, is called into question by Dio Cassius' denial of an expulsion, as it is by the fact that imperial decrees were not always obeyed. That prominent Jewish persons were affected is likely to be true. A case in point would be the expulsion of Prisca and Aquila, persons who were evidently wealthy, since they had owned homes in Asia (1 Cor 16:19; Ephesus? see also Acts 18:18), Rome (Rom 16:5), and apparently in Corinth (Acts 18:3), and would therefore have come to the attention of the authorities. Yet simply to assume that every Jewish-Christian slave and/or freed man or woman would leave because of the decree represents a kind of Roman legal fundamentalism, and strains credulity.[18] One need only consider the difficulty encountered in the attempt to expel astrologers from Rome to see that decrees were not immediately and necessarily transformed into reality.[19]

With all of this, I want simply to issue a kind of caveat against a too quick acceptance of an expulsion of all Jews from Rome by Claudius in the year 49. The questions I want to raise have to do with the year 49, and with the notion that virtually all (Christian) Jews left Rome. On that basis I question whether that historical sequence can be used safely as the basis for a hypothetical purpose of Paul's letter that is nowhere stated as such. I am not denying a decree by Claudius concerning the Jews, only its date and whether it was all-compassing in intention, to say nothing of effect. That Jews are named in chap. 16 is beside the point; if not all Jews left Rome, then the question of their return is rendered nugatory, and hence I have not felt it necessary to deal with it.

16 That seems to be the gist of Josephus, *Ant.* 19.5.2.

17 That is the force of a letter written on 10 Nov. 41; its text may be found in John L. White, *Light from Ancient Letters* (Philadelphia: Fortress, 1986) 131–136.

18 I am tempted to note that we are dealing here with Proto-Italians, who may well have reflected the same attitude to law as do their successors; e.g., the wide-spread modern Italian avoidance of income taxes.

19 Cf. Tac. *Ann* 32; Dio Cassius *Hist. Rom.* 57.8

Second, the assumption that Paul is addressing both Jewish and gentile Christians to heal the division between them is nowhere substantiated in the letter. When Paul does identify those to whom he is writing, he invariably says they are gentiles (1:5–6, 13). That is borne out in 1:14, where Paul divides those toward whom he is under obligation as Greeks and barbarians, i.e., both categories of gentiles. Had the purpose been to address both Jewish and gentile Christians, one would have expected some reference to that fact.

That Paul seeks to heal such a division is nowhere mentioned as a reason for the letter. The purpose is stated in quite different terms, as noted above. Where divisions were the problem, as in the Christian community in Corinth, Paul addresses the problem immediately and directly (beginning in 1 Cor 1:10). Again, in his discussion of the body of Christ in Rom 12:4–11, although it, like the comparable discussion in 1 Corinthians 12, deals with diversities of gifts, there is no reference to disputes among individual members as there is in that similar discussion in 1 Corinthians 12 (esp. 14–26), where we know from other indications divisions are the problem.

A further point needs to be made here, namely that one may not say "weak" refers exclusively, or even characteristically, to the Jewish Christians, while the "strong" refers exclusively, or even characteristically, to the gentile Christians. Paul, a Jew, surely belongs in the strong group, as do, because of their close association with Paul, Prisca and Aquila. Nor may one assume all gentile Christians would automatically eat any meat or drink wine, given the association of banquets with Roman cults, and the sale of meat in the public market that had been sacrificed to idols. There were almost surely both Jews and Greeks in both weak and strong groups. At most one could say that the "weak" were principally comprised of "Judaisers," while the strong refers to those who accepted Paul's gospel.

All of that in its turn tends to weaken the argument that Paul has been forced to deal with Israel in the course of his letter because of an assumed dispute between Jewish and gentile Christians that included a denigration of the importance of Israel on the part of gentile Christians. Aside from the fact that such a discussion as that found in 2:17–29 is hard to fit into an attempt to remedy a situation in which a gentile Christian majority is treating a Jewish Christian minority with contempt, it is probable, especially in light of Paul's initial description of the "divine gospel" he was called to preach in terms of Christ's relation to Israel (Rom 1:2–4), that the discussion of Israel owes more to Paul's theology as a whole than it does to the external situation of the letter.

Finally, one may ask why Paul chose to address only gentiles if, as is surely the case—see only the Jewish names in chap. 16—Jews were also present. The answer seems to be that Paul was scrupulously observing the comity arrangement of Gal. 2:7–9: Paul is to be the apostle to the gentiles (1:5, 13b). Hence he here addresses only gentiles, lest he be accused of violating his apostolic agreement (see his explicit reference to this in Rom 15:20).

II

Taking all that into account, it would probably be better to pin less faith on the purported situation of the Roman Christian community in determining Paul's theological message in Romans than has come to be customary among a number of scholars. Rather, I want to urge, the shape of Paul's argument in Romans owes more to internal than to external factors, i.e., more to Paul's own theology than to the situation he confronted. That internal factor I take to be the economy of salvation that informs Paul's understanding of God's redemption of sinful humanity enacted in Christ.[20]

By economy of salvation,[21] I mean to refer to Paul's evident conviction that the divine election of Israel through the promise given to Abraham is part of the larger plan whereby God intends to save humanity from its Adam-initiated rebellion against God, a plan whose decisive contours were revealed with the appearance of Christ, especially with his death and God-willed resurrection. That plan will culminate when the Christ who has already appeared returns in glory at the time of the last judgment and the transformation of reality. At that time immediate fellowship in the presence of God will be realized by those who withstand divine judgment, a time at which both sin and death are also eliminated.[22]

It is precisely in terms of this economy of salvation that Paul defines what he means by "gospel" at the very outset of the letter (1:2–4), namely something promised beforehand in the (Hebrew) prophets and brought to reality in God's son who was descended from the (Hebrew) David, the son who would himself rise from the dead as Lord. It is that economy that underlies the opening salvo of

20 With this emphasis on the economy of salvation, I mean to react positively to Wright's emphasis on covenant, surely one of the chief engines driving the economy of salvation, and to Keck's emphasis that Paul did not allow the immediate situation, in this instance in Rome, to govern completely what he said, but rather allowed the inner logic of his gospel to assert itself.

21 The term Paul uses to refer to what I mean by the economy of salvation is μυστήριον ("mystery"; e.g. Rom 16:25; 1 Cor 4:1; cf. Eph 1:9; 3:3; Mark 4:11 and parr.) although he can also use the term to refer to specific parts of that plan (e.g. Rom 11:25; 1 Cor 15:51; cf. Eph 5:32). The use of "economy" (οἰκονομία) as the plan encompassing part of this "mystery" is found in Eph. 3:9, however, and it is in that sense that I want to use it here.

22 While this last point owes more explicit evidence to 1 Cor 15 than to Romans, I believe it is just that kind of transformation that underlies what Paul writes in Rom 8:18–23.

Paul's discussion in Romans, an economy that reaches back to the very act of creation (1:19–20) and that includes the origin of human rebellion and sin, here in the form of idolatry. It is that economy that then leads Paul to single out the Jew for special consideration at the close of chap. 2.[23] The further incorporation of 3:1–8 in that discussion points again and clearly to the economy of salvation (esp. 3:2). The universality included in the divine economy, already manifest in the repeated phrase "both to (the) Jew first and to (the) Greek"[24] (1:16; 2:9, 10) a phrase that clearly reflects the economy, becomes thematic in the remainder of the chapter. It is that economy of salvation that clearly underlies the discussion of Abraham in chap. 4, a discussion that in its turn was prompted by the initial discussion of the law in 3:21–31. Discussion of the law then informs the chapters 6–7, after the results of faithfulness to Christ (5:1–11), and the origin of human rebellion (5:12–19) have been discussed, this last again clearly reflecting the economy of salvation in its use of Adam and Christ. Chapter eight anticipates the final spiritual reality awaiting faithful Christians, and chapters 9–11 tackle the daunting problem posed by the rejection of God's salvation by the chosen people. Paul solves the problem specifically in terms of the economy of salvation: in chap. 9 he rehearses the way God has dealt with Israel in terms of remnant, and includes a defense of the divine right to deal with creation as seems good to God. In chap. 10 Scripture is cited to show how closely related God's word to Israel is to the continuing progress of the economy of salvation, and in chap. 11 Paul describes the economy as involving first the hardening of part of the Jews (continuing the reduction of "Israel," a reduction initially described in chap. 9), then the conversion of the gentiles, and finally the return of the Jews who had been hardened. Perhaps not surprisingly, therefore, Paul concludes these chapters with comments on his ability to fathom the reasons for the economy. These comments are found in 11:32–36, that, as a climax to the first eleven chapters, form an inclusio with 1:2–4 in pointing explicitly to the economy of salvation, in the latter case to the inability of the apostle himself to discern the why of it, even after its reality has been described.[25]

23 That the "Jew" is singled out for the first time in 2:17 leads me to conclude that up to that point, the discussion of idolatry had included both Jew and gentile. Exodus 32 is evidence enough that idolatry was also a problem in Jewish history, to say nothing of the prophetic messages against it.

24 This is I think a somewhat more accurate translation than the usual "to the Jew first and *also* to the Greek"; τε—καί is more normally rendered "both—and" than "and also," although the latter is of course possible.

25 What student of Romans has not wanted to echo Paul's words in terms of trying to understand this epistle—unsearchable and inscrutable!

Two brief remarks may be included here concerning predestination in Rom 9:19–24 in light of Paul's larger scheme of the economy of salvation. 1) Paul is talking in these verses about historical events involving Israel as it moved within the larger economy of salvation. He is not discussing the fate of discreet individuals. The inclusion in the discussion of the reference to Pharaoh and the exodus, and the discussion of potter and clay derived from Jer 18:6, where it specifically refers to the house of Israel,[26] makes that clear. 2) There is in fact no *double* predestination, since even the vessels made for destruction are not destroyed, but are borne with much patience, the same patience that is intended to lead to repentance in 2:4 and that overlooked sin in 3:25b–26a. Nor is one to understand hardening (9:17–18) as the equivalent of rejection or some kind of eternal punishment. That is demonstrated when the hardening that has come upon part of Israel, whose purpose it is to allow gentiles to be saved, is eventually to be removed from Israel resulting in its own salvation. Hardening is thus not another way of saying eternal rejection, it is rather to be understood as one of the ways God moves forward the economy of salvation. The theme in this discussion is Israel within the economy of salvation, not individual Israelites or for that matter individual Christians, nor even a "new Israel," i.e., the church.

The concluding chapters apply the reality of that economy of salvation as it is embedded in the gospel to the normal lives of Christians in their traffic within and without the community of faith; its reality is to inform all that they do (12:1–15:13). Thematic is Paul's call to adjust one's life to the reality of the gospel rather than to the perceived reality that surrounds them (12:2). Paul concludes (15:14–33) by reciting his own plans for the future, perhaps showing by way of example how his life conforms to the economy of salvation and his part in it: the further evangelization of the gentiles, now in lands far to the west, after the reconciling gesture of the offering to Jerusalem.

Finally, the divine plan that underlies Paul's theology in general, and Romans in particular, clearly centers in Christ. While God's plan for the eventual inclusion of gentiles into the people of God was known to the Jews prior to Christ, the realization of that plan did not get underway until the advent of Christ, when that purpose became central: universal inclusion of all peoples within God's gracious plan. What is known of God and of the divine plan is thus confirmed and completed through Christ, up to and including the economy of salvation as it has concerned the Jews. It is precisely the Christ event

26 When Isaiah uses the same figure (29:16) it is again with reference to the people as a whole (29:13–14).

that has broadened election now to include Gentiles as well, and if that was part of God's plan from the beginning, it is being actualized fully only now in Christ. Paul's apostolic task is to bring gentiles to the obedience that is faith (1:5), and that is possible only through Jesus Christ risen and reigning (1:2–4).

The centrality of Christ for the economy of salvation is indicated in a subtler way in Paul's discussion of the way the economy of salvation proceeds in relation to the Jews. Remarkably, the fate of the Jews described in chap. 11 reflects the fate of Christ: to be rejected (Christ: crucified; Israel: hardened), thus apparently suffering divine punishment, but in the end to have the rejection itself rejected (Christ: resurrection; Israel: all to be saved), reflecting the divine vindication both of Christ and of Israel. The whole of that replication is then summed up in 11:30–31. This is the mystery that Paul announces in 11:25: that the fate of Israel reenacts the fate of Christ, its representative. That point is especially clear in 11:12,15, reflecting as it does language about Jesus in 2 Cor 8:9, that in its turn reflects Phil 2:6–11. The fate of Israel from whom the messiah came (9:5) thus reflects the fate of the messiah. The great theme of Romans (and of Paul's theology?) is that God's way of dealing with humanity is to be understood in terms of the way he has dealt with Jesus—rejected as sinner, punished as sinner, but vindicated. That is the story of gentiles as it is of Jews. That is what illumines for Paul the future of the Jews in 9–11, as it has informed his understanding of how God has dealt with gentiles in 1–8 (that is also why, e.g., suffering is a sign not of divine rejection but of divine acceptance [5:3–5], since so also Christ suffered). Within this larger scheme, Paul's task as apostle to the gentiles is to function as priest in presenting the gentiles to God as a worthy offering (15:15b–16); in that way however he also contributes to the larger scheme since his success will motivate Jews also to return (11:13–14). Thus God works in unlikely ways to bring about his salvific purposes (11:33), again a dominating theme in Paul (e.g., God's unanticipated activity in using the weak to show his strength [1 Corinthians]) but again, a theme that draws on the example of the way God's mighty salvific purpose was worked out through the weakness of a Christ rejected and killed.[27]

Yet despite such a christocentric shape to the economy of salvation as it is currently proceeding, that economy remains under the control of God, who is the one who has shaped it in such christocentric form. That is why Paul continues here as elsewhere to be primarily a theologian rather than exclusively a "christologian." It is *God's* plan that informs Paul's understanding of the

27 We have strayed from Romans, but only to show that themes discussed in Romans share in the larger framework of Paul's understanding of God's way with sinful humanity.

"gospel of God" as he has made clear at the outset. God is the one who moves it along its way, and who is also behind its defining moment that consists in the appearance of Jesus Christ.

III

If, as we have been urging, the economy of salvation informs Paul's discussion in Romans, and determines why in particular he must continue to refer to Israel and its fate, such informing by the economy of salvation also has implications for other aspects of the way Paul has shaped his argument in Romans.

A. In the first instance, it has implications for discerning the theme of Romans. The often identified theme in 1:17, now occasionally broadened to include v. 16, is too narrow to serve in that capacity. That is true, I would urge, both grammatically and substantively. Grammatically, 1:17, introduced by γάρ, serves to give the reason why Paul believes what he says in v. 16b is true, that in its turn supports what Paul says in 16a, that once more in its turn gives support to v. 14.[28] It seems unlikely on the face of it that the theme of the letter would thus be expressed in the midst of what could be termed a compound enthymeme, an enthymeme that then to all appearances continues through v. 21.[29] A more appropriate locus for such a theme would be at the beginning of the letter, and in that case 1:2–4 would be an admirable candidate, summarizing as it does the economy of salvation and leading into Paul's declaration of his own call to evangelize the gentiles (v. 5). The implied universality contained in 1:2–5 is then in fact made thematic in 1:14–16, where the universality is expressed in terms of two inclusive contrasts: Greek and Barbarian (v. 14) and Jew and Greek (v. 16). Seeing the universality of divine salvation, understood in terms of the economy of salvation, as the theme of Paul's letter receives interesting confirmation when one considers the verse that concludes the extended argument of chaps. 1–11, and that leads into Paul's hymnic celebration of the divine economy. That verse is 11:32, with its explicit declaration of the universality of purpose contained in the divine economy of salvation:

28 I take v. 15 to be parenthetical support for Paul's desire, expressed in vv. 11–12, to present his gospel to the Christians in Rome.

29 Although the conjunction γάρ ("since") is limited to vv. 18 and 20, the conjunction διότι ("because") is used to the same effect in vv. 19 and 21.

God has enclosed (συνέκλεισεν) all people in disobedience, in order to have mercy on all.[30]

In those ways, the universality of the gospel is announced, an announcement that, I would argue, lies closer to the theme of the letter than the concept of being made right with God through trust. Such "righteousness through trust" is rather the means by which the gospel of God's mercy is made available to gentile as well as Jew. That in turn is shown by the fact that v. 17 serves as clarification of the announcement in v. 16b that God's saving righteousness is now open to everyone, Jew (first) and Greek, i.e., that it is universal in scope. That the economy of salvation still underlies even that universal expression of God's mercy is shown by its being framed in terms of δικαιοσύνη, "righteousness," a term almost surely borrowed from the covenant language of Israel. One may note in passing that it is precisely this announced universality of the gospel that makes essential, and gives poignancy to, the discussion in chaps. 9–11, where that universality now appears violated by the exclusion of the Jews, rather than by the exclusion of the gentiles as had been the case prior to Christ's coming. Thus the means by which the economy of salvation proceeds, namely through God's covenants with sinful and rebellious Adamic humanity,[31] are announced in v. 17, clearly supporting the universality of the gospel announced in vv. 14–16. Obviously, getting right with God through trust is an important theologoumenon, but it is important as the means by which the theme of universality is carried out rather than as the theme of the letter itself.

B. Because the key event in the economy of salvation from the perspective of Paul's gospel is the resurrection of Christ,[32] and because the understanding of reality in which resurrection played a major role was one shaped by an apocalyptic outlook, it is evident that we cannot ignore the apocalyptic shaping

30 The strikingly similar statement in Gal 3:22, again in the context of universality—it concludes with 3:28—indicates that such phrasing may have been almost a topos for Paul when he discussed the universality of the range and application of the Gospel.

31 Although the plural αἱ διαθῆκαι may be a later "improvement" in Rom 9:4, the reference to "new covenant" in 1 Cor 11:25; 2 Cor 3:6, and to "old covenant" in 2 Cor 3:4, along with the reference to two covenants in Gal 4:24 indicates Paul did deal with the concept of multiple covenants in his theology. He was of course aware of God's promises to Abraham and Moses, but whether he understood them as two covenants within Judaism is not clear.

32 It is mentioned as the key element in what I take to be the announcement of the "theme" of Romans (1:2–4), and plays an important role in the ensuing discussion (4:24, 25; 6:4, 5, 9; 7:4; 8:11, 34; 10:9; 13:11; cf. 4:17).

of Paul's argument in this letter. Such shaping in the first three chapters can be readily recognized in the description of the present aeon as unalterably evil, followed by the decisive turning point announced with the νυνὶ δέ of 3:21. Such shaping can also be sensed in the conclusion of the discussion contained in 9–11, with its anticipation of the future resolution, under God's specific guidance, of the current problem contained within the economy of salvation, namely the return of the Jews to God's salvation willed for them. Such apocalyptic shaping is also evident in a discussion such as that contained in 8:18–23, with its anticipation of the final transformation of reality, or perhaps even in the discussion of Adam and Christ in 5:11–19, if one construe the old age as Adamic, and the new as bearing the imprint of the reality that has been shown in Christ. Yet if, as seems evident from Romans[33] as from other places in Paul's thought,[34] the Spirit is the characteristic of the age to come, with the Spirit understood in the present aeon as the presence of God, then 5:5 may well be the key to the discussion contained in chaps. 5–8: the presence of God through the Spirit now in the new age expresses itself in terms of God's love, not his wrath (cf. 1:18; hence suffering is no longer terrifying, but encouraging, 5:1–4). Perhaps indeed the transition between chaps. 4 and 5 is the passing from the old to the new aeon, announced in 3:21 and foreshadowed in Abraham, namely the age in which trust is now possible precisely because we have God's presence (Spirit) in terms of love. Thus these chapters, 5–8, describe the life of the people of God in the new age, already present through the power of the risen Christ and the outpouring of God's Spirit. To be sure, I do not want to maintain that Romans is an apocalyptic tract, but I concur with those who see an apocalyptic shaping in the contours of Paul's arguments in Romans.

Yet another indication of the way the economy of salvation shaped by an apocalyptic understanding pervades Paul's argument in Romans is Paul's adaptation of the apocalyptic two-age schema. Paul accomplished this adaptation by introducing a period during which the two ages overlapped, with the introduction of the new age accomplished by Christ's resurrection and with the conclusion of the old age postponed until the transformation of reality (probably accompanying Christ's return). During this period (the "time between the times"), both old and new aeons exercised their power over human beings, the old in the form of sin, the new in the form of the presence of God's Spirit. It is precisely in such a time, with both old and new ages present and exercising their influences, that relationships between Christians with one another,

33 E.g., 8:2, 4–6, 9, 11, 14, 17, where the Spirit's presence characterizes the new life in contrast to the former life dominated by the "flesh."

34 E.g., 1 Cor 15:42–53.

and with the larger communities outside the church, become problematic. It is that problematic that makes necessary, and is reflected in, the kind of discussion found in chaps. 13–15, where precisely such relationships become thematic, not only those relationships within the Christian community (12:3–13;[35] 14–15) but also those involving persons and groups outside the Christian community, up to and including the state (12:14–13:14).

C. A further indication of the usefulness of the way of viewing Romans for which we have been arguing concerns the way in which we are to understand the key concept of divine impartiality. Such impartiality is related both to the aspect of universality that we have urged as the theme of the epistle, and to the general economy of salvation we have found fundamental for accounting for the way Paul conducts his argument.

That God's impartiality is mirrored in the fundamental statement of the universality of God's grace shaped by the economy of salvation, i.e., Jew first and (also) Greek, is shown in the combination of the two in 2:10–11, where the twice repeated "both the Jew first and the Greek" (v. 10) is justified (γάρ! ["since"]) by the fact that God is impartial. That means that to speak of the economy of salvation is evidently also to speak of God's impartiality. Yet further, the phrase "both the Jew first and the Greek" is the expression of the universality of the divine salvific grace, as is made clear in both 1:16–17 and 10: 12–13. In an almost complementary sense, such universal salvation is made necessary by the universal sinfulness of human beings, expressly stated in 3:9, 22, and grounded in the discussion of Adam in 5:12–19. Typically, however, the discussion of Adam by whom universal sin is introduced is coupled with a discussion of Christ by whom universal righteousness and life are introduced. The result is that God's impartial judgment upon, and grace to, all people who have sinned and hence need grace, implies precisely the universality of grace that, we have urged, is thematic to Romans, and is contained within Paul's understanding of the economy of salvation.

It is thus clear, I would want to urge, that both God's impartiality and the universal scope of divine grace in Jesus Christ are functions of that economy. It is an order in which the Jews have historical, but not ontological, priority (e.g., Rom 3:2: the Jews were historically the first with whom God communicated), and hence an order in which that historical priority can be relativized by the further historical event of Christ's death and resurrection, an event that does not annul the historic priority of Israel, but rather broadens God's communication now to include the whole of humanity.

35 I take 12:1–2 to be thematic for the discussion of the final chapters: it indicates how they are to be related to God (v. 1) and to other people (v. 2).

That Paul is speaking of historical rather than ontological priority is a point of some importance for the understanding of Paul's argument in Romans. The point is that when Paul draws his examples, not to say his proofs, he draws them from the events in the story of Israel (e.g., Rom 9:17), not from the ontological realm of the constitution of being or the nature of human nature. Such use shows again Paul's background—not in the ontological categories of the philosophers but in the story of Israel. Christ cannot become for Paul, therefore, simply the illustration of a grander ontological principle concerning the nature of the divine and the human, as was the case with the Gnostics. Christ is part, indeed the culmination of, a divine plan that, directed by a free and sovereign God, works itself out within human history; he is not an illustration of the ontological structure of reality.

D. Finally some remarks on faith, and then on law. As is obvious to anyone who has paid even minimal attention to the proceedings of this Group, there is an ongoing discussion regarding the kind of genitive represented by Χριστοῦ in the phrase πίστις Χριστοῦ ("faith[fulness] in [of] Christ")[36] a phrase that occurs with greater frequency, for example, in Galatians than it does in Romans. The one occurrence of that phrase in Romans, however (3:22), bears with it all the problematic associated with its other appearances. It is helpful to note what is and is not at stake in this debate. On the one hand, that the faithfulness of Christ, primarily expressed in his obedience to the divine will, is important for Paul cannot be questioned. It is in fact precisely Christ's faithful obedience to the divine will that opens a way to regain divine favor for a humanity ineluctably participating in the Adamic disobedience to the will of God (Rom 5:12–19). That point stands regardless of how one decides the question of grammar with respect to the genitive Χριστοῦ ("Christ"). On the other hand, it is clear that our trust in, and faithfulness to, Christ, and to the God who raised him from the dead, is equally important for Paul. That is evident in the very opening remarks of Romans, where Paul defines his apostolic task as bringing gentiles into the obedience that is faith (or into faithful obedience, 1:5),[37] a task given him by the risen Christ (1:4).[38] What is at issue therefore is not whether Christ's faithfulness is of central importance for the economy of salvation, nor is the issue whether our faithfulness to the faithful Christ is essen-

36 The issue is whether it is subjective genitive (Christ's faithfulness) or objective genitive (faithfulness directed toward Christ).

37 Paul's definition of the purpose of his apostleship to the gentiles as calling forth an obedience which is faith (1:5) may indeed be modeled on Christ's obedient faithfulness.

38 Rom 15:18 confirms Paul's understanding of trust in terms of obedience as does 6:16, where in the phrase ὑπακοῆς εἰς δικαιοσύνην ("obedience which leads to righteousness") is used as a synonym for faith.

tial for our own participation in that economy. Both are essential for Paul. What is at issue is simply what is intended in any given instance of the expression πίστις Χριστοῦ.

This leads to a second observation about the Greek stem πιστ- and its translation into English. Taken as a whole, it would probably be better to translate the verb πιστεύω as "trust" rather than "believe" or "have faith," and the noun πίστις as "faithfulness." The common English use of the word "believe" in a religious sense is frequently used to mean intellectual assent to some kind of content.[39] That is, I take it, not the primary intention of Paul when he uses this vocabulary.[40] His point of directing trust toward God and Christ is not to get his readers to assent to their existence, but to place their trust in God and Christ to fulfill what they have promised. In that way, Paul wants to persuade his readers to act in accordance with the divine will for human beings. In that sense, I would urge that the vocabulary of "trust" and "faithfulness" does greater justice to Paul's intention than the vocabulary of "faith" and "belief."[41]

Finally, I would want to urge that the economy of salvation that I think underlies Paul's necessary discussion of the Jews in God's plan of salvation revealed in Jesus Christ casts light on what Paul means by the word νόμος. In neither case are the two following observations original, but I think they are substantiated and reinforced if what I have been arguing about the economy of salvation is valid.

The first of the observations is that it would be preferable, I think, both in terms of Paul's own intention, and in terms of getting a clearer picture of what he is arguing, if one were to understand νόμος in every instance in Romans as torah ("teaching"), rather than finding in some place or another some such meaning as regulations or even the principle of regulation. That is true, I would want to urge, even in such cases such as Romans 3:27, 7:21, and even 7:23–25.

In the first case (3:27), I think it better to translate the two genitives τῶν ἔργων and πίστεως that modify the word νόμος as genitives of quality or qualification, so that one reads that boasting is excluded not through the torah

39 To "believe in God" or "believe in angels" has come to mean one assents to the existence of such supernatural entities, without any notion of trust in them or commitment to be faithful to what they may desire.

40 The one exception in Romans could be 10:9, where the object of the verb is a ὅτι ("that") clause, indicating content. If on the other hand, the emphasis in the ὅτι clause is on the ὁ θεός ("God") rather than on the verb ἤγειρεν ("raised"), the added implication would be that the God who raised Christ is surely trustworthy.

41 The fact that faith is defined as obedience in 1:5 means a predisposition exists to see in uses of the πιστ- stem the notion of faithfulness which incorporates obedience, rather than faith in terms of intellectual content, i.e., an intellectual acceptance of the gospel as true.

understood as having as its chief characteristic that of functioning as a racial boundary marker, but rather through the torah understood as having as its chief characteristic that of trust. That is confirmed not only in 3:28, where being made right with God is to be understood as a matter solely of the trust that is the principal qualification of the torah, but also in 3:31, where it is precisely trust that is to be understood as that which gives to the torah its very substance.

In the second case (7:21), the phrase τὸν νόμον ("the law") is not to be construed as the object of εὑρίσκω ("I find"), since the object of that verb is supplied by the ὅτι ("that") clause: what the ἐγώ ("I")[42] has discovered is that evil lies close at hand whenever that person wishes to do the good. The phrase τὸν νόμον rather serves to qualify, as an adjectival accusative of reference,[43] when such a discovery is made, namely it is made with respect to the torah. That is, whenever the ἐγώ seeks to do the good[44] as understood and defined in the torah, the result is the opposite, namely the doing of evil.[45]

In the third case (7:23–25), we see again Paul's way of qualifying νόμος with genitives, e.g. 3:27; 8:2; cf. 9:32. That same use of the genitive is at work in 7:23 where two qualifications of the law are opposed: νόμος as qualified by its divine intent, and νόμος as qualified by sin. That after all was the point of chap. 7: to show that although the torah was good it had been overcome by sin (e.g., 7:8–11). The problem is not the inability to know and will the good, it is to do the good. In doing the good, the torah, overpowered by sin, is no help at all. That is the context, I take it, of 7:23–25, and its use of νόμος in the sense of Torah.

[42] I do not wish at this point to enter into the discussion of the person or class represented by that pronoun. I have argued elsewhere at length that it is to be understood as the Jew who seeks to do God's will relying exclusively on the torah, which then leads that person/group as a result to reject Christ, but for the purpose of the point I want to make here, the correctness of such an identification is not germane.

[43] This use of the accusative is far more common in non-Biblical Greek than it is in the NT. I need also here to acknowledge my delight when I discovered that Prof. Wright provided the same grammatical analysis.

[44] Again, I have argued elsewhere that τὸ καλόν ("the good") represents doing God's will, while τὸ κακόν ("the evil") is failing to do it, but I may further note that my point here does not depend on that identification.

[45] Paul has earlier identified such a result as due to the power of sin which has taken over the law (e.g., 7:7–11, esp. v. 11). Again, I have argued elsewhere that Paul's understanding of that take-over was based, at least in part, on his own earlier opposition to Christ which resulted from his former Pharisaic conviction that the torah functioned as the exclusive source of knowing God's will (e.g., Gal 1:13–15; Phil 3:5–11), but yet once again, that point is not substantive to what I want to argue here.

Such an understanding of νόμος as torah, I would want to urge, helps clarify how Paul can argue in Romans that trust constitutes or underlies the torah (3:31), namely because it is trust that establishes the torah as God's own teaching, and because without such trust, such divine teaching cannot function as it is intended to do. That is, as torah, it is intended not primarily to express legal responsibility, but rather is intended to provide an appropriate means for a graced people to respond to the one who has chosen them because of grace. That would mean that the contrast in Romans is not between trusting in God (through Christ) or trusting in one's own virtue, in this instance a virtue established through works of the "law" done to the virtual exclusion of grace. Rather the contrast is between two ways of being related to God: by belonging ethnically to the descendants of Abraham, or belonging to those descendants by emulating Abraham's trust in God as the One who justifies the ungodly (4:5) and brings life to the dead (4:17), to use Pauline language.

The second observation about Paul's use of the phrase ἔργα νόμου ("works of the law") as well as the word νόμος ("law"), already implied in what has already been said, is that they function primarily if not exclusively to designate the boundary markers of what it means to belong ethnically to the Jewish people, and to rely on that heritage for one's relationship to God. This is perhaps most clearly seen in Romans 3:28–29, where it is clear from the question in v. 29 ("Is God the God of the Jews only?") that Paul understands that only Jews can do works of the "law." The point of the question is this: if it were not true that a person is made righteous by trust apart from works of the "law," but rather one could be righteous by works of the "law," then God would be the God of the Jews alone, since, evidently, only Jews could then become righteous before God since only Jews can perform the "works of the law." That point Paul then expressly denies: God is indeed also the God of the gentiles.[46]

The contrast between "trust" and "works" thus again finds its proper locus in the economy of salvation, in which the phrase πίστις Χριστοῦ ("faith[fulness] in [of] Christ") refers to the eschatological work of God (i.e., the faithfulness of Christ) that makes such trust significant (i.e., our trust in, and faithfulness to, the God who sent the faithful Christ), while the phrase ἔργα νόμου refers to the institution in which such works have meaning (i.e., membership in

46 It is I think one of the ironies of interpreting Romans that the passage that most clearly points to works of the law as a Jewish boundary marker is juxtaposed to the passage (4:4–5) that seems most clearly to point to works as human accomplishment about which one may boast. Yet the juxtaposition of one who works with one who trusts points again to the contrast between those who rely on ethnic heritage and those who rely on trust for their positive relationship with God.

the chosen race that entitles them to the grace shown in the election of that people). It is precisely the figure of Abraham who anticipates that move within the economy of salvation, and that is why he is the key figure in the discussion of the relationship between "law" and "faith."

IV

Much remains to be said, both about Romans and about our discussions of it, enough, at any rate, to allow room for a lively discussion. Yet enough of the contours of what many of us have said about Romans during our discussion of this epistle have been included, I think, to mean that our lively discussion now will not be entirely unrelated to the work that has gone before. One of the things I think all Pauline scholars look forward to in heaven is attending St. Paul's Seminar on his Epistle to the Romans, where questions can finally be answered. In this "time between the times," however, our discussion in this Group on Pauline Theology will have to serve as an ἀρραβών ("foretaste") of that final consummation.

2 SEARCHABLE JUDGMENTS AND SCRUTABLE WAYS

A Response to Paul J. Achtemeier[1]

Leander E. Keck

THERE IS MUCH in Professor Achtemeier's tightly woven and vigorously argued paper with which I agree, sometimes heartily. Instead of underscoring our agreements, however, I will manifest my deep appreciation by responding to those matters which invite on-going reflection and conversation.

I

Currently, not only do all students of Romans agree that Melanchthon wrongly characterized this letter as a compendium of Christian doctrine, but many of them are also determined to liberate it from its alleged "Lutheran captivity" that confined its subject-matter to the individual's justification by faith. To do this, they seek an historical occasion that will account for the letter's content and the Apostle's purpose in sending it precisely to Rome. Because on this basis the key to a proper reading of the letter lies more in Rome than in Paul, misjudgments here will skew today's interpretation as surely as Melanchthon's. It is entirely appropriate, therefore, that Mr. Achtemeier questions the solidity of one datum that figures prominently in the common reconstruction of the letter's occasion.

Mr. Achtemeier rightly sees that there is something anomalous in this reconstruction—namely, that it confidently replaces Paul's stated purpose (1:10–13; 15:22–32) with an unstated one invented by scholars: healing the breach between Christian gentiles and those Christian Jews who had returned to Rome, having been expelled, together with other Jews by Claudius in 49 C.E.

[1] See Note 1 of Achtemeier, "Unsearchable Judgments."

The letter itself, however, is totally silent about all three points: the expulsion, the return, and the alleged tension that arose because the returnees were not welcomed.

Professor Achtemeier does not deny outright that Claudius did take some action against Roman Jews but he does examine the date, scope ("all the Jews," Acts 18:2), and the likely result. His objection to a comprehensive "ethnic cleansing" (not his phrase) relies on both analogy (Rome's difficulty in expelling astrologers) and explicit evidence—Dio Cassius' report that Claudius, realizing that the size of the Jewish community made mass expulsion problematic, merely forbade their assembling. Mr. Achtemeier might have adduced also a stylistic consideration—the tendency in Acts to magnify the size of groups (see Acts 2:47; 3:9, 11; 4:21; 8:10; 9:35; [13:44]; 17:21; 19:27; 21:30). His main concern, however, is the commonly accepted date, provided only by the fifth-century Orosius, who claims to have gotten it from Josephus, from whose extant writings the date is absent. Rather than reject Claudius' action against Jews altogether, however, Mr. Achtemeier suggests that this action occurred eight years earlier, in 41 C.E., when the emperor had problems with Alexandrian Jews. Although he cites no evidence for Claudian action against Roman Jews in 41 C.E., he does say that there was a precedent for it in the well-attested action of Tiberius against the Jews of Rome.

It is hard to see how this proposed alternative date puts us on firmer ground, for not unlike the reconstructed occasion for Romans that it is designed to replace, it asks us to substitute an event without evidence for a date that contradicts the evidence of Acts. According to Acts, Aquila and Priscilla (Prisca in Romans 16) had arrived in Corinth recently (προσφάτως)—i.e., shortly before Paul arrived for an eighteen-month stay (Acts 18:1–3, 11). During this time Paul was brought before Gallio, who was "the proconsul of Achaia" for a short time. Paul's arrival is generally dated ca. 50–51. Thus the conjunction of Paul's and Gallio's presence in Corinth, coupled with Aquila's and Priscilla's "recent" arrival supports Orosius' date (even if he was wrong about Josephus), not the date Mr. Achtemeier proposes in its place. Moreover, instead of weakening the case for gentile-Jewish Christian tensions in the Roman house churches, the alternative date has the effect of actually strengthening it, for it adds eight years to the time when Roman Christianity could have become solidly gentile, and thus inhospitable to Christian Jews who returned, presumably after Claudius' death in 54 C.E.

For some reason, Prof. Achtemeier overlooks a simpler solution, one implied in Dio Cassius' report that while Claudius did not expel the Jews he did prohibit their meeting together. Aquila and Prisca, as well as other Christian Jews, might well have regarded this prohibition as precluding their assembling in house churches, and so left the city for Corinth as their peaceful response to a now hostile environment. It would have been easy for Acts to construe this as their expulsion, inflated to include "all the Jews." Indeed, if Mr. Achtemeier is correct in surmising that this couple was wealthy enough to own their own house in whatever city they lived, their residence in Rome probably was a meeting place for Christians there before they left as it was upon their return (Rom 16:5). The departure of a few Christian Jews, who felt themselves threatened by Claudius' prohibition, would hardly have been regarded by Dio Cassius as important enough to record as an exception to his report that Claudius did not expel the Jews "because their large numbers would have caused a great tumult."

What makes these observations and speculations somewhat significant is what many colleagues inferred from the return of Jewish Christians. Mr. Achtemeier rightly notes that the presence of Jewish names in Romans 16 means nothing if all Jews, Christianized or not, had not left Rome in the first place. In fact, it should not be forgotten that only if we conclude that Romans 16 was part of Paul's letter to start with (which appears to be the majority view today, and rightly) is there any basis for speaking of Christian Jews returning at all, since Aquila and Prisca are the only persons who we know had been in Rome before. That there were others is surely a plausible inference, but no inference, no matter how valid, should ever be transfigured into evidence. In short, Mr. Achtemeier rightly pronounces "Caveat emptor!" to those who buy the widely accepted reconstruction of the occasion that Romans is to have addressed.

Without new evidence, we know very little about the demographic make-up of the Roman house churches—certainly not enough to facilely equate "the weak" with Torah-observant Christian Jews and "the strong" with the Christian gentiles; nor do we know what proportion were gentile and what percentage of the Christian Jews were returnees. Mr. Achtemeier rightly notes that, while some of Paul's readers were Jewish believers, when he identifies those to whom he writes "he invariably says they are gentiles," and that he never explicitly identifies the fault line between "the weak" and "the strong" as an ethnic one. We also know that as Paul moves toward the climax of his discussion of Israel, he pointedly says, "Now I am speaking to you Gentiles" (11:13, RSV), and that the gospel he expounds, from the initial period onward, emphasizes God's faithfulness to the covenant with Abraham and to the scriptures of the synagogue.

Assuming (as we must until evidence disallows it) that Paul thought his letter made sense not only in its argument but also in light of its task when read, the central question remains: Why is this scripture-saturated, covenant-emphasizing letter not addressed to Christian Jews in Rome but pointedly to Christian gentiles? Mr. Achtemeier suggests that "Paul was scrupulously observing the comity arrangement of Gal 2:7–9," according to which he was to be the apostle to the gentiles. That might account for the audience he had in view, but it does not explain why the content of the letter is not more like that of 1 Thessalonians or the Corinthian letters. Paul evidently was convinced that it was the Christian gentiles in Rome more than their Jewish sisters and brothers who needed to read precisely *this* discourse, *not* because there were tensions between them (though there might well have been even if we know nothing about them), but because they needed to understand more fully the gospel's meaning for humanity. This is what prompted him to plan a trip to Spain by way of Rome. Paul Achtemeier is on target when he insists that "the shape of Paul's argument in Romans owes more to internal than to external factors, i.e., more to Paul's own theology than to the situation he confronted." Such a stance need not return us to a chastened Melanchthonian view (Romans as a compendium of *Paul's* doctrine), nor need it rehire us as jailors preserving the "Lutheran captivity" of the letter; it can—and should—keep our attention on the theological content, including Paul's self-understanding as an apostle to gentiles. After all, that is what has always made Romans significant—and challenging.

II

Prof. Achtemeier's claim—which I share—that "Paul's own theology," the inner logic of his grasp of the gospel, shapes what Paul writes more than alleged animosities and resentments in Rome brings us to the heart of the matter, because here everything turns on how we understand that theology to be related to the text of the letter. It is at this point that some differences, at least in accent, between us emerge that deserve discussion.

A. Professor Achtemeier regards "the internal factor," or "Paul's own theology" as "the economy of salvation," whose convenient summary (p. 9) includes Christ's return "at the time of the last judgment and the transformation of reality." That Paul expects the parousia is clearer in 1 Thessalonians and 1 Corinthians than in Romans, however. In fact, while "transformation" is clearly in view in Rom 8:18–25, the parousia is not mentioned explicitly in Romans at all—not even in 13:11–14, which asserts that "salvation is nearer to us now than when we first believed." Because we have the other Pauline letters it is easy for us to see here an oblique allusion to the parousia, but did Paul's first readers of Romans see it as well? Nor does Paul clearly refer to it in connection with his claim that when "the full number of gentiles" has "come in" (11:25–26) "all Israel will be saved"—unless one assumes that his quotation of Isa 59:20–21 ("the Deliverer will come *from* [!] Zion," etc.) refers to Christ's coming *to* earth. These references show that Paul draws on those elements of the economy of salvation that he thinks will propel his argument, and by-passes or mutes what he deems not germane or useful.

What begs for inclusion in the interpretation of both Paul and Romans is a satisfactory explanation of what he omits or mutes precisely in those passages where an emphasis on the economy of salvation prompts us to expect what turns out to be not in the text. In Romans, this includes, among other things, the silence about the Lord's Supper (which might well have been mentioned in chap. 6 as well as in chaps. 14–15). It is not clear, to me at least, whether the absence of an explicit ecclesial reference from Mr. Achtemeier's summary of the economy of salvation is merely an oversight (admittedly noticeable because we have 1 Corinthians), or reflects the fact that this summary is largely derived from Romans itself. But if that is the case, why is the parousia more prominent in the summary than in the letter? These observations lead up to the main question that invites further work: precisely how does the eschatology of Romans compare with Paul's eschatology expressed elsewhere, and what might account for the difference?

B. Suggestive is Prof. Achtemeier's discussion of the christomorphic character of the economy of salvation, though I am not persuaded that Rom 11:12, 15 reflects 2 Cor 8:9, or that the "replication of both Christ and Israel" is summed up in 11:30–31, or that in 11:25 the "fate" of Israel "re-enacts" that of Christ. If it were the case that "the great theme of Romans (and of Paul's theology?) is that God's way of dealing with humanity is to be understood in terms of the way he has dealt with Jesus—rejected as a sinner, punished as a sinner, but vindicated"—one must ask why Paul never makes this pattern manifest and explicit. That Paul could say that Christ was rejected as a sinner might be inferred from his reference to the crucified as cursed (Gal 3:13) but is scarcely consonant with Rom 3:25, which declares that God "put forward" Christ as an expiation for sin. So too, that Christ was "punished as a sinner" is more in accord with 2 Cor 5:21 (God "made him to be sin") than with anything said about Christ in Romans. Rather than speaking of the "replication" of Israel and Jesus, it would be better to talk of the faithfulness of God in his *modus operandi,* for that allows one to see more clearly that the theology of justification in Romans 1–8 is repeated and applied to Israel in chaps. 9–11, from which references to Jesus are noticeably absent.

Mr. Achtemeier sees clearly that "the economy remains under the control of God" who gave it "christocentric form," and that Paul therefore remains a *theo*logian instead of becoming a "christologian." In fact, future study of Paul's theology would do well to probe deeply the implications of Rom 5:8, that "*God* shows his love for us in that while we were yet sinners *Christ* died for us." This challenges the more easily digested view that in his dying Christ showed *his* love for God and/or for us. The God of Rom 5:8 is the One who "justifies the ungodly" (4:5) because his faithfulness, actualized as rectifying rectitude manifested apart from law, is the obverse of the faithfulness of Jesus. Unless, and until, this bold challenge of Paul's theology runs clear as a mountain stream, his economy of salvation is in danger of becoming a reassuring doctrine of providence or a philosophy of history.

C. Because Mr. Achtemeier sees that the universality of the gospel announced at the outset is closer to the actual theme of the letter than justification by faith ("the means by which the gospel of God's mercy is made available to gentile as well as to Jew") the logic of the projected mission to gentile Spain deserves more consideration than it generally receives. Indeed, Prof. Achtemeier's contention that a particular economy of salvation, one that begins with Adam and not with Abraham, underlies Romans can be strengthened. As already implied, Paul thought that the largely gentile Christian community in Rome needed to understand that his mission to Spain in no way implies that he had concluded that God has "rejected his people," and that as a consequence he was setting out to found a Jesus cult for gentiles. On the contrary, by going to Spain, he was actively advancing the day when the number of gentiles will be complete and "all Israel," now temporarily "hardened," will be "saved." Romans 9–11 is not designed to instruct Jewish believers so much as gentile Christians because it is they who need to understand themselves rightly in relation to God's commitment to Israel, for only so will they be the "acceptable offering" that Paul, the λειτουργός (minister) of Christ will present (15:16). It is not accidental that after interpreting his vocation Paul goes on to explain why he is going first to Jerusalem with funds raised by his gentile churches. This gift expressed monetarily their spiritual obligation to the first church, one that Paul assumes consisted of Jewish believers. In other words, just as the funds gathered in Macedonia and Achaia acknowledge these gentile Christians' "share in their [Jerusalem's] spiritual blessings," so Paul's mission to Spain is designed to be a way of "grafting" the gentile believers there into Israel (11:17).

By no means does this "grafting" make gentiles proselytes to Judaism, a possibility before and apart from Christ. More important, a proselytizing mission would imply that the answer to the gentile condition is found in Moses and the law. But Paul takes great care to show that the law, while "holy" (7:12), is nonetheless not able to deal with Sin and Death, the hallmarks of the Adamic situation in which Jews are as imprisoned as gentiles, as Mr. Achtemeier sees. So it is not Moses but Abraham who epitomizes the answer to Adam, because he trusted God, and "gave glory to God" (4:20), the alternative to the root sin of humanity: the refusal to honor God as God (1:21). So it is Abraham who is "the father of us all, as it is written, 'I have made you the father of many nations.'" (4:16–17). It is therefore only by Abrahamic faith/trust that Jews as well as gentiles truly call him "father." It is not surprising that Abraham's faith/trust is portrayed in terms taken from the faith-response to the gospel: he believed in/trusted the God "who gives life to the dead." In his case, it was the "deadness" of his body and of Sarah's womb (4:19); in the case of Jews and gentiles it is the deadness of Jesus, "who was put to death for our trespasses and raised for our justification" (4:25) that God overcame. The "root" that supports believing Jew and believing gentile alike is not Moses but Abraham, and Jews, "if they do not persist [in unbelief] will be grafted in" (11:23), namely into Abraham, for "not all are children of Abraham because they are his descendants" (4:17).

Mr. Achtemeier is quite right in insisting that for Paul "to the Jew first" is a matter of "historical rather than ontological priority" (p. 18), and that "universal salvation is made necessary by the universal sinfulness of human beings, expressly stated in 3:9, 22, and grounded in the discussion of Adam in 5:12–19." From beginning to end in Romans, it is the shared *human* condition that Paul has in view, for unless that is resolved by trusting the God whose rectifying rectitude in the Christ-event is manifest "apart from the law" (i.e., apart from Moses) there is no reason why gentiles should pay attention to the gospel at all. Likewise, unless God's rectifying rectitude apart from the law is consistent with God's action vis-a-vis Abraham and Sarah, then Isaac and Rebekah (9:6–13), Moses himself (10:5–13), Elijah (11:2–6) as well as with the words of Hosea and Isaiah (10:25–30)—and thus "attested by the law and the prophets" (3:21)—there is no reason why Jews should heed the gospel either.

Since it is the common *human* condition that Paul probes and expounds in Romans, it is inevitable that he also emphasizes both God's impartial wrath against all "ungodliness and wickedness" (1:18) and the one requisite but wholly adequate *human* response—available to Jew and gentile alike—to what God has done in Christ to deal with it—πίστις (faith/trust). Mr. Achtemeier rightly sees that this is more a matter of trust than of "belief" or "assent." Still, that this trust in God does not preclude assent to a specified content ("that . . .") is clear not only in 10:9 ("that God raised him from the dead"), which Mr. Achtemeier regards as an exception, but is surely implied also in 4:25. It is of course correct that Paul's "point of directing trust toward God and Christ is not to get his readers to assent to their existence," but the "point" is skewed by the claim that Paul wants them to "place their trust in God and Christ to fulfill what they have promised" (p. 18). This generalization is indeed consonant with

Phil 1:6, which refers to God completing the good work begun in the readers,[2] and with the portrayal of Abraham's πίστις in Rom 4:19–22, where the patriarch's response is to God's promise and so necessarily points to the future, to what has not yet happened. But trust in God's future promise-keeping is not the characteristic or constitutive dimension of Paul's use of πίστις in Romans. Apart from 6:8 ("if we have died with Christ, we believe that we shall also live with him"), I find no instance in Romans where Paul uses πίστις language to write about God's future deed; rather, this terminology is used consistently to refer to what God has already done in Christ, as in 4:25. When Paul refers to the Christian stance toward the future (8:24–28) he uses "hope." I call attention to this distinction not to quibble but to emphasize that in Romans πίστις is a response to the news of what God has already done in Christ. Indeed, Paul deserves to be considered a theologian because he thought through the meaning of the Christ-event—God's sending, "putting forth as expiation," and raising the Son—as a real occurrence. Paul's theology reflects his *ex post facto* thinking.[3]

D. An essential element in that occurrence was "the faithfulness of Jesus." That both Christ's faithfulness (πίστις Χριστοῦ) and "our faithfulness to the faithful Christ," expressed in his obedience, are "essential" for Paul is rightly emphasized by Prof. Achtemeier (p. 18). Nonetheless, to say that what is at issue in the continuing debate over the right way to render πίστις Χριστοῦ is "simply what is intended in any given instance of the expression" is unsatisfactory. Granted, Paul's own usage in 3:26 is more elliptical than in v. 22, which asserts that God's rectitude apart from law is manifested (perfect tense!) "through [διά] the faithfulness of Christ for all who believe/respond with trust." Since this verse has already been discussed, the focus here is on the relation between our πίστις and Christ's, which v. 26 expresses as God δικαιοῦντα τὸν ἐκ πίστεως Ἰησοῦ. The NRSV, like its predecessor, renders this clause in the traditional way: God "justifies the one who has faith in Jesus," but its alternative is, to put it mildly, even more problematic: "who has the faith of Jesus." The variant readings show that we are not the first to stumble over Paul's cryptic formulation.[4] Here, understanding requires thinking theologically with Paul about the subject matter itself.

2 In Phil 1:16, however, Paul's confidence is not expressed as a matter of trust or belief (πίστις) but of conviction, of being persuaded (πεποιθώς).

3 For a fuller discussion, see my "Paul as Thinker," in *Interpretation* 47.1 (January, 1993), 27–38, especially pp. 29–33, "Paul's Ex Post Facto Thinking." All the essays in that issue were prepared in honor of Paul J. Achtemeier.

4 The most interesting variant changes the genitive to an accusative; as a result God "justifies Jesus on the basis of faithfulness" (δικαιοῦντα τόν ἐκ πίστεως Ἰησουν); so D L Ψ 33 *et al.*

The key, I suggest, is in Paul's use of ἐκ (of, out of, etc.), which initially appears twice in the christological statement in 1:3–4. The first (ἐκ David's seed) is not problematic, but the second (ἐξ ἀναστάσεως νεκρῶν) is, though it is customary to take it to mean "by [his] resurrection from the dead." If this is right, then here ἐκ (ἐξ) refers to the ground, the basis of Christ's designation as Son of God in power. Similarly, in the pivotal quotation of Hab 2:4 in 1:17 ἐκ πίστεως (usually rendered as "from faith") refers to πίστις as the ground or basis, whether it refers to "the one who is righteous" or to "shall live." In 3:20, Paul says that no one will be rectified ἐξ ἔργων νόμου, that is, "on the basis of works of [the] law." In 3:29 he says that God will rectify the Jew ἐκ πίστεως and the gentile διὰ πίστεως, showing that Paul can use both prepositions interchangeably. Consequently there is no solid basis for distinguishing the διὰ πίστεως Ἰησοῦ Χριστοῦ from the ἐκ πίστεως Ἰησοῦ of v. 26, where ἐκ means "on the basis of" or simply "by." In other words, v. 26 says that God rectifies the person who lives by, or on the basis of, the faithfulness of Jesus, a fidelity epitomized by his obedience made concrete in his death.

If this is what Paul's clause intends to say, what does it mean? Surely not "having" Jesus' faith, his own relation to God. According to 5:19, "through the obedience [= faithfulness] of the one [Christ] the many will be made righteous." How that occurs is not stated, unfortunately, but may well be implied in chap. 6, where Paul explains that being baptized into Christ is being baptized into his death (6:3). This suggests that it is by being baptized into Christ's death, the capstone of his obedience, that one lives by, on the basis of, the faithfulness of Jesus. Moreover, because it was *his* fidelity that manifests God's rectitude apart from law, that same rectitude rectifies whoever lives by, grounds his/her existence in the faithfulness of Jesus. To live by, on the basis of, Jesus' faithfulness is for Paul not to lionize the devotion of "the Jesus of history" into a model to be imitated (being a "disciple" is foreign to Paul's understanding of the believer's relation to Jesus), but rather, and solely, to entrust oneself to God whose rectitude is now proclaimed as rectifying apart from [the] law because the Christ-event occurred for us while we were sinners in order to deal with our sin by freeing us from it instead of punishing us for it. The occurring of this event is for Paul as definitive a disclosure as the Abraham-event of God's freedom—the unstated theological axiom of Romans. It is this freedom that makes it possible for Paul to write of a disclosure of God's rectitude apart from the law.

E. Paul's understanding of the law (νόμος) continues to generate heated debate. Prof. Achtemeier proposes that it would be preferable, "both in terms of Paul's own intention, and in terms of [our] getting a clearer picture of what he is arguing, if one were to understand νόμος in every instance in Romans as torah ("teaching")." This is not the context to test such a sweeping proposal. It must suffice to say that this would scarcely illumine what Paul means in 7:23–25. What could he possibly mean by writing, "I see in my members another torah/teaching at war with the torah of my mind and making me captive to the torah of sin which dwells in my members"? To be sure, the "torah of my mind" is the "torah of God" in which Paul's inner self delights (v. 22). But what is the torah in his members, a "teaching" so powerful that it imprisons him in the teaching of sin/sinful teaching in his members? Does not here νόμος refer to a constraint, a compulsion he cannot resist successfully, a compelling factor so strong and so persistent that it functions as a law that must be obeyed (perhaps the "evil impulse")? And when he follows the statement that the νόμος is holy by adding "and the commandment is holy and just and good" does that not imply that νόμος is "law" rather than "teaching"? Surely it is preferable to recognize that νόμος serves Paul well precisely because it has multiple meanings, including Pentateuch, torah, and rule or principle.

In any case, Mr. Achtemeier has many colleagues who cast their discussion of νόμος in terms of torah, instead of law, and it is this current practice that deserves more critical reflection than it has received. To a large extent, the current practice of substituting torah for law reflects an understanding of Judaism as something that cannot be put down as "legalism," and so lets us think of Paul in relation to what we respect, torah. And that is surely a gain, long overdue. Nonetheless, there are other considerations about Paul himself.

To begin with, it is obvious that even if Paul thought "torah" he did not write διδαχή ("teaching") or παιδεία ("training, instruction, discipline") but νόμος because he thought it was the right word for what he had in mind. Romans gives no evidence that he sensed that the word νόμος was inadequate or misleading because his readers would take it to mean "law." Hellenistic, Septuagint-using Jew that he was, it was the natural word to use. At this point it is useful to recall what Samuel Sandmel wrote nearly four decades ago, and which—to my knowledge—has not been refuted. He is worth quoting extensively.

> Greek Jews focused their attention on Judaism as though it was both in essence and as a totality *law* and nothing but *law*. . . . for Hellenistic Judaism, the casualness with which the Hebrew word Torah was translated by the Greek word *nomos* . . . is apparent on every page of the surviving literature. Greek Jews nowhere raised the question of whether Torah really means *nomos,* law! And whenever they defended their Jewish convictions, it was always on the premise, startling to modern Jewish students, that *nomos* did adequately translate *Torah.* To Palestinian Jews, and their spiritual descendants, the word Torah never had so restricted a connotation; they equated *Torah* with

> our word "revelation" . . . which *included* "law" [but] they would probably have denied that revelation and "law" were interchangeable.[5]

The fact that Sandmel did not reckon sufficiently (in this passage) with Hellenistic Judaism in Palestine does not annul his point about Hellenized Jews' view of torah as law. His view, somewhat akin to that of H. J. Schoeps and others, is in disfavor, I suspect, because it has the effect of explaining Paul in terms of an error, on the one hand, and because, on the other, it calls into question his pre-Christian Pharisaism which, in turn, is commonly portrayed by appealing to post-70 Tannaitic Judaism. That during Second Temple Judaism many Palestinian Jews were Hellenized only suggests that if Paul had been a Pharisee in Jerusalem he could just as easily have understood torah as law there as at home in Tarsus. In any case, just what do we know about diaspora Jews who became Pharisees in Palestine before the disastrous war disrupted the Judaism Paul knew first hand?

The matter need not be pursued farther just now. Enough has been said, I trust, to suggest that there are significant historical and hermeneutical problems in claiming that we can understand Paul better by substituting a transliterated Hebrew word for the Greek one he used.

Above all, I hope to have shown that Prof. Achtemeier's paper has given all its readers much to think about. And for that we, and surely Paul as well, are grateful.

5 Samuel Sandmel, *The Genius of Paul: A Study in History.* (Philadelphia: Fortress Press, 1979; first published in 1958): 46–47.

Part II

Faith in or of Jesus Christ

3 ΠΙΣΤΙΣ AND PAULINE CHRISTOLOGY

What Is At Stake?

Richard B. Hays
Duke Divinity School

WERE THERE A Purgatory—though those of us who live and work in Paul's theological world have reason to suppose there is not—sinful scholars would surely be assigned the purifying ordeal of reading their own dissertations. Those who had especially many sins to atone for would be given the task of reworking their dissertations (perhaps, Sisyphus-like, ever anew) to conform to the wisdom conferred by experience. For my many sins, the Pauline Theology Group has given me a foretaste of purgatorial fire by asking me to revisit the question of how to interpret Paul's notoriously enigmatic expression πίστις Ἰησοῦ Χριστοῦ ("faith of/in Jesus Christ").

The discussion has moved forward significantly in the years since I completed my book *The Faith of Jesus Christ,*[1] and there have been several important new contributions to the debate.[2] Many interpreters of Paul have become convinced that the genitive in πίστις Ἰησοῦ Χριστοῦ should be understood to be

1 R. B. Hays, *The Faith of Jesus Christ: An Investigation of the Narrative Substructure of Galatians 3:1–4:11* (SBLDS 56; Chico: Scholars, 1983).

2 Especially noteworthy are D. M. Hay, "*Pistis* as 'Ground for Faith' in Hellenized Judaism and Paul," *JBL* 108 (1989) 461–76; M. D. Hooker, "ΠΙΣΤΙΣ ΧΡΙΣΤΟΥ," *NTS* 35 (1989) 321–42 [her 1988 SNTS Presidential Address]; L. E. Keck, "'Jesus' in Romans," *JBL* 108 (1989) 443–60; D. Campbell, *The Rhetoric of Righteousness in Romans 3.21–26* JSNTSup 65 (Sheffield: JSOT Press, 1992); S. K. Stowers, *A Rereading of Romans: Justice, Jews, & Gentiles* (New Haven: Yale University Press, 1994); I. G. Wallis, *The Faith of Jesus Christ in Early Christian Traditions* (SNTSMS 84; Cambridge: Cambridge University Press, 1995; a series of important articles by S. K. Williams: "Again *Pistis Christou,*" *CBQ* 49 (1987) 431–47; "Justification and the Spirit in Galatians," *JSNT* 29 (1987); "*Promise* in Galatians: A Reading of Paul's Reading of Scripture," *JBL* 107 (1988) 709–20; and "The Hearing of Faith: ΑΚΟΗ ΠΙΣΤΣΩΣ in Galatians 3," *NTS* 35 (1989) 82–93; and the detailed studies of D. Campbell: "The Meaning of ΠΙΣΤΙΣ and ΝΟΜΟΣ in Paul: A Linguistic and Structural Perspective," *JBL* 111 (1992) 91–103; "Romans 1:17—A *Crux Interpretum* for the ΠΙΣΤΙΣ ΧΡΙΣΤΟΥ Debate," *JBL* 113 (1994) 265–85.

subjective,[3] but others, such as J. D. G. Dunn, remain unconvinced, preferring instead the objective genitive interpretation: that πίστις Ἰησοῦ Χριστοῦ refers to "faith in Jesus Christ," the Christian's act of "faith directed toward Christ as the object."[4]

3 Without presuming to offer a comprehensive bibliographical survey, I note the following supporters of this view who have taken a position on the question since 1981 (for earlier literature, see Hays, *Faith of Jesus Christ,* 139–91, and G. Howard, "On the 'Faith of Christ'," *HTR* 60 [1967] 459–65; idem, "The Faith of Christ," *ExT* 85 [1974] 212–15): L. T. Johnson, "Romans 3:21–26 and the Faith of Jesus," *CBQ* 44 (1982) 77–90; B. Byrne, *Reckoning with Romans* (Wilmington, DE: Glazier, 1986) 79–80; T. L. Donaldson, "The 'Curse of the Law and the Inclusion of the Gentiles: Galatians 3.13–14," *NTS* 32 (1986) 94–112; L. Gaston, *Paul and the Torah* (Vancouver: University of British Columbia Press, 1987), especially p. 12; M. L. Soards, "Assessing Paul's 'Faith' Talk in Galatians," (paper read in SBL Pauline Epistles Section, 1989); S. K. Stowers, 'Ἐκ πίστεως and διὰ τῆς πίστεως in Romans 3:30," *JBL* 108 (1989) 665–74; idem, *A Rereading of Romans: Justice, Jews and Gentiles* (New Haven: Yale University Press, 1994),194–226; B. Witherington III, "The Influence of Galatians on Hebrews," *NTS* 37 (1991) 146–52; idem, *Paul's Narrative Thought World* (Louisville: Westminter/John Knox, 1994) 267–72; G. Howard, *Paul: Crisis in Galatia,* 2nd ed. (SNTSMS 35; Cambridge: Cambridge University Press, 1990); idem, "Faith of Christ," *ABD* 2.758–60; C. B. Cousar, *A Theology of the Cross: The Death of Jesus in the Pauline Letters* (Minneapolis: Fortress, 1990) 39–40; G. N. Davies, *Faith and Obedience in Romans* (JSNTS 39; Sheffield: JSOT, 1990) 107–12; R. N. Longenecker, *Galatians* (Word Biblical Commentary; Dallas: Word, 1990) 87–88, 93–94, 145; B. R. Gaventa, "The Singularity of the Gospel: A Reading of Galatians," in J. Bassler (ed.), *Pauline Theology, Volume I* (Minneapolis: Fortress, 1991), 147–59; J. L. Martyn, "Events in Galatia: Modified Covenantal Nomism versus God's Invasion of the Cosmos in the Singular Gospel: Response to Dunn and Gaventa," in J. Bassler (ed.) *Pauline Theology, Volume I,* 160–79; P. T. O'Brien, *The Epistle to the Philippians* (NIGTC; Grand Rapids: Eerdmans, 1991); F. J. Matera, *Galatians* (Sacra Pagina 9; Collegeville, MN: Liturgical Press, 1992); B. W. Longenecker, "ΠΙΣΤΙΣ in Romans 3.25: Neglected Evidence for the 'Faithfulness of Christ'?" *NTS* 39 (1993) 478-80; C. A. Davis, *The Structure of Paul's Theology* (Lewiston, NY: Mellen, 1995), 62–72; N. T. Wright, "Romans and the Theology of Paul," in D. M. Hay and E. E. Johnson (eds.), *Pauline Theology, Volume III* (Minneapolis: Fortress, 1995), 37–38; also the articles of Hooker, Keck, Williams, and Campbell (see n. 2 above). The NRSV has now given "the faith of Jesus Christ" a place in the footnotes as an alternative translation.

4 Dunn, *Romans 1–8,* (Word Biblical Commentary; Dallas: Word, 1988) 178. Others continuing to assert the "traditional" (since Luther) objective genitive interpretation include J. Barclay, *Obeying the Truth: A Study of Paul's Ethics in Galatians* (Edinburgh: T. & T. Clark, 1988); F. F. Bruce, *Commentary on Galatians* (NIGTC; Grand Rapids: Eerdmans, 1982; G. F. Hawthorne, *Philippians* (WBC 43; Waco, TX: Word, 1983); M. Silva, *Philippians* (Wycliffe Exegetical Commentary; Chicago: Moody, 1988); R. Y. K. Fung, *The Epistle to the Galatians* (NICNT; Grand Rapids: Eerdmans, 1988); G. W. Hansen, *Abraham in Galatians* (JSNTSup 29; Sheffield: JSOT Press, 1989); A. Hultgren, "The *Pistis Christou* Formulations in Paul," *NovT* 22 (1980) 248–63; W. Johnson, "The Paradigm of Abraham in Galatians 3:6–9," *TrinJ* 8 NS (1987) 179–99; S. Westerholm, *Israel's Law and the Church's Faith* (Grand Rapids: Eerdmans, 1988); V. Koperski, "The Meaning of *Pistis Christou* in Philippians 3:9," *LS* 18 (1993) 198–216; R. A. Harrisville, "ΠΙΣΤΙΣ ΧΡΙΣΤΟΥ: Witness of the Fathers," *NovT* 36 (1994) 233–41. Of course, all the older standard commentaries on Romans and Galatians represent the objective genitive interpretation, and this continues to be the majority view among European scholars.

Indeed, at the 1988 meeting of the Pauline Theology Group, Prof. Dunn, observing the pronounced shift in North American scholarship towards the "faith of Jesus Christ" position, compared this movement to the headlong rush of the Gerasene swine into the sea. In response, I likened him to the Gerasene swineherds who begged Jesus to go away and leave them alone. Clearly, rhetorical tensions were rising, and the *kairos* for judgment was at hand. The steering committee of the Pauline Theology group decided to ask Professor Dunn and me to elucidate our disagreement in a manner somewhat more exegetical and somewhat less dependent on typological interpretation of Mark 5. Hence, the present essay.

I. FRAMING THE QUESTION

Upon rereading *The Faith of Jesus Christ* ten years later, I remain unrepentant concerning the central thesis of my earlier work[5]: Paul's theology must be understood as the explication and defense of a *story.* The narrative structure of the gospel story depicts Jesus as the divinely commissioned protagonist who gives himself up to death on a cross in order to liberate humanity from bondage (Gal 1:4, 2:20, 3:13–14, 4:4–7). His death, in obedience to the will of God, is simultaneously a loving act of faithfulness (πίστις) to God and the decisive manifestation of God's faithfulness to his covenant promise to Abraham. Paul's uses of πίστις Ἰησοῦ Χριστοῦ and other similar phrases should be understood as summary allusions to this story,[6] referring to Jesus' fidelity in carrying out this mission. Consequently, the emphasis in Paul's theology lies less on the question of how we should dispose ourselves towards God than on the question of how

A mediating position is taken by B. Dodd ("Romans 1:17—A *Crux Interpretum* for the ΠΙΣΤΙΣ ΧΡΙΣΤΟΥ Debate?" *JBL* 114 [1994] 470–73), who is sympathetic to subjective genitive ("christological") readings of some of the key texts but who argues that each instance must be considered individually. C. H. Cosgrove (*The Cross and the Spirit: A Study in the Argument and Theology of Galatians* [Macon, GA: Mercer University Press, 1988], 57–58) takes a different tack, arguing that πίστις Χριστοῦ should be understood as metonymy for Paul's gospel of God's apocalyptic work in Christ: "Christ-Faith means God's eschatological action in Christ toward those who believe." This position is close to that of W. Schenk ("Die Gerechtigkeit Gottes und der Glaube Christi," *TLZ* 97 [1972] 161–74), who saw more clearly than most subsequent interpreters that Ernst Käsemann's apocalyptic interpretation of "the righteousness of God" also required a reinterpretation of Paul's understanding of πίστις.

5 I am, however, somewhat repentant about the methodological overkill of the piece. Some of the methodological preliminaries I would now gladly consign to the flames.

6 In the terminology of the dissertation (following Northrop Frye), the summarizing phrase πίστις Ἰησοῦ Χριστοῦ encapsulates the *dianoia* of the story: its overall sense, in contrast to its *mythos* (plot line).

God has acted in Christ to effect our deliverance. Indeed, this last sentence is a tolerable summary of the message of Paul's letter to the Galatians.

I must, in all candor, confess some puzzlement that these theses can be regarded as controversial. Nevertheless, many learned readers of Paul disagree vigorously with some or all of these claims. How is the disagreement to be resolved? Should my earlier arguments be revised, supplemented, or improved? What is at stake in the debate?

The ongoing discussion of Pauline theology—within this group and elsewhere—has brought several matters into clearer focus since the writing of *The Faith of Jesus Christ,* and I have learned a number of things from specific critiques of my work. It has become increasingly evident that the interpretation of πίστις Ἰησοῦ Χριστοῦ must be placed within the wider sphere of Paul's theology as a whole and—at the same time—within the sphere of the contingent argumentation of the letters in which this phrase appears.

With the wisdom of hindsight, I see six areas in which my earlier presentation of the evidence requires refinement and elaboration. They are as follows:

(1) The cultural/semantic background of Paul's πίστις language: how would Paul's uses of this terminology have been understood by his readers within the ancient Mediterranean world?
(2) The contingent circumstances of the letters to the Galatians and to the Romans: how does the πίστις Χριστοῦ language function within Paul's response to the politically sensitive Jew/Gentile issues that elicited these letters?
(3) Pauline christology: what is Paul's conception of the significance of Jesus' death, and how do other christological passages in his letters shed light upon the interpretation of Paul's πίστις Χριστοῦ expressions?
(4) The apocalyptic character of Paul's thought: how does the πίστις Χριστοῦ motif relate to Paul's conviction that God has acted through Christ to inaugurate the turn of the ages?
(5) Intertextual echoing of the OT as a generative factor in Paul's theology: does Paul's use of OT texts shed light on the passages in which the πίστις Χριστοῦ motif appears?
(6) Paul's insistence that the gospel constitutes the fulfillment of God's covenant promises to Israel[7]: what does πίστις Χριστοῦ have to do with the theme of God's faithfulness, which is particularly dominant in Romans?

7 See the important essays by N. T. Wright, *The Climax of the Covenant* (Edinburgh: T. & T. Clark, 1991).

When our question is located within the framework of these broader considerations, it becomes possible to give a more complete and satisfying account of the meaning of πίστις Ἰησοῦ Χριστοῦ in Pauline theology. In the present essay, I do not attempt a systematic discussion of the above six topics (to do so would produce another book at least as long as the dissertation); instead, I offer a programmatic sketch of the way in which I now believe the question should be approached, considering the handful of πίστις Χριστοῦ passages in a way that is attentive to these factors. I shall concentrate primarily on Romans, for two reasons: (1) Because I dealt with Romans only glancingly in *Faith of Jesus Christ,* a fuller treatment of the problem there may be illuminating; (2) Romans—with its extended theological argument addressed to readers unfamiliar with Paul's teaching—gives us the best chance of placing the contested phrase in its proper theological context.

Little is to be gained by rehearsing the familiar arguments about syntax. I stand by my earlier judgment that the balance of grammatical evidence strongly favors the subjective genitive interpretation and that the arguments for an objective genitive are relatively weak.[8] Such syntactical arguments are, however, finally inconclusive. The objective genitive *is* a possible construal, and there are at least two passages where Paul does use the verb πιστεύειν with Χριστὸν Ἰησοῦν (or the equivalent) as its object (Gal 2:16, Phil 1:29; cf. also Rom 10:12 and Col 2:5).[9] (It is an interesting fact—not always fully appreciated by defenders of the objective genitive interpretation—that such passages are relatively rare in Paul; more characteristically, he speaks of God [Rom 4:3,5,17, 24; Gal 3:6; cf. 2 Tim 1:12, Tit 3:8] or of the content of the proclaimed *gospel* [Rom 6:8; 10:9,16, 1 Cor 15:11, 1 Thess 4:14] as the object of faith, or he uses the verb absolutely, with no expressed object.) Our interpretative decision about the meaning of Paul's phrase, therefore, must be governed by larger judgments about the shape and logic of Paul's thought concerning faith, Christ, and salvation. Indeed, rather than defining the debate as a dispute between subjective genitive and objective genitive readings, we would do better to speak—as some recent essays have suggested—of a distinction between the *christological* and *anthropological* interpretations of πίστις Χριστοῦ. The christological reading highlights the salvific efficacy of Jesus Christ's faith(fulness) for God's people;

8 See *Faith of Jesus Christ,* 164. For detailed evidence, see Howard's early essays on the topic (n. 3, above). The recent exchange between Hultgren ("*Pistis Christou* Formulations") and Williams ("Again *Pistis Christou,*") demonstrates again how strongly the lexical and syntactical arguments weigh in favor of the subjective genitive.

9 This has always been the strongest evidence in favor of the objective genitive interpretation. See now, however, Williams' very provocative discussion of Gal 2:16 ("Again *Pistis Christou,*" 442–44).

the anthropological reading stresses the salvific efficacy of the human act of faith directed toward Christ.

What is required is an attempt to understand how πίστις Ἰησοῦ Χριστοῦ functions within the construction of Paul's arguments. The following survey, then, is offered not as a definitive exegesis of the pertinent passages but as a "reading," seeking to show how the subjective genitive makes sense out of the texts.

II. ΠΙΣΤΙΣ ΧΡΙΣΤΟΥ IN ROMANS

For methodological reasons, the investigation should begin with Paul's Letter to the Romans.[10] Because Paul had not founded the Roman church(es?) and had not previously taught there, his letter must set forth a relatively self-explanatory exposition of the gospel. Though he presupposes that the Romans do know a number of things about Jesus and the gospel[11]—he is, after all, writing to Roman Christians to whom he can say ἡ πίστις ὑμῶν καταγγέλεται ἐν ὅλῳ τῷ κόσμῳ (Rom 1:8)—he cannot rely upon the signifying power of the compressed, allusive formulations that he employs in Galatians to remind his readers of his own earlier preaching. Thus, we have a better chance of grasping Paul's πίστις language if we "take our seat in the Roman congregation," as J. Louis Martyn might recommend, and listen to the way in which the discussion unfolds.

Faith-Obedience (1:5)

In Rom 1:5, we encounter the thematic phrase ὑπακοὴ πίστεως ("obedience of faith"), which is to be understood as an epexegetical construction virtually equating the two nouns. Paul has received his apostleship from Jesus Christ "to bring about faith-obedience among all the Gentiles," who are called—as Paul explains later—to present their bodies as a living sacrifice (12:2) in obedience to God. Thus, from the letter's first sentence we find obedience and faith closely correlated. We also find that ὑπακοὴ πίστεως evidently describes a particular response to the proclaimed gospel. This supposition is confirmed by Paul's thanksgiving in 1:8 that "your faith," (i.e., the faith of the

10 In *Faith of Jesus Christ,* I deliberately undertook to discuss Galatians because it seemed the more difficult case (cf. p. 170). Here I pursue a different tack.

11 See the discussion in Keck, "'Jesus' in Romans," for a reconstruction of what Paul assumes they do know.

Roman Christians) is widely known. (It is worth noting that in the expression ἡ πίστις ὑμῶν the genitive is clearly subjective: Paul's sentence does *not* mean, "Faith in you Romans is proclaimed in the whole world.") Similarly, in 1:12, where Paul hopes that "we may be mutually encouraged by each other's faith," Paul thinks of πίστις, whatever its precise nuance, as an attribute or disposition characterizing the members of the church. Similar usages are to be found in 11:20, 14:1, and throughout chapter 4 (re: Abraham).

By Faith for Faith (1:17)

The next reference to πίστις, a crucial one for our purposes, appears in Paul's programmatic formulation of the gospel (1:16–17), where it is anchored by his citation of Hab 2:4. The fundamental assertion comes first: the gospel is "the power of God for salvation to everyone who believes (πάντι τῷ πιστεύοντι), to the Jew first and also to the Greek." Paul here articulates four key motifs: (a) the gospel as God's saving power, (b) the importance of human response in faith, (c) the priority of Israel in God's saving design, and (d) the inclusion of the Gentiles. Following in v. 17 is the warrant for the claims of the previous verse: the righteousness of God is being revealed ἐκ πίστεως εἰς πίστιν, καθὼς γέγραπται· ὁ δὲ δίκαιος ἐκ πίστεως ζήσεται ("by faith for faith, just as it is written, 'the Righteous One will live by faith'").

For the purposes of our present discussion, I do not need to argue the case that the ἐκ πίστεως in 1:17a refers to God's faithfulness eschatologicially revealed in the gospel, so that the phrase ἐκ πίστεως εἰς πίστιν means "from (God's) faithfulness for (our) faith." Dunn has already marshalled compelling arguments for this interpretation.[12] God's πίστις is his covenant-faithfulness (cf. 3:3), which endures and overcomes all human unfaithfulness. When Paul affirms that the righteousness of God is revealed ἐκ πίστεως, he is pointing to the source of the revelation. The phrase "from faith for faith" then becomes a rhetorically effective slogan to summarize the gospel message of a salvation that originates in God's power and is received trustingly by the beneficiaries of

[12] *Romans 1–8,* 44. Campbell ("Romans 1:17—A *Crux Interpretum,*" 269), declaring that Rom 1:17 is "'the Thermopylae' of the πίστις Χριστοῦ debate in Romans," contends that it must be held "with blood and tears" by defenders of the christological interpretation and suggests (269 n. 16) that my concurrence with Dunn here constitutes premature surrender of a crucial point. This overstates the issue. Romans certainly is—as Dunn and I agree—about the eschatological faithfulness of God. To allow this interpretation of 1:17a does not necessarily determine all subsequent uses of πίστις in the letter, nor does it preclude a christological interpretation of 1:17b.

that power. As J. Haussleiter remarked over a century ago, the Greek πίστις does not require the writer or reader to make the distinction between "*Treue*" and "*Glaube*": both ideas are contained in the single term.[13] The difficulty of appreciating this semantic nuance contributes to the confusion surrounding the whole discussion of the meaning of πίστις in Paul. (A similar reciprocal interplay of divine and human πίστις is found also, e.g., in Philo, *De Abr.* 273: ὅς τῆς πρὸς αὐτὸν πίστεως ἀγάμενος τὸν ἄνδρα πίστιν ἀντιδίδωσιν αὐτῷ, τὴν δι' ὅρκου βεβαίωσιν ὧν ὑπέσχετο δωρεῶν ["(God), marvelling at Abraham's faith towards him, repaid him with faith by confirming with an oath the gifts which he had promised"]. Here, however, Abraham's faith seems to elicit the divine πίστις rather than, as in Paul, vice versa.)

The Function of the Habakkuk Citation

Rom 1:17 provides decisive evidence that Paul's use of the peculiar locution ἐκ πίστεως is derived from Hab 2:4. When Paul first introduces the phrase, he explicitly cites the text to show the Romans where it comes from. As Douglas Campbell has pointed out, ἐκ πίστεως occurs in Paul's letters *only* in Romans and Galatians, that is, only in the two letters where he quotes Hab 2:4.[14] This observation supports my earlier suggestion that ἐκ πίστεως is an exegetical catchphrase that alludes to the Habbakuk text.[15] Once the phrase is established within the theological vocabulary of a particular letter, it can be used in contexts that have nothing to do with the exegesis of Habakkuk (e.g., Rom 14:23)[16], but it surely originates in Paul's reading of the prophetic passage.

Equally crucial, and certainly more controversial, is the suggestion that Paul understands Hab 2:4 as a messianic prophecy now brought to fulfillment through the death and resurrection of Jesus.[17] This is one interpretative proposal in *Faith of Jesus Christ* that has encountered much skepticism, even from critics who otherwise found the book's argument persuasive. It seems to me, however,

[13] J. Haussleiter, "Der Glaube Jesu Christi und der christliche Glaube," *NKZ* 2 (1891) 136.

[14] Campbell, "Πίστις and Νόμος," 100–101.

[15] *Faith of Jesus Christ,* 150–57.

[16] In the discussion of this issue in the Pauline Theology Group in Kansas City, Robert Jewett raised the interesting possibility that passages such as Rom 14:22–23 might reflect a formula or slogan of one group in Rome, presumably the "strong" in faith. It is difficult to know how this intriguing hypothesis might be tested. In the absence of other evidence, it is simpler to treat the expression ἐκ πίστεως as Paul's own formulation, derived from his reading of Habakkuk.

[17] This position is now also defended by Campbell, "Romans 1:17—A *Crux Interpretum,*" 281–85.

that in Romans 1 a number of factors encourage us to give this messianic hypothesis a serious hearing.

Paul's quotation of Hab 2:4 in Rom 1:17 supports his assertion that the righteousness of God is revealed in the gospel (taking the antecedent of αὐτῷ ["it"] to be τὸ εὐαγγέλιον ["the gospel"] in 1:16). How, we should ask ourselves, is the righteousness of God revealed in the gospel? In the opening of the letter, Paul declares that the εὐαγγέλιον θεοῦ was "prepromised (προεπηγγείλατο) through his prophets in holy writings concerning his Son, . . . Jesus Christ our Lord" (1:1–4).[18] Thus, when we find a prophetic holy writing (Hab 2:4) quoted as the epigraph to Paul's exposition of the gospel, it is not unreasonable to suppose that Paul regards this text as a prefiguration of God's Son. If so, then Jesus Christ would be the means of the revelation of God's righteousness ἐκ πίστεως ["by faith"]. (See below on Rom 3:21–26).

This interpretation would be particularly attractive if it could be shown (1) that Hab 2:4 was already understood in first-century Judaism as a messianic prophecy and/or (2) that ὁ δίκαιος ("the Righteous One") was an established epithet for the eschatological deliverer.

(1) The first of these proposals was defended in *Faith of Jesus Christ* (pp. 151–56); to my arguments there should be added the observations of August Strobel, *Untersuchungen zum eschatologischen Verzögerungsproblem auf Grund der spätjudisch-urchristlichen Geschichte von Habakuk 2,2ff,*[19] and now also D.-A. Koch, "Der Text von Hab 2.4b in der Septuaginta und im Neuen Testament,"[20] both of whom accept the position, already taken by T. W. Manson, C. H. Dodd, and A. T. Hanson, that the LXX has rendered the text of Hab 2:2–4 in a way that shows unmistakable signs of a messianic interpretation.

(2) The second proposal, that ὁ δίκαιος is a common messianic title, seems to me to be beyond dispute. In addition to the clear NT evidence (Acts 3: 14, 7:52, 22:14, 1 Pet 3:18 [echoing Isa 53:11], and 1 John 2:1—I leave aside the disputed Pauline passages), we have evidence in the Similitudes of Enoch (see 1 Enoch 38:2, 53:6; cf also 39:6, 46:3, 48:2, 62:5ff.) of a figure called the Righteous One who appears at the scene of eschatological judgment as a revealer and executor of divine justice. Since I have gathered these texts and

[18] Most commentators prefer to connect the phrase περὶ τοῦ υἱοῦ αὐτοῦ (v. 3) directly back to εὐαγγέλιον θεοῦ (v. 1). This is a highly artificial interpretation, apparently influenced by the fact that Paul, unlike Matthew and John, does not usually argue that Jesus is the fulfillment of OT prophecy. But this objection fails to reckon with the fact that Paul is probably employing traditional language here. In any case, no hearer of the text of Rom 1:1-4, read aloud, would fail to connect περὶ τοῦ υἱοῦ αὐτοῦ with the immediately preceding phrase ἐν γραφαῖς ἁγίαις.

[19] (NovTSup, 2; Leiden: Brill, 1961) especially pp. 47–56.

[20] *ZNW* 76 (1985) 73 n.25.

discussed their exegesis in an essay elsewhere,[21] I will not repeat my arguments here. The point is simply that first-century Jews and Christians were well acquainted with the use of "the Righteous One" as a title for the agent of God's eschatological justice.[22]

These arguments suggest that a messianic interpretation of Hab 2:4 is both historically possible and contextually meaningful in Rom 1:17. It remains to be seen whether the development of Paul's argument will sustain the hypothesis that God's righteousness is somehow revealed through the πίστις of the Righteous One, Jesus Messiah.

The Faith of Jesus Christ Manifests God's Righteousness (3:21–26)

In Rom 1:18–3:20 Paul depicts, in stark contrast to the righteousness of God, the ungodliness and unrighteousness of God's human creatures. Gentile and Jew alike, they have failed to glorify God. With or without the Law, they have turned away into rebellion and delusion. The whole world stands under the wrath of God, subject to God's righteous judgment. In the midst of this devastating indictment of human unrighteousness, Paul pauses to reflect plaintively on the situation of God's chosen people (3:1-20), those who were supposed to be "a priestly kingdom and a holy nation" (Exod 19:6). Tragically, despite the privileges with which they were entrusted (3:2: ἐπιστεύθησαν—note the continuing wordplay), they too have fallen under the power of sin (3:9), as Israel's own Scriptures forcefully attest (3:10–20).

All of this ineluctably forces the critical question that surfaces in 3:3: "Will their faithlessness (ἀπιστία) nullify the faithfulness of God (τὴν πίστιν τοῦ θεοῦ)?" Will God's election of a people turn out to be fruitless? Of course, Paul's question (introduced by μὴ) demands a negative answer. The faithfulness

21 "'The Righteous One' as Eschatological Deliverer: A Case Study in Paul's Apocalyptic Hermeneutics," in J. Marcus and M. L. Soards (eds.), *Apocalyptic and the New Testament: Essays in Honor of J. Louis Martyn* (JSNTSup 24; Sheffield: JSOT Press, 1988) 191–215.

22 For a different, non-messianic interpretation of Hab 2:4 in later rabbinic Judaism, see Ecclesiastes Rabbah on Eccl 3:9 ("What gain has the worker from his toil?"): "Solomon said: Since there are times for all things, what advantage has the labourer in his work and the upright man in his uprightness? . . . R. Isaac b. R. Marion said: *But the righteous shall live by his faith* (Hab. II, 4) means that even the Righteous One who lives for ever lives from His faith" (*Midrash Rabbah* VIII, trans. A. Cohen [London: Soncino, 1939], 83). Here "the Righteous One" is interpreted as a reference to God, not the Messiah. This is in keeping with the well-known tendency of rabbinic literature to deemphasize messianic themes. Nonetheless, if the rabbis could speak of God himself as living by faith (even though this is admittedly an unusual text), the early Christians might have found no awkwardness in speaking of the faith of Jesus the Christ.

of God—his resolute adherence to his covenant—demands that he be true even if everyone be false. In 3:3–8, Paul emphatically rejects the notion that God's faithfulness can be thwarted, and he asserts three apparently synonymous attributes of God: ἡ πίστις τοῦ θεοῦ, θεοῦ δικαιοσύνη, and ἡ ἀλήθεια τοῦ θεοῦ ("the faithfulness of God, God's righteousness, and the truthfulness of God," 3:3,5,7).[23] He does not yet, however, explain *how* God is to prevail over human unrighteousness. Is it merely through the act of pronouncing condemnation, as 3:9–20 might suggest?

The answer at last comes in Rom 3:21–26. How does God's πίστις/δικαιοσύνη prevail? The righteousness of God has been made manifest (note the perfect tense πεφανέρωται) διὰ πίστεως Ἰησοῦ Χριστοῦ ("through the faithfulness of Jesus Christ"), whom God put forward to demonstrate his own righteousness. This notoriously dense passage contains dozens of exegetical difficulties, but I propose the following interpretation. God has solved the problem of human unrighteousness and Israel's unfaithfulness by putting forward as a sacrifice the one perfectly faithful human being, Jesus. Though others rebelled and refused to give glory to God, he remained faithful. His death is an act of πίστις: human πίστις—the counterweight to Israel's ἀπιστία ("unfaithfulness")—because it is an act of perfect obedience through which many will be made righteous vicariously (5:19), and divine πίστις because it affirms God's unbreakable love: "God proves his love for us in that while we still were sinners Christ died for us" (5:8). (Here we might want to give serious consideration to David Hay's suggestion that πίστις can mean "pledge" or "objective basis for faith": "Jesus is a pledge or assurance from God that makes human faith possible."[24]) Christ's death is—mysteriously—an act of divine love and faithkeeping (cf. 15:8).

The pivotal point in this discussion is the meaning of δικαιοσύνη θεοῦ. As long as interpreters maintained the notion that this phrase signified a status of righteousness imputed by God to believers, it was possible to make sense of Ἰησοῦ Χριστοῦ in 3:22 as an objective genitive: the status of righteousness is

23 See the analysis of this passage in R. B. Hays, "Psalm 143 and the Logic of Romans 3," *JBL* 99 (1980) 107–15.

24 Hay, "*Pistis* as 'Ground for Faith'," 472. I differ from Hay's proposal because it seems to me to accord insufficient attention to the way in which Rom 3:1–8 functions to define πίστις θεοῦ as God's covenant-faithfulness. Still, it makes far better sense of Rom 3:22 than does the objective genitive interpetation. One problem with Hay's article is that he fails to give sufficient weight to his own observation that "In the LXX, which uses *pistis* fifty-seven times, the "evidence" sense is generally absent" (462). Given the importance of the LXX in constituting Paul's theological vocabulary, this fact deserves more attention, especially since in Romans and Galatians Paul seems to be grounding his discussion of faith in Genesis and Habakkuk.

conferred through the believer's faith in Jesus Christ. (This reading leaves the phrase εἰς πάντας τοὺς πιστεύοντας ["for all who believe"] as a peculiar redundancy and renders the choice of the verb πεφανέρωται ["has been made manifest"] puzzling, but I let these issues pass for now.) However, it should be beyond dispute that the "righteousness" in question in 3:21–22 is God's own righteousness (subjective genitive), just as in 3:3–7 and 3:25–26.[25] Paul is framing an argument concerning theodicy, insisting that God's way of dealing with humanity through the gospel is a manifestation of his justice, not an arbitrary dissolution of his promises to Israel. Romans 3 is a defense of God's justice.[26] Once that point becomes clear, the objective genitive interpretation of πίστις Ἰησοῦ Χριστοῦ becomes virtually unintelligible. What would it mean to say that God's justice has been made manifest through our act of believing in Jesus Christ? This, if it means anything at all, verges on blasphemous absorption in our own religious subjectivity. God's eschatological justice can only have been shown forth by an act of God: Paul's claim is that the death of Jesus is just such an apocalyptic event.

In light of these observations, it is still not easy to decide whether the difficult διὰ (τῆς) πίστεως ("through faith") in 3:25 refers to God's faithfulness (probably not directly), Christ's faithfulness in accepting death on the cross (the likeliest option),[27] or the faith whereby hearers of the gospel receive the atoning benefits of Christ's death (since δικαιοσύνη θεοῦ ["God's righteousness"] is, after all, manifested εἰς πάντας τοὺς πιστεύοντας ["for all who believe," 3:23]). If Paul means the last of these three possibilities, he certainly has not made himself very clear. The emphasis of the whole passage is on God's action in putting forward Jesus Messiah who enacts the faith-obedience that Israel failed to render, who thereby glorifies God as faithless human creatures had failed to do and constitutes, through his resurrection, the beginning of a new humanity (cf. chaps. 5 and 6),[28] whom God has "predestined to be conformed to the image of his Son" (8:29). Because this manifestation of God's saving righteousness has taken place χωρὶς νόμου ["apart from law"], through Christ's action, the new humanity includes Jews and Gentiles without distinction.

25 Cf. Hays, "Psalm 143." I would now contend—on the basis of OT sources of the language—that δικαιοσύνη θεοῦ means God's covenant faithfulness. See my article on "Justification," *ABD* 3.1129–33.

26 For a fuller exposition of this interpretation, see R. B. Hays, *Echoes of Scripture in the Letters of Paul* (New Haven: Yale University Press, 1989) 36–54.

27 I am persuaded on this point by S. K. Williams, *Jesus' Death as Saving Event* (HDR 2; Missoula: Scholars Press, 1975) 41–51.

28 The discussions of Keck, Hooker, and Wright, though differing in emphasis from one another, are particularly alert to these themes.

Nonetheless, the faithfulness of Jesus is also at the same time the manifestation of God's covenant-faithfulness (here again, the wordplay on πίστις is important) to Israel, as Paul will argue in Romans 9–11 and 15:8–9.

The paragraph concludes in 3:26 with the affirmation that God's act of putting forth Jesus Christ was undertaken "so that [God] himself might be just precisely by justifying[29] the one who shares the faith of Jesus." I continue to resist the temptation of reading, with D L Ψ 33 614 et al., δικαιοῦντα τὸν ἐκ πίστεως Ἰησοῦν (="by justifying Jesus ἐκ πίστεως"). This manuscript tradition shows that a significant number of interpreters in the church later found no difficulty with the idea that Jesus was justified by faith, but the meaning of Paul's expression (reading τὸν ἐκ πίστεως Ἰησοῦ ["the one who shares the faith of Jesus"]) is better illuminated by the parallel expression in Rom 4:16: τῷ ἐκ πίστεως Ἀβραάμ ("to the one who shares the faith of Abraham"). The parallelism between 3:26 and 4:16 is a fatal embarassment for all interpreters who seek to treat Ἰησοῦ as an objective genitive.

The Faith of Abraham (4:1–25)

One argument frequently urged against understanding πίστις Ἰησοῦ Χριστοῦ as "faith of Jesus Christ" is that when Paul wants to offer a "model" of faith, he points not to Jesus (as does the Letter to the Hebrews—see especially Heb 12:2), but to Abraham. This argument, however, neglects the contextual argumentative purpose of Paul's appeals to the figure of Abraham.

In the case of Galatians, Paul does not pick Abraham out of the air as an example. We should probably accept the suggestions of C. K. Barrett[30] and J. Louis Martyn[31] that Abraham was introduced into the Galatian discussion by Paul's opponents, the Jewish-Christian "Teachers" who were urging the Galatians to receive circumcision as Abraham did. Paul, seizing the opportunity afforded by Gen 15:6, offers a subversive counterreading of the Abraham story that seeks to enlist Abraham against the Teachers (see especially Gal 4:21).

In the case of Romans 4, Paul brings Abraham into the argument neither because he is looking for models of faith, nor because he is seeking in some general way to explain how justification takes place. Rather, he appeals to Abraham

29 I take the καί to be epexegetical.

30 "The Allegory of Abraham, Sarah, and Hagar in the Argument of Galatians," in J. Friedrich et al. (eds.) *Rechtfertigung: Festschrift für Ernst Käsemann* (Tübingen: J. C. B. Mohr [Paul Siebeck], 1976 and Göttingen: Vandenhoeck & Ruprecht, 1976) 1–16.

31 "A Law-Observant Mission to Gentiles: The Background of Galatians," *SJT* 38 (1985) 307–24.

in defense of the claim that his gospel does not nullify the Law (Rom 3:31). The structure of the argument positively requires him to produce evidence *from Scripture* that will demonstrate the continuity between Torah and gospel. To cite kerygmatic traditions about Jesus here would not serve his purpose at all. His argument requires a *scriptural* warrant for the claim that God will justify Jews and Gentiles alike ἐκ πίστεως/διὰ τῆς πίστεως ("by faith/through faith," 3:30).[32]

Consequently, the fact that he points to Abraham rather than Jesus as a paradigm for faith proves nothing one way or the other about the meaning of πίστις Ἰησοῦ Χριστοῦ. Abraham appears in Paul's exposition because his story provides an analogically provocative set of *Biblical* images that Paul can use to reinforce his gospel story.

Indeed, much critical discussion of Paul's use of the Abraham story—and here I include my own analysis of Galatians 3 in *Faith of Jesus Christ*—goes subtly astray by failing to appreciate that Paul is working backwards from his gospel into a typological/literary interpretation of the OT text. Abraham is of interest to Paul not as a "historical" figure but as a metaphorical figure in Paul's symbolic world. He is theologically valuable to Paul because his story prefigures certain aspects of the gospel that Paul preaches.[33] So, for example, Paul claims that Abraham received circumcision after faith was reckoned to him as righteousness (Gen 15:6), not before, in order that he might be the symbolic father figure both of Gentile believers and of circumcised believers (Rom 4:9–12). Likewise, Paul writes that Gen 15:6 was "written not for [Abraham's] sake alone, but for ours also, to whom it is going to be reckoned, to those who place their trust in the one who raised Jesus our Lord from the dead" (Rom 4: 23–24). Abraham typologically prefigures Christian believers, whose faith—note carefully—is said to be directed not toward Jesus but toward the God who raised Jesus.

Adam and Christ (5:12–21)

The final crucial passage in Romans for assessing the meaning of Paul's references to the "faith of Jesus Christ" is the typological contrast between Adam and Christ in Rom 5:12–21. Adam is "a type of the coming one" [i.e.,

32 Against Stowers ("Ἐκ πίστεως and διὰ τῆς πίστεως"), I continue to regard these expressions as synonymous. To posit a distinction here would be to undo the whole point of Paul's argument, which is to insist that "there is no distinction," that Jews and Gentiles are now related to God on precisely the same terms through the grace of Jesus Christ.

33 A similar point could be made about Adam in Romans 5 and Moses in 2 Corinthians 3.

Jesus][34] in that he is the progenitor, the typological embodiment, the ἀρχηγός ("captain," to borrow a term from Hebrews) of a people. His sin carries vicarious consequences (condemnation) for all who are "in" him. Jesus Christ, on the the other hand, by his act of righteousness (δικαίωμα, 5:18), his obedience (ὑπακοή, 5:19), effects justification for all who are "in" him. Of course, the act of obedience in view here is Christ's death (5:6-11). The passage does not use the word πίστις, but in light of the virtual synonymity established in 1:5 between πίστις and ὑπακοή, it is difficult to suppose that this terminological difference is particularly significant.[35] Luke Johnson's cogent argument that Rom 5:15–21 is the plain explication of "the faith of Jesus" in Rom 3:21–26 has never been seriously countered.[36] In any case, Romans 5 shows unmistakably that Paul regards Jesus' death as an act of obedience that carries the destiny of many; furthermore, Romans 6 goes on to contend that his death is not merely vicarious but that through baptism we have entered a union with Christ in such a way that his death and resurrection define a pattern for our obedience as well. If—as I have been contending—πίστις Ἰησοῦ Χριστοῦ is a summary description of Christ's faithful death, then those who are "conformed to the image of God's Son" (8:29), crying as he did "Abba, Father" (8:14) will also share in his πίστις, being conformed to it. That is surely the sense of the expression τὸν ἐκ πίστεως Ἰησοῦ ("the one who shares the faith of Jesus," 3:26).

One of the liabilities of the traditional interpretation of justification through believing in Jesus, as Schweitzer perceptively noted, is its inability to explain how Romans 5–8 are related to Romans 1–4. E. P. Sanders reemphasized this point, of course, in *Paul and Palestinian Judaism.* Whereas Schweitzer and Sanders both attributed the disjunction to a lack of internal systematic coherence in Romans, I would suggest that the difficulty lies in the "objective genitive" (i.e., *anthropological*) misinterpretation of πίστις Χριστοῦ—hence, more in Luther than in Paul. A great strength of the subjective genitive (i.e., *christological*) construal is that it allows us to read Romans 1–8 as a theologically coherent discussion in which Paul's christology and soteriology are correlated in such a way that "justification by faith" and "participation in Christ" are virtually syn-

34 Note the way in which Paul here applies the messianic epithet ὁ μελλῶν ("the coming one") to Jesus Christ without explanation or comment; the usage is analogous to his equally casual use of ὁ δίκαιος ("the righteous one"). In both cases, he expects the reader to recognize the epithet as a term of reference to the Messiah.

35 *Contra* Cosgrove, *Cross and Spirit,* 55–56; idem, "Justification in Paul: A Linguistic and Theological Reflection," *JBL* 106 (1987) 665 n.32.

36 Johnson "Romans 3:21–26," 87–89. See also R. Longenecker, "The Obedience of Christ in the Theology of the Early Church," in R. Banks (ed.), *Reconciliation and Hope* (Grand Rapids: Eerdmans, 1974) 142–52; Keck, "'Jesus' in Romans," 457.

onymous. As Morna Hooker formulates it, "Justification is a matter of participation; so, too, is believing: . . . . even the believer's initial response—his faith—is a sharing in the obedient, faithful response of Christ himself."[37] Of course, this suggestion would have to be worked out much more fully than is possible here.[38] In any case, the foregoing sketch at least begins to demonstrate how the "faith of Jesus Christ" construal helps us to make sense out of the letter to the Romans as a whole. After surveying the evidence, Leander Keck concludes that ". . . in every case, construing πίστις Ἰησοῦ as the fidelity of Jesus not only removes unwarranted awkwardness from Paul's statements but clarifies the key point—the role of Jesus in salvation."[39]

III. OTHER TEXTS: SOME OBSERVATIONS

Besides the passages in Romans, some form of the πίστις Χριστοῦ formulation occurs in Gal 2:16, 2:20, 3:22, in Phil 3:9, and—for what it may be worth—in Eph 3:12. Space limitation precludes a full discussion of these passages here. I have already written rather extensively on Galatians, and we already have in print other excellent discussions of the material. On Phil 3:9, see Hooker, "ΠΙΣΤΙΣ ΧΡΙΣΤΟΥ," 331–33. On the Galatians passages, see Sam Williams, "Again *Pistis Christou*."[40] For the record, let it be said that I agree with Williams that there is a remarkable convergence of our conclusions, despite our different approaches and some differences in detail. (I do still hope, for example, to convince him that Paul understands Hab 2:4 as a messianic prophecy.) His treatments of Gal 2:16 and 3:23–25 are particularly helpful. For the purposes of discussion I would like to highlight a couple of points where Williams' analysis seems particularly illuminating, before adding a few thetic remarks of my own (along with one significant retraction of my earlier position) concerning these texts.

Williams's Exposition of ΠΙΣΤΙΣ ΧΡΙΣΤΟΥ in Galatians

Rather than conceding that ἡμεῖς εἰς Χριστὸν Ἰησοῦν ἐπιστεύσαμεν ("we believed in Christ Jesus," Gal 2:16) designates Christ as the "object" of faith—

37 Hooker, "ΠΙΣΤΙΣ ΧΡΙΣΤΟΥ," 341. Concerning the relation between justification and participation, see my comments in *Faith of Jesus Christ,* 250–54.

38 Another important part of the interpretative task would be to show how my interpretation of πίστις Ἰησοῦ Χριστοῦ fits—or fails to fit—the discussion of Christ, faith, and Israel in Rom 9:30–10:21. But that is a project for another day.

39 L. Keck, "'Jesus' in Romans," 454.

40 *CBQ* 49 (1987) 431–47.

as exegetes on both sides of this question have almost always done—Williams notes the parallel expression εἰς Χριστὸν ἐβαπτίσθητε ("you were baptized into Christ," Gal 3:27) and proposes that εἰς Χριστὸν Ἰησοῦν ἐπιστεύσαμεν should be understood, in the same way, as "transfer terminology."

> Just as Paul can say that one comes to be "in Christ" by being baptized into Christ, so he can say that one *believes* into Christ. In this second expression, too, *eis* implies movement, change, the transfer from one order of existence into another. Thus, to "believe into Christ" is the *means* by which one comes to be "in Christ." That means is adopting the life-stance, *pistis,* which marked Christ's own relationship to God, the life-stance of which he is the eschatological exemplar. To adopt this stance is to trust and obey Him who raised Jesus from the dead, to believe *like* Christ, and thereby to stand *with* Christ in that domain, that power field, created through his death and resurrection.[41]

The value of this interpretation is evident in the good sense it enables Williams to make out of Gal 3:23–25, where πίστις is said to be something that "has come" and can be "revealed." Williams explains as follows: "Faith comes in that Christ, the single *sperma* of Abraham, actualizes and exemplifies faith. In his trusting obedience, his complete reliance on God as trustworthy and true, Christ *reveals* faith." Consequently, "Christian faith is Christ-faith, that relationship to God which Christ exemplified, that life-stance which he actualized and which, because he lived and died, now characterizes the personal existence of everyone who lives in him. Christ is not the 'object' of such faith, however, but rather its supreme exemplar—indeed, its creator."[42]

Williams would concede, I think, that his explanations of the passages are broadly paraphrastic, intended to "unpack" the connotative freight of Paul's metaphorical language.[43] One might translate ἡμεῖς εἰς Χριστὸν Ἰησοῦν ἐπιστεύσαμεν in a less theologically loaded way, such as "we have placed our trust in Christ Jesus." It seems to me, nonetheless, that Williams's proposals have considerable heuristic power. Among other things, this approach helps to account for the way in which Paul's frequent appeals to the pattern of Christ's death and resurrection function in Pauline ethics.[44]

I would want, however, to engage Williams in discussion at several points. First of all, his way of describing πίστις Ἰησοῦ Χριστοῦ leans heavily towards what he calls a "minimal reading" of Paul's metaphorical language of participa-

41 Ibid.," 443.

42 Ibid., 438, 446.

43 See Williams' useful comments on the metaphorical character of Paul's language (ibid., 439).

44 On this theme in Paul's ethics, see R. B. Hays, *The Moral Vision of the New Testament: Community Cross, New Creation* (San Francisco: HarperSanFrancisco, 1996) 27–32.

tion in Christ, with the result that he downplays the vicarious elements of Paul's story of salvation. I would prefer to speak less of Jesus as "exemplar" and somewhat more of Jesus as the σπέρμα ("seed") whose apocalyptic destiny of death and resurrection reshapes the destiny of those who are now "in" him. (Note, for instance the remarkable claim of Gal 2:19b–20a: "I have been crucified with Christ; it is no longer I who live, but it is Christ who lives in me." Or again, Gal 6:14–15: ". . . the world has been crucified to me and I to the world. For neither circumcision nor uncircumcision is anything—but new creation!" One hardly does justice to this sort of language by speaking of Christ merely as an exemplar of faith.) This is, I think, a matter of emphasis rather than a substantive disagreement with Williams. Secondly, I would emphasize more firmly than Williams does that Paul's πίστις language is thematically intertwined with his exegesis of OT texts (especially Hab 2:4 and Gen 15:6) and with the affirmation of God's faithfulness to his covenant promises. But these are, again, points for ongoing discussion between interpreters who are in substantial agreement.

A Retraction

In *Faith of Jesus Christ,* I argued that Galatians 3 "depicts Abraham not as an exemplary paradigm for faith but as a representative figure in and through whom others are blessed."[45] This now seems to me to be an overly precise and rationalistic distinction; it may have a certain heuristic usefulness, but it posits a dichotomy where I suspect Paul saw none. I still hold that Gal 3:8–9 presents Abraham as a representative figure "in" whom the word of Scripture blesses those who are his children. But those who are his children stand in this relationship to him precisely insofar as they share his orientation towards God in faith (3:6–7). If we accept (for the sake of argument) Williams' reading of πίστις Ἰησοῦ Χριστοῦ, it becomes clear at once that there is a sense in which Abraham is the prefiguration both of Christ and of those who are in Christ. Christ is Abraham's σπέρμα ("seed," 3:16), and those who are Christ's are τοῦ Ἀβραὰμ σπέρμα ("seed of Abraham," 3:29). Abraham is the Biblical type to whom the promise was given, Christ the eschatological antitype through whom the promise becomes effectual for those who are "children of promise" (4:28), Abraham's sons (3:7).

This way of putting the matter resolves my concern about the fact that Abraham's theocentric faith is not properly analogous to christocentric Chris-

[45] *Faith of Jesus Christ,* 205–06.

tian faith. In fact, on this understanding, *both* Abraham and Jesus are paradigms for Christian faith and Christian faith itself is—properly understood—theocentric. If the analogies still do not work out in a neatly systematic fashion, that is because Paul's use of the Abraham story remains metaphorical in character. Abraham is a metaphor for the truth now disclosed in the faith of Jesus Christ.[46]

Observations on Gal 2:20 and 3:22

I would reiterate for the Group's attention a few exegetical points that must be addressed in any decision about the interpretation of πίστις Ἰησοῦ Χριστοῦ. For the sake of brevity I will formulate these as thesis statements.

Gal 2:20—

(1) The syntax of the sentence poses a difficulty for the objective genitive interpretation. The definite article τῇ sets the whole phrase to the end of the sentence (τοῦ υἱοῦ τοῦ θεοῦ . . . ὑπερ ἐμου ["the Son of God . . . for me"]) in apposition to πίστει ("faith"). The sentence should therefore be translated as follows: "I no longer live, but Christ lives in me; and the life I now live in the flesh I live by faith—that is, by the faith of the Son of God who loved me and gave himself for me." If Paul intended to designate "the Son of God" as the *object* of the verbal idea in the noun πίστει, he certainly chose a very odd way to do it.

(2) The aorist participles modifying τοῦ υἱοῦ τοῦ θὲοῦ ("the Son of God") serve to specify what Paul means when he refers to "the faith of the Son of God." Keck comments, "if Paul is writing about the *Son's* πίστις, then the christological clause exegetes this πίστις as Christ's self-giving."[47] The purpose of the sentence as a whole is to emphasize Christ's agency in shaping Paul's life.

(3) The syntactical parallelism between this sentence and Rom 5:15 should be carefully observed.

46 I hasten to head off protests by insisting that metaphor is constitutive of all thought and that to describe an assertion as "metaphorical" is not to denigrate its seriousness or truth. See, e.g., G. Lakoff and M. Johnson, *Metaphors We Live By* (Chicago: University of Chicago Press, 1980). For a particularly helpful treatment of metaphors in Pauline theology, see S. Kraftchick, "A Necessary Detour: Paul's Metaphorical Understanding of the Philippian Hymn," *HBT* 15/1 (1993) 1–37.

47 Keck, "'Jesus' in Romans," 455.

Rom 5:15 ἐν χάριτι τῇ (τοῦ ἑνὸς ἀνθρώπου Ἰησοῦ Χριστοῦ)
Gal 2:20 ἐν πίστει τῇ (τοῦ υἱοῦ τοῦ θεοῦ)[48]

In Rom 5:15, the grace of God is manifested in the grace of Jesus Christ; in Gal 2:20, the life of God is manifested in the faithfulness of Jesus Christ. The subjective/christological interpretation of the genitive in Gal 2:20 brings this theological parallelism into sharper focus: in both texts, Jesus' death is interpreted as the means through which God's lifegiving power is made effective in those for whom Jesus died.

Gal 3:22—

(1) The RSV made hash of this sentence by translating ἐκ as "to": ". . . that what was promised *to* faith in Jesus Christ might be given to those who believe." The NRSV offers only minimal improvement by changing "to" to "through." The sense of the passage is significantly clarified, however, if we read the phrase ἐκ πίστεως Ἰησοῦ Χριστοῦ ("by the faith of Jesus Christ") as a modifer of δοθῇ ("given") and translate, ". . . so that what was promised might be given through the faithfulness of Jesus Christ [i.e., his death on the cross for us, as in 2:20] to those who believe."

(2) This kerygmatic pattern, beginning from Christ's πίστις as source of salvation and moving to the human response of πίστις in return, corresponds precisely to the interpretation given above of Rom 1:17 (ἐκ πίστεως εἰς πίστιν ["by faith for faith"]) and Rom 3:22 (διὰ πίστεως Ἰησοῦ Χριστοῦ εἰς πάντας τοὺς πιστεύοντας ["through the faithfulness of Jesus Christ for all who believe"]). It also corresponds to the sequence of exposition in Gal 2:16, where the affirmation that a person is justified only διά πίστεως Ἰησοῦ Χριστοῦ ("through the faith of Jesus Christ") precedes the account of the answering response, καὶ ἡμεῖς εἰς Χριστὸυ Ἰησοῦν ἐπιστεύσαμεν ("we also placed our faith in Christ Jesus").

In sum, though the evidence of Galatians, taken by itself, is less compelling than the evidence of Romans, it appears that Paul's allusive formulations in Galatians are intended to recall his preaching to them about a Jesus who was "publicly exhibited as crucified" (Gal 3:1) in obedience to the will of the the Father (1:4, 4:4) in order to set free those who had been slaves (4:3–7, 5:1) and to bring them, in unity with him, into the blessing that had been promised

48 Rom 5:15: *by grace, that is of the one man Jesus Christ*
Gal 2:20: *by faith, that is of the Son of God*
For discussion of this parallelism, see Hays, *Faith of Jesus Christ,* 168.

to the children of Abraham (3:13–14, 29). Jesus' act of giving himself up to death is precisely the act of burden-bearing to which Paul refers when he speaks of "the πίστις of the Son of God who loved me and gave himself for me" (2:20).

IV. WHAT IS AT STAKE?

What difference does it make whose faith is meant in Paul's compressed πίστις formulations? Clearly, we keep having the argument not only because the evidence is sufficiently ambiguous to sustain vigorous disagreement but also because there are serious theological issues at stake here. It may be useful to articulate precisely what we take these issues to be, so that we can see what we are really arguing about. In conclusion, I offer a sketch of the theological questions that I see as critical consequences of the present debate.

(1) The relation between Christology and soteriology in Pauline theology. One of the driving motivations of my work on the πίστις Χριστοῦ question has been the desire to understand *how* the death of Jesus can be understood to be the source of salvation. In the standard Lutheran-Reformation accounts of justification by faith, there was always a puzzling arbitrariness, a lack of "inner connexion between Christology and the doctrine of justification."[49] I still cannot, I am sorry to say, offer a satisfactory elucidation of this mystery. George Lindbeck reminds me that it is not without reason that the church has never formally dogmatized any particular theory of the atonement. It does seem to me, however, that the christological interpretation of πίστις Ἰησοῦ Χριστοῦ offers a more promising approach to the problem than does the now-traditional anthropological (objective genitive) exegesis. Williams puts the point aptly: "Christians are justified by that faith which derives its very character from [Jesus'] self-giving obedience, that faith which was first his and has now become theirs."[50] That is what it means to say that the righteousness of God is revealed by faith for faith. By no means should this be understood to mean that Christians are saved by their own Herculean faithfulness; indeed, the central emphasis of the christological interpretation of πίστις Ἰησοῦ Χριστοῦ is precisely that we are saved by Jesus' faithfulness, not by our own cognitive disposition or confessional orthodoxy.

(2) The humanity of Jesus. Some opposition to the christological interpretation may be rooted in an implicitly docetic Christology. If Jesus was a real

49 G. Ebeling, *Word and Faith* (Philadelphia: Fortress, 1963) 203. A larger section of this passage is quoted as an epigraph to Chapter IV in *Faith of Jesus Christ.*

50 Williams, "Again *Pistis Christou,*" 444.

human being, it is hardly scandalous or inappropriate to speak of his faith/fidelity towards God. Did Paul think of the Jesus who died on the cross as a human being? Formulas such as Gal 4:4–5, Rom 1:3–4, and Phil 2:6–8 suggest that he did.

(3) Experiential-expressive vs. "narrative" theology. The besetting danger of the anthropological ("objective genitive") interpretation, with its emphasis on the salvific efficacy of individual faith, is its tendency to reduce the gospel to an account of individual religious experience, or even to turn faith into a bizarre sort of work, in which Christians jump through the entranceway of salvation by cultivating the right sort of spiritual disposition. (Luther no doubt stirs and curses in his tomb whenever his seed commit this theological blunder). The narrative account of salvation as won ὑπὲρ ἡμῶν ("for us") through the faithfulness of Jesus attempts to preclude this theological misstep, emphasizing not only the *extra nos* of salvation but also its public, corporate character. Bultmannians past and present fret, of course, that this emphasis on the narrative character of the gospel will objectify the word and render it inert.

(4) The cruciform character of Christian obedience. The particular interpretation of "the faith of Jesus Christ" that I have promulgated has the effect of stressing the pattern of correspondence between Jesus and the believing community: those who are in Christ are called to live the same sort of faith-obedience that he revealed. From a theological point of view, this has the distinct advantage of explaining how Pauline ethics is christologically grounded (Philippians, not discussed in this essay, is a lovely illustration of the point—see especially Phil 1:27–2:13); from a practical point of view, this has the distinct disadvantage of summoning us to live lives of costly self-sacrificial burden-bearing.[51]

(5) The righteousness of God as covenant-faithfulness. A theological judgment on this issue is not strictly tied to one's exegetical decision about πίστις Χριστοῦ, but I would suggest that there is some positive correlation between the christological ("subjective genitive") construal and an affirmation of the centrality of Israel/covenant themes in Paul's theology.[52] The key is to recognize that Paul's defense of God's faithfulness to Israel in Romans 3:3–5 (ἡ πίστις τοῦ θεοῦ = θεοῦ δικαιοσύνη) is linked to his affirmation that the righteousness of God (δικαιοσύνη θεοῦ) has been manifested through the faithfulness of Jesus Christ (διὰ πίστεως Ἰησοῦ Χριστοῦ, 3:21–22). The issues here are complicated, and their systematic interrelation still must be sorted out more

51 For a more extensive discussion, see R. B. Hays, "Christology and Ethics in Galatians: The Law of Christ," *CBQ* 49 (1987) 268–90; idem, *Moral Vision of the New Testament,* 27–32, 197.

52 For a preliminary attempt to articulate this correlation, see Wright, "Romans and the Theology of Paul" (in Hay and Johnson [eds.], *Pauline Theology, Volume III*), 37–38.

clearly: Dunn, with whom I am in agreement about the covenant-faithfulness motif, rejects the "faith of Christ" interpretation. Martyn, on the other hand, who emphatically disagrees with Dunn's account of Paul as a covenant theologian,[53] agrees with me about πίστις Ἰησοῦ Χριστοῦ. Future analysis of the πίστις Χριστοῦ problem should seek to show how the various interpretive options are related to these other major themes in Paul's proclamation.

So, as the debate continues, advocates of each position must pursue not only critical exegesis but also constructive theological work. The fire will test what what sort of work each has done.

POSTSCRIPT: REFLECTIONS ON THE DEBATE

The Pauline Theology Group's discussion of the πίστις Χριστοῦ issue was—seen in retrospect—not a trip through the purgatorial flames but rather a foretaste of the eschatological feast: friends and colleagues gathered at table, reflecting on Scripture together. Rarely have I found an academic *Auseinandersetzung* so enjoyable. J. D. G. Dunn's paper (in this volume) represents the best attempt I have seen to *argue* the case for the objective genitive interpretation (usually it is simply asserted apodictically). I remain unconvinced by his arguments, but the whole discussion has been advanced by this serious and edifying exchange of views. Thanks are due also to Paul Achtemeier for focusing the issues in a helpful way that facilitated the discussion. Looking back on the discussion, I would like to add several concluding comments to clarify issues that arose during the debate.

Responses to J. D. G. Dunn

(1) If Paul takes the expression ἐκ πίστεως from Hab 2:4—as we can infer from his citation of this text in Rom 1:17 and Gal 3:11—then Dunn's entire discussion of the presence or absence of the definite article in this expression is irrelevant. I note for the record that in the Group's discussion Dunn conceded this point.

(2) Dunn contends that Paul wants "to argue that Abraham's πίστις meant his faith . . . and therefore *not* his 'faithfulness.'"[54] If that is the case, why does he refer to Abraham in Gal 3:9 as ὁ πιστὸς Ἀβραάμ ("the faithful Abraham")?

53 "Events in Galatia," in Bassler (ed.), *Pauline Theology, Volume 1,* 160–79.

54 See below, p. 75.

(3) Indeed, Dunn's whole argument depends on making a clear distinction between "faith" and "faithfulness." I challenge him, however, to show that it was semantically possible in Hellenistic Greek to make such a conceptual distinction. The single word πίστις carries both connotations. Therefore, Dunn's distinction is anachronistic, a semantic fallacy.[55]

(4) Dunn asks "where is the other evidence outside the Pauline corpus" that the faithfulness of Jesus was "a recognized and central theme of early Christian preaching?"[56] This is a very odd question. Dunn's own paper sketches out the evidence of this theme in James, Revelation, and Hebrews. I would add Eph 3:12 and the Pastorals, and Ian G. Wallis has now provided extensive documentation for the prevalence of this motif in early Christianity, including patristic sources.[57] In light of this evidence, it appears that Paul would be exceptional if the theme were absent from his theology. (I would have expected the opposite critique: that the christological interpertation of πίστις Χριστοῦ reads the christology of these other texts, such as Hebrews, back into Paul!) Indeed, it seems to me that the force of Dunn's question can be turned back upon him: where is the NT evidence *outside* the Pauline corpus for an *objective* genitive usage of the expression πίστις Χριστοῦ = "faith in Christ"?

(5) Dunn asks whether I would accept any of the πίστις references in Galatians as denoting human believing in Christ. Since I have already noted that the verb ἐπιστεύσαμεν in Gal 2:16 is used to refer to "human believing in Christ," Dunn's question pertains to constructions using the noun. This is an interesting question, and not as easily answered as Dunn supposes. Let us for the moment set aside the contested constructions with 'Ιησοῦ Χριστοῦ or equivalent (2:16,20; 3:22) and consider the other appearances of the noun πίστις in Galatians. In several cases, πίστις functions by metnoymy for "the gospel," referring to the content of what is preached and believed (1:23; 3:2,5; 3:23,25; 6:10). In one case, the noun appears in a list of "the fruit of the Spirit" (5:22). All of the other occurrences appear in the prepositional phrases ἐκ πίστεως (3:7–9, 11–12, 24; 5:5) and διὰ τῆς πίστεως (3:14,26). To be sure, several of

55 A similar reservation may be lodged against Paul Meyer's careful attempt (in Group discussion) to distinguish between "trust" and "faithfulness." Meyer wants to resist the notion of Jesus as "Promethean believer" by interpreting Paul's language to refer to Jesus as sufferer: his πίστις is his steadfast trust in God in the face of death on a cross. This formulation no doubt captures an important part of the meaning of πίστις Χριστοῦ for Paul, but I do not understand either how such an interpretation can be construed as dissonant with the christology of Hebrews (as Meyer suggested it was) or how one can limit the semantic range of πίστις to *exclude* the connotations of fidelity/faithfulness.

56 See below, p. 70.

57 Wallis, *Faith of Jesus Christ in Early Christian Traditions* (see n. 2, above).

these passages do refer to what Dunn calls "human believing"; this is clearest in 3:7–9, 3:14, 26, 5:5, and 5:26. In none of these cases, however, is an "object" of faith designated, although the linkage between 3:6 and 3:7 suggests that οἱ ἐκ πίστεως ("those of faith") must, like Abraham, be those who have faith in *God*. Nothing is said in 3:7–9—or in any of these other passages—about "faith in Christ." Thus, to respond directly to Dunn's question, I would say that there are no cases in Galatians where the noun πίστις unambiguously denotes "human believing *in Christ*." The fact that Paul repeatedly uses the noun without a specified object suggests—as I have argued above—that he is thinking primarily of the trust toward God that was prefigured by Abraham and definitively enacted by Jesus Christ in such a way that it now shapes the life of all who are "in Christ." As Paul writes in Gal 3:22, the fulfillment of the promise is given "*by* the faith(fulness) of Jesus Christ (ἐκ πίστεως Ἰησοῦ Χριστοῦ) *to* those who believe (τοῖς πιστεύουσιν)." The faith(fulness) of Jesus Christ is the means of the transmission of the blessing to others who now participate in his life and therefore reflect the same trusting relationship to God that broke into human experience through his death and resurrection (3:23,25).[58]

(6) The most crucial difference between Dunn and me lies in the extent to which we are willing to read Paul's language as *multivalent* and *metaphorical*. Whereas Dunn wants to press at every point for a univocal sense, I see Paul using language with connotative complexity. Some of Paul's πίστις expressions are multivalent; for example, if we ask whether in Gal 3:14 Paul means that we receive the promise through Christ's faithfulness or through our faith, the best answer is probably, "Yes, both." The expression διὰ τῆς πίστεως enfolds both semantic possibilities.

Furthermore, the noun πίστις does not have precisely the same sense in every case. Πίστις θεοῦ, πίστις Χριστοῦ, πίστις Ἀβραάμ, and πίστις ἡμῶν ("the faithfulness of God, the faith[fulness] of Christ, the faith of Abraham, and our faith") are not identical; rather, they are *analogically* related to one another. The "mapping" of one concept onto the other is not strictly isomorphic, because the correspondences are metaphorical.[59] As πίστις is predicated of us rather than of Christ, its meaning shifts slightly because the relation between Christ and believers is one of analogy rather than simple identity. Similarly, when Paul uses the language of crucifixion with Christ (Gal 5:24, 6:14), carrying the dying of Jesus (2 Cor 4:10–12), having the mindset of Christ Jesus (Phil

58 It should be said clearly that for Paul, πίστις Χριστοῦ refers to Jesus' obedience to death on the cross: in other words, the meaning of the phrase is focused on the kerygma's narration of his self-giving death, not on the whole ministry of Jesus of Nazareth. This narrower punctiliar sense—focused on the cross—is the only meaning supported by Paul's usage.

59 For a helpful discussion of metaphorical "mapping," see Kraftchick, "Necessary Detour."

2:5–11), and imitation of Christ (1 Cor 11:1, 1 Thess 1:6), he does not mean that our actions mimic the example of Jesus in a woodenly literal way; rather, he means that there is a significant metaphorical correspondence between the life-pattern defined by Christ's death and the suffering experienced by those who are in Christ. The precise nature of this correspondence must be discerned in the contingent circumstances of each believing community. The relation between our faith and the faith of Christ is similarly metaphorical: our faith answers and reflects his—indeed, *participates in* his—because according to Paul it is God's design for us "to be conformed to the image of his Son" (Rom 8:29).

4 ONCE MORE, ΠΙΣΤΙΣ ΧΡΙΣΤΟΥ

James D. G. Dunn
University of Durham

1. INTRODUCTION

THE REVITALISATION of the old debate on the meaning of the Pauline phrase πίστις Χριστοῦ, and particularly as a transatlantic debate, has been one of the most stimulating features of the renewed interest in Pauline theology. The earlier phase was largely an in-house German debate, though W. H. P. Hatch was a prominent contributor.[1] The view that it meant "faith in Christ" (objective genitive) was the dominant opinion. But among advocates of the subjective genitive ("faith of Christ") was G. Kittel.[2] And notable variations included J. Haußleiter's genitivus auctoris (faith effected by Christ), A. Deissmann's genitivus mysticus (faith experienced in mystical communion with Christ), E. Wißmann's genitivus confessionis (confessing faith, acceptance of the Christian message), and O. Schmitz's "characterizing genitive" ("Christ-faith").[3]

The opening blast of a new round of debate was sounded in Britain in the 1950s, initially by A. G. Hebert, on the basis of the Hebrew equivalent of πίστις = אֱמוּנָה "faithfulness" (hence the "faithfulness of Christ"),[4] followed by T. F. Torrance,[5] responded to by C. F. D. Moule,[6] and squelched by

1 W. H. P. Hatch, *The Pauline Idea of Faith in its Relation to Jewish and Hellenistic Religion* (HTS 2; Cambridge, MA: Harvard University Press, 1917).

2 Most recently H. W. Schmidt, *Der Brief des Paulus an die Römer* (THKNT 6; Berlin Evangelische, 1963) 66.

3 See the brief review of the debate in K. Kertelge, '*Rechtfertigung' bei Paulus* (NtA 3; Münster: Aschendorff, 1967, ^{2}1971) 162–6; also R. B. Hays, *The Faith of Christ* (SBLDS 56; Chico: Scholars Press, 1983) 158–62.

4 A. G. Hebert, "'Faithfulness' and 'Faith,'" *Theology* 58 (1955) 373–9.

5 T. F. Torrance, "One Aspect of the Biblical Conception of Faith," *ExpT* 68 (1956–57) 111–4, 221–2.

6 C. F. D. Moule, "The Biblical Conception of 'Faith'," *ExpT* 68 (1956–57) 157, 222.

J. Barr.[7] But the cudgels were taken up again on behalf of a subjective genitive reading in the 1960s, particularly on the north American side of the Atlantic, initially by R. N. Longenecker, G. M. Taylor and G. Howard,[8] and with a substantial wave of support in the 1980s,[9] which has swept the interpretation back across the Atlantic.[10]

It would be natural at this point to note and review the main arguments in favour of the renewedly popular "faith(fulness) of Christ" interpretation. But that is another's brief. Mine is to restate the case for the objective genitive interpretation—"faith in Christ"—though in so doing I will naturally have to address at least the principal arguments brought in favour of a subjective genitive reading. To this task I therefore turn. But first a reminder of the basic data.

As is well known, the phrase itself appears seven times in three of the Pauline letters

πίστις Ἰησοῦ Χριστοῦ—Rom 3:22; Gal. 3:22;
πίστις Ἰησοῦ—Rom 3:26;
πίστις Χριστοῦ Ἰησοῦ—Gal 2:16;
πίστις Χριστοῦ—Gal. 2:16; Phil 3:9;
πίστις τοῦ υἱοῦ τοῦ θεοῦ—Gal 2:20.

We should mention also Eph. 3:12—". . . Christ Jesus our Lord, in whom we have boldness and access in confidence διὰ τῆς πίστεως αὐτοῦ."

We will proceed by looking first at the form of the phrase itself. And since there is some danger of treating it in too isolated a fashion, we will then look

7 J. Barr, *The Semantics of Biblical Language* (London: Oxford University Press, 1961) 187–205.

8 R. N. Longenecker, *Paul, Apostle of Liberty* (New York Harper & Row, 1964) 149–52; G. M. Taylor, "The Function of πίστις Χριστοῦ in Galatians," *JBL* 85 (1966) 58–76; G. Howard, "On the 'Faith of Christ,'" *HTR* 60 (1967) 459–65; note also M. Barth, "The Faith of the Messiah," *Hey J* 10 (1969) 363–70, with further bibliography 364–5 n.2; D. W. B. Robinson, "'Faith of Jesus Christ'—A New Testament Debate," *Reformed Theological Review* 29 (1970) 71–81.

9 S. K. Williams, "The 'Righteousness of God" in Romans," *JBL* 99 (1980) 272–8; also "Again *Pistis Christou*," *CBQ* 49 (1987) 431–47; L. T. Johnson, "Romans 3.21–26 and the Faith of Jesus," *CBQ* 44 (1982) 77–90; Hays, *Faith* ch. 4; S. K. Stowers, "'Εκ πίστεως and διὰ τῆς πίστεως in Romans 3.30," *JBL* 108 (1989) 665–74; L. E. Keck, "'Jesus' in Romans," *JBL* 108 (1989) 443–60, here 452–7; R. N. Longenecker, *Galatians* (WBC 41; Dallas Word, 1990) 87–8; otherwise D. M. Hay, "Pistis as 'Ground for Faith' in Hellenized Judaism and Paul,'" *JBL* 108 (1989) 461–76, here 473–5. The issue came to the fore in the Pauline Theology Group at the SBL meeting in 1988 but was postponed for full discussion to the 1991 meeting.

10 M. D. Hooker, "Πίστις Χριστοῦ," *NTS* 35 (1989) 321–42, the Presidential Address delivered in Cambridge at the 1989 SNTS meeting, reprinted in *From Adam to Christ. Essays on Paul* (Cambridge University, 1990) 165–86; G. N. Davies, *Faith and Obedience in Romans. A Study of Romans 1–4* (JSNTS 39; Sheffield: JSOT, 1990) 106–10; and now I. G. Wallis, *The Faith of Jesus Christ in Early Christian Traditions* (SNTSMS 84; Cambridge: University Press, 1995).

at the way the phrase functions within the context and flow of the argument of each of the three undisputed Pauline letters in which the phrase (πίστις plus genitive referring to Christ) occurs. We will take the letters in their most likely chronological sequence—Galatians, Romans, Philippians. As a shorthand I will use πίστις Χριστοῦ throughout when referring as a whole to the five variations listed above.

2. THE FORM OF THE PHRASE

There are three grammatical or formal points which should be clarified and put in their proper perspective at the beginning.

2.1 *The force of the genitive construction.* There is, of course, something seductively attractive about taking the phrase in its most literal English translation—"the faith of Christ." But here the seeming univocal meaning of the English genitive in no way reflects the inherent ambiguity of the Greek when the phrase is taken on its own. If lingering doubts remain we need simply recall various related instances. (1) The parallel phrase, ἡ γνῶσις Χριστοῦ Ἰησοῦ, is used in close proximity to one of the seven occurrences of our phrase (Phil 3: 8–9). No one would think to take "the knowledge of Christ Jesus" as any other than an objective genitive.[11] In this case the English form allows the objective force which seems to be excluded from "the faith of Christ." Similarly with ζῆλος θεοῦ in Rom 10:2, which clearly means "zeal *for* God."[12] (2) In Mark 11:22 we read ἔχετε πίστιν θεοῦ, which can hardly be taken in the sense, "Hold the faith of God," and must mean "Have faith *in* God" (cf. the parallel in Matt 21:21—ἐὰν ἔχετε πίστιν καὶ μὴ διακριθῆτε).[13] Here again, despite the attractiveness of a literal English rendering, no one would think to take the "faith of God" as anything other than an objective genitive;[14] compare also

11 But see now Wallis, *Faith,* 122–3.

12 C. F. D. Moule, *An Idiom Book of New Testament Greek* (Cambridge University, 1953) 40.

13 But Wallis, *Faith,* 71 nevertheless asserts that there are no unambiguous cases in the NT where πίστις + genitive must be interpreted objectively.

14 Hays, *Faith,* 164, rightly notes that Mark 11:22 clearly establishes that πίστις plus objective genitive is NT, first-generation Christian usage. LSJ's failure to note any instance of πίστις plus objective genitive (Robinson 71–2) is of no consequence, since from the beginning Christianity developed its own distinctive "faith" vocabulary—πιστεύειν ἐπί/εἰς. The question, then, is whether and in what way πίστις plus genitive reflects that development. Hays is somewhat disingenuous when he argues that πίστις plus genitive meaning "faith in" cannot be demonstrated in the Pauline corpus (*Faith,* 164), since "faith in Christ" is the only form in which we might expect to find this distinctive Christian usage in Paul, and that is the very phrase which is at issue. More serious for Hays's case is the absence of a verbal equivalent to his understanding of πίστις Χριστοῦ, i.e., "Christ believed"; see further §3.3 below.

Acts 3:16, ἐπὶ τῇ πίστει τοῦ ὀνόματος αὐτοῦ, "by faith in his name," and 2 Thess 2:13, ἐν ἁγιασμῷ πνεύματος καὶ πίστει ἀληθείας, "by sanctification of the Spirit and faith in the truth."

We must therefore not be misled by the inflexibility of the literal English translation of our phrase, the "faith of Christ." And no one I assume would wish to argue on this basis.[15] There is, then, presumably, no dispute that the syntactical relation of the two words, πίστις and Χριστοῦ, tells us nothing to resolve our disagreement.

2.2 *The absence of the definite article.* What is the significance of the lack of the definite article in the phrase—πίστις Χριστοῦ, rather than ἡ πίστις Χριστοῦ.[16] I have in mind here the observation of E. D. Burton that when πίστις is accompanied by a subjective genitive "the article is . . . almost invariably present."[17] The point is weakened since the great bulk of the phrases cited by Burton speak of "your faith."[18] But we should note three cases which may give Burton's point force for us. (1) James 2:1—ἔχετε τὴν πίστιν τοῦ κυρίου ἡμῶν. In this classic example of Jewish Christian paraenesis (James), it is very plausible to read the phrase as a subjective genitive—"you hold the faith which our Lord Jesus Christ himself displayed."[19] (2) Rev 2:13—"you do not deny my faith (οὐκ ἠρνήσω τὴν πίστιν μου)," says the exalted Christ. (3) Rev 14:12—"those who keep the commandments and the faith of Jesus (τὴν πίστιν Ἰησοῦ)." In each case we need to remind ourselves that the faithfulness of Christ (ὁ πιστός) is a particular theme of the seer (Rev 1:5; 3:14; 19:11), as, it would appear, of the more characteristically Jewish Christian documents in the NT (Heb 2:17; 3:2; 12:2).[20] So once again it is very likely that in each case the genitive is, if anything, subjective.

15 For further examples of the objective genitive see J. H. Moulton, *A Grammar of New Testament Greek,* Vol. III by N. Turner (Edinburgh: T. & T. Clark, 1963) 211–2.

16 The lack of a second definite article, τοῦ Χριστοῦ, can be adequately explained by the fact that Χριστός by this stage, in Greek-speaking Christianity, regularly functioned as a proper name.

17 E. D. Burton, *Galatians* (ICC; Edinburgh; T. & T. Clark, 1921) 482. The point is taken up by A. J. Hultgren, "*The Pistis Christou* Formulation in Paul," *NovT* 22 (1980) 248–63, here 253, though with a less cautious formulation ("invariably present").

18 This is the basis of the main critique of Hultgren by Williams, "Again," 432–3.

19 It may be argued that ἔχετε is more naturally translated, "you hold on to your (own) faith in our Lord" (cf. 2:18), and that the definite article refers back to the previously mentioned "faith" (1.3, 6). On the other hand, our third example (Rev 14:12) speaks of "those who keep . . . the faith of Jesus," where "keeping" is closely parallel to "holding."

20 This consideration has to be weighed against Hays, *Faith,* 187 n.113, who follows Robinson in regarding the genitives of these texts as "broadly adjectival," denoting "the (Christian) faith."

We should also simply mention Rom 3:3, τὴν πίστιν τοῦ θεοῦ, "the faithfulness of God," a clear example of the definite article with the subjective genitive. And perhaps we should include Col 2:12, διὰ τῆς πίστεως τῆς ἐνεργείας τοῦ θεοῦ, which Hebert translates "through the faithfulness of the working of God."[21]

It would appear, then, that Burton's observation has some force. (a) The genitive phrase, "the faith of Christ" *was* used within earliest Christian circles in reference to "the faith(fulness) of Christ" (subjective genitive). But in the three arguably most clear examples which we have, the phrase takes the form, "*the* faith of Christ," where quite properly and naturally the definite article denotes the particular faith(fulness) referred to—that of Christ. Just as in the regular usage which Burton noted—"the faith, that is, of you." (b) In contrast, it is probably more significant than at first appears that *all* the phrases which come into dispute in Paul *lack* the definite article. The fact that it is *all* the disputed cases does suggest that we are confronted by a regular pattern of speech, where the lack of the definite article is in itself almost sufficient to indicate that what is in view is *faith* (that is, faith as exercised by believers in general), rather than *the faith* (that is, the particular faith of Jesus himself).[22]

There are, however, two exceptions to the above patterns. One is Eph 3:12, cited above. Here it may be significant, even decisive, that the definite article *is* used—διὰ τῆς πίστεως αὐτοῦ. Should we therefore translate, "through the faith of him," that is, through Christ's faithfulness?[23] If so, it would simply confirm that Burton's observation is sound and that the definite article was the accepted way of indicating that the genitive was subjective in force. But in that case it may be all the more significant that the undisputed, or earlier (if you prefer) Pauline usage is so consistently anarthrous—a recognized way of signalling that the accompanying genitive is objective.

The other exception is potentially more disruptive of the pattern which seems thus far to have emerged. In Rom 4:16 Paul speaks clearly of "the faith of Abraham," where the Greek is again anarthrous—"the one who is ἐκ πίστεως Ἀβραάμ." Here is a key example which indicates that Burton was

21 Hebert, "Faithfulness," 377.

22 Whether it is also significant that the clearest references to Christ's faithfulness come in the more characteristically Jewish writings of the NT (James, Hebrews and the Apocalypse of John), and that, in contrast, the anarthrous Pauline phrase comes in passages where Paul is in contentious dialogue with Jewish Christian views, is a point to which we will have to return.

23 So particularly M. Barth, *Ephesians* (AB 34; New York: Doubleday, 1974) 347; Wallis, *Faith,* 128–32. But note the following reference to "the faith" in 3:17, where the definite article points back to the already mentioned faith of 3:12, and where the reference can hardly be other than to the believers' faith through which Christ dwells in their hearts.

right to qualify his conclusion that the definite article "almost invariably" denotes the subjective genitive.[24] Whether it merely weakens the force of Burton's point ("almost invariably"), however, or disrupts it entirely, remains unclear. A factor of substantive importance in this case (Rom 4:16) is bound to be the fact that the phrase ἐκ πίστεως is a major *leit motiv* in Romans.[25] It must be judged quite likely that Paul unconsciously slipped into (or maintained) the anarthrous use, because in his train of thought in this letter that was his principal prepositional phrase for "justifying faith."[26] It may well be, therefore, that Rom 4:16 should be regarded as a genuine exception (for understandable reasons) to what otherwise was an almost invariable rule within earliest Christian speech.

2.3 *Equivalent phrases.* Finally, we need to clarify the possible significance of potentially synonymous phrases. The deutero-Paulines seem to have developed the formula, "faith *in* Christ Jesus (πίστις [anarthrous] ἡ ἐν Χριστῷ Ἰησοῦ)" (1 Tim 3:13; 2 Tim 1:13; 3:15). An earlier version of it is Eph 1:15—"your faith in the Lord Jesus (τὴν καθ' ὑμᾶς πίστιν ἐν τῷ κυρίῳ Ἰησοῦ)—the definite article in this case required, of course, to indicate the particular faith (καθ' ὑμᾶς) in view. This could be significant, since it might indicate that a different phrase was current to denote "faith in Christ," and thus suggest that by "faith of Christ" Paul must have meant something else (Christ's faith). The difficulty of course is precisely that all the instances of the "in" phrase belong to the deutero-Pauline corpus and thus provide no evidence of Paul's own usage or of usage current at the time of Paul.[27] The deutero-Pauline usage therefore gives us no assistance in resolving the force of the genitive constructions in Paul.[28]

24 The issue does not hang on the genitive construction (see §2.1), as Keck, "'Jesus,'" 456 unwisely argues, but on the significance of the absence of the definite article.

25 Rom 1:17 (twice); 3:26, 30; 4:16 (twice); 5:1; 9:30, 32; 10:6; 14:23 (twice).

26 I use "justifying faith" as the shorthand for the faith summed up in Rom 5:1—"Therefore, having been justified ἐκ πίστεως . . .". The alternative, διὰ πίστεως, appears only four times, and all in the one section of the argument—Rom 3:22, 25, 30, 31.

27 The apparently close parallel of Gal 3:26 is almost certainly to be taken as sequential rather than as integrated prepositional phrases—"for you all are sons of God, through faith, in Christ Jesus," rather than in the deutero-Pauline sense, "through faith in Christ Jesus" (πάντες γὰρ υἱοὶ θεοῦ ἐστε διὰ τῆς πίστεως ἐν Χριστῷ Ἰησοῦ); so most, e.g., H. Schlier, *Der Brief an die Galater* (KEK; Göttingen: Vandenhoeck & Ruprecht, [4]1965) 171 and Hays, *Faith,* 169–70. Similarly with the phrasing in Rom 3:25—ἱλαστήριον διὰ (τῆς) πίστεως ἐν τῷ αὐτοῦ αἵματι—"an atonement, through faith, in his blood"; διὰ (τῆς) πίστεως is usually taken now as a Pauline insertion into a pre-Pauline formula (see e.g., the bibliography and discussion reviewed in my *Romans* [WBC 38; Dallas: Word, 1988] 161–4). It may indeed be the case that a casual reading of these texts was what gave rise to the deutero-Pauline use. See further below nn. 43 and 64.

28 The double variation from standard Pauline usage, in Eph 1:15 and 3:12, is typical of the slight distance from Pauline thought which convinces most scholars that Ephesians stems from the circle of Paul's (immediate) associates, after his death, rather than from Paul himself.

Much the same is true of the further variation Col 2:5—"the firmness of your faith in Christ (τῆς εἰς Χριστὸν πίστεως ὑμῶν)". The problem is that ἡ εἰς Χριστὸν πίστις is a hapax legomenon in Paul, and though the verbal equivalent is used in the undisputed Paulines (Rom 10:14?; Gal 2:16; Phil 1:29), the issue of the Pauline authorship of Colossians muddies the discussion and makes it difficult to place much weight on the Col 2:5 usage either way.[29]

The only other variation is Phlm 5—τὴν πίστιν, ἥν ἔχεις πρὸς τὸν κύριον Ἰησοῦν. But it is difficult to know how much weight to put on this isolated example.

All we can say, then, is that the deutero-Paulines developed a way of speaking of "faith in Christ" which Paul had not used. The absence of such usage from the undisputed Paulines, with the exception of Phlm 5, may, however, suggest that Paul did not need to use such forms because he had his own form—πίστις Χριστοῦ.[30] If faith was such an important motif for Paul, the absences of such phrases leaves the proponents of the subjective genitive with a somewhat surprising conclusion: *either* πίστις Χριστοῦ is Paul's way of speaking of "faith in Christ," *or* Paul, for some yet to be explained reason, seems to have *avoided* speaking of "faith in Christ."

2.4 In short, not too much significance can be read out of the form of the phrase; though the lack of the definite article does seem to give some support to the inference that whoever's the faith in view in the Pauline phrase, πίστις Χριστοῦ, it would *not* be understood in earliest Christian circles as "the faith of Christ"; and the relative absence from the undisputed Paulines of other phrases denoting "faith in Christ" may indicate that πίστις Χριστοῦ filled that function for Paul.

3. GALATIANS

3.1 If I understand the arguments in favour of the subjective genitive reading of πίστις Χριστοῦ aright, there are two principal grounds for taking it as a reference to "the faith of Christ" in Galatians. Here and in the following section I refer particularly to the treatments of Hays and Hooker, the two most recent

29 Elsewhere in the NT it occurs only in Acts 20:21, 24:24 and 26:18 (cf. 1 Pet 1:21).

30 Hultgren "The *Pistis Christou* Formulation," 254. Williams, "Again" 433–5, surprisingly argues that Paul does not see Christ as the object of faith; but see the two preceding paragraphs, and Williams's attempt to turn πιστεύειν εἰς Χρίστον to his own account (442–3). See also below n. 60.

and thoroughgoing expositions of the view.[31] (1) In three of the four occurrences in Galatians there is reference also to the act of believing, using the verb πιστεῦειν (Gal 2:16; 3:22); "another reference to the faith of believers would be redundant in a sentence which already refers to those who believe."[32] (2) The parallel with Abraham which dominates Gal 3:6–9 strongly suggests that πίστις Χριστοῦ is intended as a parallel to the reference to Abraham's faith. Hays develops the point in terms of a representative-christology—". . . Jesus Christ, like Abraham, is justified ἐκ πίστεως and . . . we, as a consequence, are justified *in* him."[33] For Hooker (followed by Wallis) the logic of Paul's argument is clear. The talk is of a sonship of Abraham understood in terms of sharing Abraham's faith. The logic indicates that *the* son of Abraham, Christ (Gal 3:16), also had faith, and that for others to share in that sonship they must share in the faith of the one true seed. This, she maintains, is the force of Gal 3:22: that the promise made to Abraham on the basis of faith is now fulfilled on the basis of Jesus Christ's faith.

3.2 Hays's argument is in danger of overkill. On the surface it seems that he merely wishes to deny that the other references in Galatians 3 point to Christ as the object of faith. In 3:2 and 5, πίστις denotes the Christian faith.[34] In 3:6–9 οἱ ἐκ πίστεως probably has the connotation, "those who are given life on the basis of (Christ's) faith."[35] In 3:11, ὁ δίκαιος ἐκ πίστεως ζήσεται (Hab 2:4), the reference is once again to Christ's faith,[36] the implication being (though Hays does not spell it out clearly) that this conclusion carries with it the ἐκ πίστεως of 3:12 and the διὰ τῆς πίστεως of 3:14.[37] In 3:23, 25 the "coming of the faith" is virtually identified with the coming of Christ himself,[38] with the consequence that the ἐκ πίστεως of 3:24 (as also 5:5) is best understood as referring, once again to "the faith (that is, of Jesus Christ)."[39]

31 Hays, *Faith,* 164–70; Hooker, "πίστις Χριστοῦ," 170–5. See also particularly Barth, "Faith of Messiah," 367–8, Williams, "Again," and Wallis, *Faith.*

32 Hooker "πίστις Χριστοῦ," 173. So also, e.g., Williams, "Righteousness," 273–4; Keck "'Jesus,'" 454, though I am puzzled at Keck's claim that "faith in *Christ*" (my emphasis) "separates Christ from justification, which now depends solely on human believing"; Wallis, *Faith,* 71 (three references in as many lines would be "strained").

33 Hays, *Faith,* 165–6; he argues back from Eph 3:12, without raising the issue of the significance of the definite article (see §2.2 above).

34 Hays, *Faith,* 143–9. Cf. 1:23.

35 Hays, *Faith,* 200–2.

36 Hays, *Faith,* 150–7; similarly Wallis *Faith,* 111–2.

37 Hays, *Faith,* 206–12.

38 Cf. 3:26 (Hays, *Faith,* 169–70).

39 Hays, *Faith,* 228–32.

Thus, almost without realising it, we find that every reference to πίστις in the body of Galatians has been swept up into the defence of the subjective genitive. On Hays's logic even 3:2, 5 and 5:6 would most obviously be taken as a reference to Christ's faith: "the message of faith," that is, of Christ's faith (3:2, 5; also 1:23); "faith working through love," that is, Christ's faithfulness coming to effect through his (or God's) love (5:6).[40] More to the point, on Hays's thesis we have no clear reference to the "faith" of believers. There are two such references using the equivalent verb (2:16 and 3:22). But Hays leaves us with no noun counterpart, no noun to denote the Galatians' act of believing. Hays's thesis vacuums up every relevant reference to "faith" in Galatians in order to defend the subjective genitive reading of 2:16, 20 and 3:22.[41] This is nothing short of astonishing. It now appears that a text (Galatians), which has provided such a powerful charter of "justifying faith" for Christian self-understanding, *nowhere* clearly speaks of that "faith."[42]

Two questions cannot be avoided. (1) If "faith" as a reference to *Christ's* faith filled such an overwhelmingly prominent role in Galatians, why does it appear at best fleetingly elsewhere?[43] On Hays's thesis Paul could speak of it as something well known, which would require no explanation when first mentioned in what is at least potentially ambiguous phrasing (2:16), an understanding of

40 "Through love" is occasionally taken as referring to God's love (G. S. Duncan, *The Epistle to the Galatians* [Moffatt; London: Hodder, 1934] 157–8), despite the obvious elaboration in 5:13–14 of the thought in 5:6.

41 Only 5:22, where πίστις is normally taken as denoting "trustworthiness" rather than "faith," would be exempt.

42 To argue that the phrase includes reference both to Christ's faith and to faith in Christ (so particularly Williams, "Righteousness," 276–8; "Again," 437, 443–6) is surely to overload it; to be meaningful to his readers such a phrase would have to be unpacked by Paul not only in terms of Christians believing (which he does) but also in terms of Christ believing (which he does not).

43 "Nowhere does the apostle speak plainly of Jesus as believing, trusting, or displaying *pistis* as 'faithfulness'" (Hay, "Pistis," 474). So far as Romans is concerned, Hays limits his case to Rom 3:21–26 (*Faith,* 170–4). If Rom 3:25 includes a pre-Pauline formulation, of which διὰ τῆς πίστεως was an integral part (so particularly S. K. Williams, *Jesus' Death as Saving Event* [Missoula: Scholars, 1975] 41–51; though see above n.27), it could be argued that πίστις there (in the pre-Pauline formula) referred to the well-known concept of Christ's faith (but see below n. 66); though once again the thesis assumes an established and widespread usage which surpisingly (if so established and widespread) is otherwise hardly attested. And at the level of *Paul's* use of the formula, the echo of the διὰ τῆς πίστεως in 3:30 and 31 hardly encourages the suggestion that Paul referred the πίστις in any case to *Jesus'* faith (despite Stowers; see below n. 63), since the "faith" in question is clearly the medium by which justification comes to the believer, as in the case of Abraham (Rom 4). We should perhaps note that Hays does *not* take the "faith" references in 3:30–31 as referring to Christ's faith in his "'Have we found Abraham to be our forefather according to the flesh?' A Reconsideration of Rom 4:1," *NovT* 27 (1985) 76–98.

the Christian message which could be summed up simply in the word "faith," that is, the faith of Christ (1:23; 3:2, 5, 23, 25). But where is the other evidence from outside the Pauline corpus that this was a recognized and central theme of early Christian preaching and self-understanding?[44] Where in the Gospel tradition, by means of which the first Christians maintained the memory of Christ's ministry, is there any emphasis on "the faith of Christ?" The fact that Hays's thesis makes Galatians stand out as so exceptional within the wide sweep of earliest Christianity must surely sound a warning note; the thesis is in danger of self-condemnation by *reductio ad absurdum.*

(2) Too little asked is the further question What does "the faith of Christ" mean? To what does it refer? The answer is hardly clear.[45] The ministry of Jesus as a whole? The death of Christ in particular? The continuing ministry of the exalted Christ in heaven? Neither the first nor the last of these are prominent themes in Paul. And while a reference to the death of Christ would fit well within Paul's theology, it is not clear how that would explain the διά forms of the phrase in 2:16 and 3:14, 26. What would Paul mean by saying "through Christ's faithfulness" in his life and/or on the cross? A more likely expression of the point would be διά plus accusative ("on account of"), equivalent to ἐκ plus the genitive ("on the basis of"), rather than διά plus genitive ("through" the medium of). It is true that Paul has a concept of the death of Christ as in some sense an ongoing event, if that is the right way to put it (cf. 2:19; 6:14), but he never expresses it in a διά formula. And if the reference is to the exalted Christ, then we would expect Paul to speak of Christ directly, rather than of his faith:

44 The verses reviewed in §2.2 (James 2:1 apart) do not provide strong evidence for first-generation Christian usage. Hooker, "πίστις Χριστοῦ," 178–9 suggests that the πίστις of 2 Cor 4:13 refers to Christ's faith. But a reference back to Christ's death and resurrection under that motif would be surprising here. (1) The "belief" is more naturally linked to the immediately associated Psalm quotation, "I believed"; elsewhere it is Paul's custom to quote scripture *after* an assertion, to back up that assertion. (2) The fuller phrase is "the same Spirit of faith" and is more naturally referred to the Spirit inspiring (or the spirit inspired to write) the words of the psalm. (3) The belief in the first clause is presumably the believing of the last clause; "the same spirit/Spirit" is the inspiring Spirit (inspired spirit) which brings belief to speech and witness. See further, e.g., V. P. Furnish, *2 Corinthians* (AB 32A; New York: Doubleday, 1984) 257–8.

45 Williams, "Again," illustrates the vagueness of the phrase as used in the current debate. At 444 he takes it to refer to "Christ's own openness to God," "the mode of personal existence which Christ pioneered" (thus unconsciously slipping into the language and motifs of Hebrews rather than of Paul). But in commenting on Gal 2:19–20 he takes "the faith of the Son of God" as defined by the relative clauses, "who loved me and gave himself for me" (445). And later on he defines it as "that relationship to God which Christ exemplified, that life stance which he actualized" (446)—but is this Paul?

thus in 6:14, δι' οὗ referring to Christ ("through whom"), as also in Rom 1:5 and 5:11.

I therefore find myself quite unconvinced by Hays's thesis.

3.3 Hooker does not try to be so ambitious, limiting the thrust of her exposition to the key reference 3:22 in context. For her the pressure to read 3:22 as a reference to Christ's faith grows out of the argument of 3:15ff. that Christ is the one true seed of Abraham. For her the logic is that Christ must therefore have shared Abraham's faith, have believed as Abraham believed. But is this Paul's logic? I think not.

Had it been so, Paul must surely have brought it out more clearly, that is, by saying directly that Christ believed as Abraham believed. Had that indeed been Paul's point, that Christ as Abraham's seed believed as Abraham believed, he could have said so quite straightforwardly. In 3:26 in particular rather than the potentially confusing "You are all sons of God through faith in Christ Jesus," Paul could have said so much more clearly, "You are all sons of God in Christ Jesus who believed." The lack of a verbal equivalent to the noun phrase, "the faith of Christ," is as weakening to Hooker's case as is the loss of a noun equivalent to the act of 'justifying faith' (πιστεύειν) in Hays's case.[46]

More to the point, Paul's logic is manifestly different from that which Hooker follows. Paul's problem was to demonstrate that *non*-Jews could be counted Abraham's children. His answer was in terms of Gentiles believing as Abraham believed; they were his children because they shared his faith—"sons of" = sharing the same characteristic attitude and status before God (3:7).[47] But Jesus as a Jew did not require this special concession. And as Messiah he could be regarded as the "seed" of Abraham in a pre-eminent sense. Paul signals this difference in status between Christ and Christians by defining Christ's relation to Abraham solely in terms of the word "seed"; as "son" Christ is only to be understood as "God's son" (1:16; 2.20; 4:4, 6).

The logic of Paul's argument is that Christians are Abraham's children by a *twofold* action—by sharing in Abraham's faith (3:7), and by being "in Christ" (3:28–29). The climax of the argument in 3:26ff. is quite clear "you are all sons/children of God, (1) through faith, (2) in Christ Jesus."[48] The first phrase

46 See also above, n.14.

47 "Son of" as denoting share in a particular characteristic or quality would be familiar particularly to those familiar with semitic thought (BDB, בן 8), but it was also a Greek idiom (BAGD, υἱός 1cδ).

48 See above, n. 27.

(1) sums up the line of argument in the first half of the chapter, the first half of the two-fold action (3:1–14). The second phrase (2) sums up the force of the argument in the second half of the chapter (3:15ff). "Sons of Abraham" *through faith* are also "seed of Abraham" *in Christ* (3:28–29).

Hooker has thus merged the two strands of Paul's argument and her thesis arises from the resulting confusion.[49] It does *not* follow that because Christ was Abraham's seed therefore he shared Abraham's faith. By allowing that the οἱ ἐκ πίστεως of 3:6–9 refers to believers who share Abraham's faith,[50] Hooker has weakened her case regarding 3:22. For ἐκ πίστεως referring to Gentiles' faith, like that of Abraham in 3:6–9, probably has the same reference in 3:22: now that the promise has been fulfilled, the faith which "justified" in 3:6–9 can be defined more accurately as "faith in Jesus Christ" (the promised seed). In fact, as Hays seems to have appreciated, for the subjective genitive thesis to carry weight in regard to 3:22 it really does need to draw in all the other πίστις references with it. But that pushes us back into the *reductio ad absurdum* argument already exposed.

3.4 In pointed contrast to both Hays and Hooker, I would have to say that on the more natural reading, the text does speak precisely and consistently of "justifying faith," including the disputed πίστις Χριστοῦ passages.

a) In Gal 2:16 the antithesis between "works of the law" and πίστις Χριστοῦ is central, and is most naturally understood as Paul's way of posing the alternatives on the human side on the basis of which, ἐκ, (according to the opposing Christian views) one might hope to be justified.[51] To speak of the redundancy of expression (one verb phrase, two noun phrases) is to miss the point. This is Paul's first clear statement on this theme so central to his own understanding. We should not be surprised, then, if he repeats himself in two synonymous formulations for the sake of emphasis and clarity. After all, he has no hesitation in emphasising the correlated (οὐκ) ἐξ ἔργων νόμου no less than three times. So we can fairly translate ". . . knowing that a person is *not* justified by works of the law *but only* through faith in Jesus Christ,[52] we too *have* believed

49 Williams, "Again," 437–47, and Wallis, *Faith,* 105–15 are open to the same criticism.

50 Hooker, "πίστις Χριστοῦ," 170–1.

51 Cf. B. L. Martin, *Christ and the Law in Paul* (NovTSupp 62; Leiden: Brill, 1989) 116. The choice of the hitherto unusual phrase πίστις Χριστοῦ may be simply explained by the rhetorical desire to have a simple two word antithesis to ἔργα νόμου. The unusual parallel between πνεῦμα δουλείας and πνεῦμα υἱοθεσίας in Rom 8:15 is probably to be explained in the same way.

52 The argument here is not dependent on my understanding of the flow of thought between 2:15 and 16; see my "The New Perspective on Paul," *Jesus, Paul and the Law* (London: SPCK/ Louisville: Westminster, 1990) 204 n.25, 208–9, 212.

in Christ Jesus, *precisely* in order that we might be justified by faith in Christ, and *not* by works of the law . . .".

b) In Gal 2:20 the πίστις τοῦ υἱοῦ τοῦ θεοῦ form is defined by the relative clauses, "who loved me and gave himself for me." But these are versions of the standard pistis-formula (confessional formula);[53] that is, they are most naturally understood as describing confessional faith, rather than the act of Christ's faithfulness.

c) In 3:2 and 5 ἐξ ἀκοῆς πίστεως is best understood as "hearing with faith" or "the hearing which is faith,"[54] on the parallel not least with ὑπακοὴ πίστεως (Rom 1:5).[55]

d) The implication of 2:16 (synonymous formulations repeated for emphasis) is borne out in 3:6–9 where again it is most obvious to see the verbal and noun phrases used interchangeably.

> 3:6—Abraham believed (ἐπίστευσεν) God, and it was reckoned to him for righteousness (εἰς δικαιοσύνην).
>
> 3:8—God justifies (δικαιοῖ) the Gentiles by faith (ἐκ πίστεως).

The parallel is straightforward: God justifies on the basis of faith, whether the faith of Abraham or that of Gentiles. Abraham provides the pattern of faith. Those who express the same faith (3:6, 9) thus share in the same blessing (justification), are blessed with Abraham, the man of πίστις (3:9), and thus are truly his sons (3:7).[56] In contrast, to argue that the references here could only be understood in the light of the subsequent portrayal of Christ as alone the "seed" of Abraham (3:16) would mean that the crucial argument of 3:6–9 was likely to be lost on the Galatian audiences.

e) Likewise in 3:14—". . . in order that we might receive the promise of the Spirit through faith." Here too it is most natural to take the phrase διὰ τῆς πίστεως as a reference to the medium on the human side through, or to which (cf. 3:2) the Spirit was given.[57] Had Paul wished to specify the divine medium through which the Spirit was given we would have expected something like "through whom,"[58] that is, through Christ himself. A reference to Christ's faith is much less natural.

53 W. Kramer, Christ, *Lord, Son of God* (London: SCM, 1966) 118 (§26b).

54 See now S. Williams, "The Hearing of Faith ΑΚΟΗ ΠΙΣΤΕΩΣ in Galatians 3," *NTS* 35 (1989) 82–93.

55 Martin, *Christ,* 118. Contrast Wallis's laboured formulation "the Spirit is received within or under the auspices of the dispensation of faith fulfilled in Christ" (*Faith,* 107–8).

56 See above, n. 47.

57 The usual view, including now Williams, "ΑΚΟΗ ΠΙΣΤΕΩΣ," 88, arguing against Hays.

58 See above §3.2(2).

f) In 3:22 once again it is at least as plausible to take the double reference to faith/believing as Paul's way of reinforcing the importance of his argument—"in order that the promise which is by faith in Jesus Christ might be given (precisely) to those who believe." Apart from anything else, the reading is quite natural grammatically (§2.2) and avoids the problems posed by the sudden injection of thought of Jesus' faith already noted (§3.3).

g) Proponents of "the faith of Christ" interpretation seem to forget that Paul *has* a way of speaking of the divine source, medium, resource by means of which his saving power comes to effect. It is the word which in traditional Christian theology has always stood as the counterpart on the divine side to the human exercise of faith—"grace." 1:6—God "who called you in the grace of Christ"; 1:15—God "who called me through his grace"; 2:21—"I do not annul the grace of God"; 5:4—"you have fallen away from grace." The most natural reading throughout Galatians is summarized in the classic formulation—justified by grace through faith.

3.5 The irony of the subjective genitive reading of πίστις Χριστοῦ, therefore, is that in order to sustain it, other unqualified references to "faith" have to be taken as echoing or pointing forward to that meaning, "(Christ's) faith." Which leaves Paul's teaching on how Gentile and Jew receive the blessing of divine acceptance with a very large and unexplained hole in it. Conversely, if even a few of these intermediate references are taken as referring to human faith, the act of believing, the noun version of the verb phrase, it becomes increasingly difficult to maintain that the particular πίστις *Χριστοῦ* references point to something different.

4. ROMANS

4.1 Here the arguments are if anything more straightforward and focus on the double use of the phrase in 3:22 and 26.[59](1) Again there is the problem of redundancy in 3:22—διὰ πίστεως Ἰησοῦ Χριστοῦ εἰς πάντας τοὺς πιστεύοντας. (2) There seems to be a close parallel between πίστις Ἰησοῦ and πίστις Ἀβραάμ (3:26; 4.16). (3) Hays notes also the parallel with πίστις θεοῦ (3:3). (4) And Hooker presses the parallel between Christ and Adam; "if men and women are faithless, we may expect Christ to be faithful."[60]

59 On 3:25 see above, n.43 and below §4.4.

60 Hays, *Faith,* 170–2; Hooker, "πίστις Χριστοῦ," 168–70. Hays also rightly notes that Romans is thoroughly theocentric, but draws the dubious conclusion that Christ is never unambiguously

4.2 (1) On the problem of redundancy the matter is simply resolved. "Why would Paul need to add εἰς πάντας τοὺς πιστεύοντας?" asks Hays. Precisely in order to emphasize the πάντας, is the obvious answer: "the righteousness of God through faith in Jesus Christ to *all* who believe." Students of Romans will not need to be reminded that this "all" is a thematic word in the letter, being used again and again, often with varying degrees of redundancy, and precisely as a means of emphasis (see particularly 1:5, 16; 2:10; 4:11, 16; 10:4, 11–13). The usage in 3:22 is simply part of a sustained motif.[61]

4.3 (2) The failure to be clear on whether Paul meant the "faith of Christ" or the "faithfulness of Christ" is a good deal more critical than has been appreciated by the proponents of the subjective genitive thesis. For in fact just such a distinction seems to have been crucial to Paul's exposition of Abraham's faith in chap. 4. The point which has been wholly ignored in the debate thus far is that Paul was in effect attacking the traditional Jewish understanding of Abraham which saw him as the archetype of *faithfulness*. As passages like Sir 44:19–21 and 1 Macc 2:52 (not to mention James 2:21–23) clearly show, Abraham was held up in Jewish piety as one of the supreme examples of "faithfulness" under trial, in his willingness to offer up Isaac. More to the point for Paul, as the same passages also show, Gen 15:6 was typically interpreted in Jewish circles by reference to Abraham's faithfulness thus displayed.[62]

Paul's response was twofold. First to insist that Gen 15:6 had to be understood prior to and independent of the later accounts both of Abraham's circumcision (4:9–15), and, by implication, of Abraham's offering of Isaac. And second, in consequence, to argue that Abraham's πίστις meant his faith, his naked trust in God's promise (4:16–22), and therefore *not* his "faithfulness." We must see then, that for Paul's πίστις Χριστοῦ to be understood of Christ's faithfulness would be to play into the hands of his Jewish-Christian opponents: Abraham's faith (= faithfulness) was a prototype of Jesus' faithfulness and so could continue to serve as a model of Jewish-Christian covenant faithfulness. In sharp contrast Paul insists that Abraham was a model of *faith* = trust. But where then does that leave the parallel between 3:26 and 4:16? Did Paul intend to present Christ as an example of that same sheer naked trust? To what would he be referring, since a reference to Christ's faithfulness to death (the more natural parallel if parallel was sought) seems to be excluded? And why again does Paul

---

presented as an object of faith (as Williams, "Again," above, n. 30); this is surely to treat 9:33 and 10:11, 14 in too cavalier a fashion. Similarly the difficulty of making sense of the idea of God's righteousness being revealed through faith (in Jesus Christ) is greatly exaggerated in view of 1:17.

61 Keck "'Jesus,'" 456 conveniently misses out the πάντας τοὺς in his quotation of 3:22.

62 See further my *Romans,* 200–1.

fail to bring out the parallel more clearly? In point of fact he ends his exposition of Abraham's faith in the way that makes most sense of the objective genitive reading "faith was reckoned for righteousness to Abraham on our account also, to those who believe (as did Abraham—4:17) in him who raised Jesus our Lord from the dead" (4:22–24). What is in view throughout is faith in the life-giving power of God (manifested in the conception of Isaac, and in the resurrection of Christ), not faithfulness (either of Abraham or of Christ).[63]

We may pursue the point a little further. For if Paul's intention had been to parallel Abraham's faith and Christ's, we would have expected a rather fuller and rather different treatment of Abraham, focusing precisely on Abraham's faith(fulness) in offering Isaac and paralleling it to Christ's faith(fulness) in offering himself on the cross. Now there is a generally recognized allusion to the offering of Isaac in 8:32—"he who did not spare his own son . . .".[64] The difference is that the parallel is between *God* and Abraham, not between Jesus and Abraham. This underlines the conclusion just drawn, that the point of chap.4's exposition is to demonstrate what "justifying faith" is, to draw a parallel between Abraham's faith and the faith of all who believe in God's life-giving power, not to draw a parallel between Christ and Abraham.

4.4 (3) The reference to God is a reminder that Paul *has* a concept in Romans of what we might call simply "divine faith." Indeed, it is one of the major themes of the letter, often underestimated in significance because talk of "God's faith" is explicit as such only at 3:3. What is too easily missed is the fact that for a Jew like Paul talk of "the truth of God" carried the same connotation, since אֱמוּנָה and אֱמֶת could be translated equally by ἀλήθεια or πίστις. Hence the theme is actually very prominent in 3:3–7, a passage which is a railway junction for most of Paul's main lines of thought in the letter, and in the climax of 15:8.[65] In my judgment it is also present in the ἐκ πίστεως of 1:17, possibly in the διὰ (τῆς) πίστεως of 3:25,[66] and implicit in the quotation of 15:11,[67] as

63 This also undermines Stowers's attempt to take the ἐκ πίστεως and διὰ πίστεως of Rom 3:30, 31 as references to Christ's faithfulness: "the heroic merit of Jesus was the means by which God provided an expiation" (670); "because of Abraham's faithfulness God established a covenant of righteousness for all his descendants" (673). But this interpretation cuts right against the grain of Romans 4.

64 See, e.g., my *Romans,* 501 and those cited there.

65 Δικαιοσύνη θεοῦ (3:5) overlaps with but is not synonymous with ἡ πίστις τοῦ θεοῦ and ἡ ἀλήθεια τοῦ θεοῦ (3:3, 7) the first phrase is the more general, embracing God's relationship as Creator to the world as a whole (3:5–6), hence its characteristic anarthrous form; whereas the last two phrases refer specifically to God's covenant faithfulness, hence the definite article.

66 This is more likely than a reference to the faithfulness of Christ, since what is being described is the action of God; but see above nn. 27 and 43, and B. W. Longenecker, "ΠΙΣΤΙΣ in Romans 3.25: Neglected Evidence for the 'Faithfulness of Christ,'" *NTS* 39 (1993) 478–80.

well as underlying the whole thrust of chaps. 9–11. What is noticeable in all this theme is the variety of ways in which Paul refers to it and draws it in.

Of course it is arguable that πίστις Χριστοῦ is an equivalent reference to the faithfulness of Christ. But in contrast to the anarthrous πίστις Χριστοῦ, it is noticeable that the reference in 3:3 has the definite article (τὴν πίστιν τοῦ θεοῦ), in line with the "almost invariable" practice noted above (§2.2). And if, *ex hypothesi,* the faithfulness of Christ is so important for Paul, why then is it referred to only in the two grammatically ambiguous phrases in 3:22 and 26, in contrast to the far richer theme of God's faithfulness? Why no reference to Christ as πιστός, as he has to God elsewhere too (1 Cor 1:9; 10:13; 2 Cor 1:18; 1 Thess 5:24)?[68] We could push the argument still further. To understand πίστις Χριστοῦ as referring to *Christ's* faithfulness would not only weaken the emphasis on human faith (like that of Abraham) but also confuse and even divert attention from the emphasis on *God's* faithfulness. What Paul is calling for throughout Romans is for faith in God's faithfulness, faith like that of Abraham, faith in the one who now embodies in eschatological fulness that faithfulness, *God's* faithfulness, not Christ's.[69]

4.5 (4) Finally as to the parallel between Christ and Adam (Hooker).[70] Perhaps all we need to note here is what Paul does *not* say. According to Hooker's statement of the subjective genitive thesis, the logic is simply crying out for Paul to make the precise antithesis which Hooker herself makes—between Adam's faithlessness and Christ's faithfulness. But Paul does not make it.[71] The sequence of antitheses in 5:15ff. was the ideal point at which to make clear beyond doubt that he was thinking of Christ as the prototype of faith. What would have been more natural, on Hooker's thesis, than that Paul should add to the antitheses between παράπτωμα and χάρισμα, between Adam's παρακοή and Christ's ὑπακοή, the further antithesis between Adam's ἀπιστία and Christ's πίστις? But he fails to do so. Does this not suggest that Hooker's logic has once again diverged from Paul's? The parallel/contrast between Adam and Christ is rich and resonant, but it evidently did *not* include the thought of Christ undoing Adam's faithlessness by means of his own faith in God.[72]

67 See my *Romans* on each passage.

68 2 Thess 3:3 and 2 Tim 2:13 are the only exceptions in the Pauline corpus.

69 The same is true of 2 Cor 1:17–22—a reference to *God's* faithfulness, not Christ's (*pace* Hooker, "πίστις Χριστοῦ," 177–8), though we might speak of God's faithfulness incarnated in Christ (as Torrance, "One Aspect," 114, elaborating Hebert, "Faithfulness," 375–6).

70 So also particularly Barth, "Faith," 366–7.

71 Despite Johnson, "Romans 3:21–26," 88–9.

72 Perhaps indicative of the state of the question is Hooker's expostulation, "If Paul does not use this idea, then he ought to!" ("Πίστις Χριστοῦ," 168). Since in Rom. 5:14–21 Paul resisted that

4.6 For all these reasons I find myself being pushed strongly to the conclusion that the subjective genitive reading of πίστις Χριστοῦ in Romans is simply an example of mistaken exegesis.

5. PHILIPPIANS

The one remaining example, in Phil 3:9, can be treated briefly. Hooker's arguments are simply the application of considerations we have already encountered. (1) The redundancy of two mentions of faith—"not having my own righteousness which is ἐκ νόμου, but that which is διὰ πίστεως Χριστοῦ, the righteousness ἐκ θεοῦ ἐπὶ τῇ πίστει."[73] (2) The parallel with Adam. In 3:7–8 Paul speaks of the reversal of values which marked his conversion. Hooker finds in the threefold use of ἡγέομαι ("I considered loss/rubbish") an echo of Christ's *kenosis* in 2:6–7 (ἡγήσατο), and suggests that the pattern of interchange between Christ and the believer, which she finds elsewhere in Paul, reappears here in another version. Christ's *kenosis* provides a model for Paul's own experience. This suggests that the διὰ πίστεως Χριστοῦ "ought to refer to the obedient self-surrender of Christ, that is, to his faithfulness."[74]

The parallel with Adam at this point, however, is rather remote, and the argument ignores the distinctiveness of the section in which the phrase occurs—3:2–16. For the more immediate context is dominated by the same issues which have featured so strongly in the earlier passages. How is it that God reckons righteousness to humans? Is it because they are Jews, circumcised, of the race of Israel (3:4–5), live fully "within the law" (3:6)? That was Paul's old view and status. It is that which he had reacted against. And once again the contrast he poses is in terms of faith—the righteousness which is through faith in Christ, the righteousness which is from God to that faith.

Three considerations strongly support this reading. (1) The repetition of both "righteousness" and "faith"; Paul was evidently concerned to emphasize a point here. Once again it is a matter of emphasis rather than of redundancy. (2) The lack of the definite article with the first reference to "faith" (διὰ πίστεως Χριστοῦ) once again probably tells against the reading "the faith of Christ" and indicates an objective genitive, "faith in Christ." (3) Conversely, it is also to be noted that the second reference to faith is *not* anarthrous—ἐπὶ τῇ πίστει. This

---

inviting "ought" the implication is rather that he did *not* wish to speak of Christ's faith, even in one of the two most explicit Adam/Christ parallels.

73 So also Keck, "'Jesus,'" 455–6.

74 Hooker "πίστις Χριστοῦ," 175–7; so also Wallis, *Faith,* 118–24.

must mean that Paul was referring to the same faith both times—"the faith," that is, the faith just mentioned. His Greek would be scarcely intelligible if he meant the first πίστις to refer to Christ's faith and the second πίστις to "justifying faith." Once again, then, the subjective genitive reading overshoots the mark. In order to sustain the claim that the first reference is to Christ's faith, the second must be so interpreted as well; *both* of the crucial references must be referred to Christ's self-surrender on the cross. And at the crucial point in the brief polemic we find the same hole as before; the vital means by which the righteousness actually comes to the individual is left unexplained.

In short, here too a subjective genitive reading of the text begins to look more and more like a forced reading rather than the most natural reading of the text.

6. CONCLUSION

I should make it clear that the *theology* of the subjective genitive reading is powerful, important and attractive. For anyone who wishes to take the humanness of Jesus with full seriousness "the faith of Jesus" strikes a strong and resonant chord. Moreover, as a theological motif, it seems to me wholly compatible with Paul's theology; that is, not a component of Paul's theology but consistent with other emphases. As Hooker has noted, it follows naturally when we bring together the thought of God in Christ and the thought of God's faithfulness. It is an attractive variant on the Adam motif of Christ's obedience. None of this, however, is to the particular point at dispute. That focuses on the meaning Paul intended when he dictated the phrase πίστις Χριστοῦ. And on this point I remain wholly convinced that Paul intended his audiences to hear that phrase in the sense "faith in Christ".

This conclusion is based on the three major findings of the above discussion. (1) There are good grammatical grounds for affirming the objective genitive reading and denying the subjective genitive reading of πίστις Χριστοῦ. (2) The traditional "faith in Christ" makes consistently good sense of the line of thought in each case, with repetition serving to reinforce the claim being made. Whereas, insistence on reading πίστις Χριστοῦ as a subjective genitive runs the risk of throwing other, clear lines of Paul's argument in some confusion. (3) Outside the phrase in dispute there is nothing that can be called a clear reference to Christ's faith (as such). At this point the agency of Christ in Paul is consistently described in other ways ("in/through/to Christ"), but nowhere else in terms of Christ's own faith or faithfulness. A thesis built solely on a disputed phrase is usually likely to be wrong.

In consequence I find myself rather puzzled as to why the subjective genitive interpretation is being pushed with such fervor. In line with the above findings, the simplest and most coherent exegesis of the disputed phrase is surely to conclude that Paul did *not* intend to be understood as speaking of Christ's faith, but only of "faith in Christ."

Additional note:

In the debate at Kansas City my chief criticisms of Hays's paper were as follows.

Hays all the while seems to be working from what he perceives to be the narrative underlying Paul's theology as set out in his letters (his main thesis in *Faith*), *rather than from the actual argument of the letters themselves, and to do so in a way which ignores the terms and thrust of the argument actually used.* It is against the background of that underlying narrative that he reads *pistis Christou* as a reference to Christ's faith/faithfulness. The trouble is that neither Galatians nor Romans are narratives but arguments. And it is the specific terms of these arguments themselves which determines the sense of *pistis Christou* as denoting faith in Christ.

a) Most striking is the way in which Hays treats Rom 3:21–26 in isolation from its immediate context—3:19–20 and 3:27–31 (see above, pp. 44–47). (i) Thus he ignores the fact that the alternative against which Paul is polemicizing is *erga nomou* (3:19–20)—*pistis* as the opposite of *erga nomou*. The clear implication is that *pistis* is something on the human side of the salvation process. (ii) And when we look at the other end of the sequence (3:19–31) it is surely clear beyond dispute that *pistis* in 3:27–31 means human believing. How odd, then, if *pistis* in the central section should be so (exclusively for Hays) focused on Christ's faithfulness, whereas the follow through is exclusively focused on human faith. Something jars here. Hays has evidently taken his understanding of *pistis Christou* from the hypothesized underlying narrative rather than from the sequence and logic of the argument actually used by Paul.

b) The same is true with his treatment of Romans 4. When we understand the Jewish evaluation of Abraham and the context of the exposition of Gen 15:6 offered by Paul, it becomes clear how Abraham's *pistis* = trust offers a genuine and direct alternative to *erga nomou* (= works of the law, such as, not least, his circumcision and offering of Isaac). To argue that *pistis* = Abraham's faithfulness cuts quite against the grain of the argument. And for Abraham's *pistis* to be understood as a prefiguration of Christ's faithfulness would undermine Paul's argument, since it would be playing directly into the hands of those who opposed Paul (by maintaining the traditional view of Abraham as counted righteous because of his faithfulness when tested in the matter of Isaac).

c) The same problem arises for Hays from his reading of Galatians. A crucial factor is the consistency in the *pistis/pisteuein* references—a consistency demanded by the actual argument used. Hays seems to recognize this since, as I pointed out in my paper, the logic of his exposition virtually forces him to draw in *all* the *pistis* references to his thesis as denoting Christ's faith. But the most straightforward reading of the bulk of the *pistis/pisteuein* passages in Galatians is surely as references to the act/attitude of (human) believing. So that the coherence of the flow of the argument actually used pushes strongly for the conclusion that all the *pistis* references (including *pistis Christou*) denote human faith. I do not recall Hays responding to one of my questions to him on this point: whether he would accept any of the *pistis* references in Galatians as denoting human believing in Christ. I'm still waiting for an answer.

The problem confronting Hays at this point is, once again, that he can sustain his interpretation of Galatians 3:22 in particular only by reading it against the underlying narrative which he reconstructs, rather than from the actual course of Paul's argument in Galatians 3. And in so doing he throws the actual argument of Galatians 3 into some confusion: what *is* the human response to the gospel to be if it is not *erga nomou*? According to Hays, and despite the most obvious reading of Galatians 3, Paul does not actually answer that question.

5 APROPOS THE FAITH OF/IN CHRIST

A Response to Hays and Dunn

Paul J. Achtemeier
Union Theological Seminary in Virginia

1. INTRODUCTION

1.1 There is no point, at this stage of the discussion, for me to rehearse seriatim the data and arguments presented in the papers by Prof. Richard Hays and Prof. James Dunn. As their long list of publications attests, they both write well and have orderly minds (!), and their papers reflect that. In addition, those who have read the papers do not need such a summary; those who have not read the papers will not be helped by the brief summary remarks I could make. What I propose to do is raise questions, including those both stated and implied in the papers, and make such additional comments as I think useful for the debate.

1.2 In one sense, the question of whether or not the phrase πίστις Χριστοῦ can mean the faith(fulness) Jesus exercised is of critical importance. As both Prof. Hays and Prof. Dunn make clear, how this issue is resolved has important implications for the understanding of a whole range of Pauline theological positions. In another sense, however, as both the authors also make clear, the fundamental tenets of Paul's theology bear the same freight however one may decide this particular issue. In that sense, what we have is merely an interesting exegetical exercise, since either position allows for the full range of Pauline theological positions contained in those letters of his that we have. Yet clarity of some passages is at stake, and for that reason the debate is a useful one.

2. GRAMMAR AND SYNTAX

Facing the question of how the genitive case is used, one would think first of a solution on the basis of grammar and syntax. We may begin there.

2.1 There is first the matter of grammar. Prof. Hays asserts that on balance, the grammatical evidence strongly favors the subjective genitive interpretation since the arguments for the objective genitive are relatively weak, but he goes no further than that. Prof. Dunn cites the work of E. D. Burton, who found that when a subjective genitive is intended, the article is "almost invariably present" with the modified word. Prof. Dunn notes that *all* disputed examples of πίστις Χριστοῦ lack the definite article. A look at the Deutero-Pauline usage shows that there are formulae other than πίστις Χριστοῦ to express faith in Christ but that they post-date Paul, and thus provide no help.[1]

The weakness of the argument based on the presence of the article signifying the subjective genitive is that the rule works *almost* all the time. A grammatical rule like that in the face precisely of disputed passages lacks a certain reliability; the disputed passage may be one that falls outside the "almost." As a result, Prof. Dunn and Prof. Hays agree that in this matter arguments based on grammar are finally inconclusive.[2]

2.2 There is secondly the matter of syntax—more specifically, the question of a certain redundancy were one to understand Χριστοῦ as an objective genitive. For example, Prof. Hays argues that in a verse like Gal 2:20, to understand τοῦ υἱοῦ τοῦ θεοῦ as an objective genitive makes the syntax difficult, since it sets the whole final phrase in apposition to πίστει and thus makes an awkward construction if the final phrase gives the content of that faith.[3] Prof. Dunn, on the other hand, finds the phrase typical of elements of the standard πίστις (i.e., confessional) formula, and thus does not find the awkwardness. One might also note that the final phrase works quite well as an adjectival description of precisely *why* it is appropriate to live by trust in that Christ: because he loved me and gave himself up for me.

Again, Prof. Dunn fails to be troubled by a redundancy Hays finds introduced into Gal 2:16 by an objective genitive, since again such redundancy simply reinforces the point Paul is making. One may note that the ABB'A' construction of the first four elements of that verse would argue for just such reinforcing emphasis. Similarly, Prof. Dunn finds the claimed redundancy imposed by an objective genitive in Rom 3:22 to function instead as an emphasis on the πάντας in that verse, an emphasis which is surely a major note sounded in Romans. Finally, the redundancy found in Phil 3:9 Prof. Dunn finds to be

1 Prof. Dunn feels that such phrases are not necessary in Paul since it was precisely the phrase πίστις Χριστοῦ that served that purpose (67, paragraph 2.4).

2 Hays, 39; Dunn, 67.

3 Hays, 53.

rather a matter of emphasis. It may also be noted that Phil. 3:9 is redundant whether the genitive be understood as subjective *or* objective, since the second phrase concerning faith surely modifies the first.

One may note further that Paul frequently employs redundancy to make an important point; that is, he repeats a point he wants to emphasize (e.g., Rom 5: 18-19; 2 Cor 5:18-19). On that basis, the discovery of redundancy can cut both ways; it could commend as well as question an interpretation relative to its being appropriate to the Pauline style.

3. THE LARGER CONTEXT

Failing decisive arguments based on grammar and syntax, it becomes apparent that the issue will have to be decided, as Prof. Hays notes, "by larger judgments about the shape and logic of Paul's thought . . ."[4] It is to some of those larger issues we must now turn our attention.

3.1 There is, for example, the matter Paul's use of covenantal language, an issue that bulks larger in Prof. Hays's presentation that it does in Prof. Dunn's. Indeed, Prof. Hays's basic thesis argues that Jesus' death, done in obedience to God's will, is simultaneously a loving act of faithfulness (πίστις) to God and the decisive manifestation of God's faithfulness to his covenant promise to Abraham. It is as summary allusions to this "story" that Paul's use of πίστις Χριστοῦ and other similar phrases should be understood.[5]

That the language of faith, obedience and righteousness are fundamentally covenantal in origin and significance I agree. That the fundamental meaning of δικαιοσύνη is to be seen in terms of God's covenant faithfulness I also agree. For that reason I am puzzled when Prof. Hays argues that Paul in Romans 3 is concerned to show that "God's way of dealing with humanity through the gospel is a manifestation of his *justice*."[6] The whole point of the argument in the beginning of that chapter, as Hays urges, is to show that God's righteousness is to be understood in terms of faithfulness (3:3, 5). If one uses justice in a distributive sense, that is just what Paul is *not* talking about, any more than he is talking about an attribute imputed to God or to humans. It is precisely the covenantal framework that protects one from such a misunderstanding. Similarly, it is the covenantal framework, I would urge, that makes it unlikely that

4 Hays, 39.

5 Hays, 37.

6 Hays 46; emphasis added.

the καί in Rom. 3:26 is epexegetic. It is precisely the death of Christ that opens the way to the new covenant; by that death which forgives sins, God shows his own (righteous) faithfulness by sustaining his covenant promises, and allows those who trust him through that act (διὰ τῆς πίστεως ἐν τῷ αὐτοῦ αἵματι, v. 25) to enter into that covenant. Thus Romans 3:26b describes the way in which Christ is both the means whereby God sustains his covenantal promises and the means whereby sinful humanity may enter that covenant. It is precisely the covenantal framework of the language that argues here against rather than for a subjective genitive. That such a covenant is now a matter of faith, not law, is an important point in this context, and it is a point to which we must return below.

3.2 Closely related to all of that is the matter of faith. Critical to Prof. Hays's thesis for the subjective genitive is Rom 1:17 with its quotation of Hab 2.4, which Prof. Hays in turn understands as a messianic prophecy fulfilled in Jesus: Jesus, the righteous one, lives from or by his faithfulness.[7] On this point I remain skeptical, not only because Paul uses the OT in ways other than messianic prophecy, but also because the immediate context centers on the universality of a divine salvation open to faith (1:16); it is that point, as the γάρ shows, v. 17 is to illustrate. Incidentally, Paul himself shows how the phrase ἐκ πίστεως εἰς πίστιν is to be understood when he uses the identical construction in 2 Cor 2:16, where the meaning is clearly "arising from (or "taking its origin from") and leading to." It is surely that sense in which Paul means it here: God's righteousness, revealed in the gospel, originates in faith(fulness) and leads to faith(fulness), but a faith(fulness), in this context, open to everyone, whether Jew or Greek. On that basis, I do not think the reference here is to the faith(fulness) of Christ.

Also to be included here is the relationship of faith to obedience, and hence the significance of the comparison between Christ and Adam in Rom 5. I agree that the genitive in the phrase in Rom. 1:5—εἰς ὑπακοὴν πίστεως—is epexegetic: faith(fulness) defines what Paul means by obedience.[8] I suspect there would be little disagreement on that point.[9] If that be granted, however, the case for the subjective genitive is strengthened, Prof. Hays argues, because then the contrast between Christ and Adam, involving as it does obedience (ὑπακοή) and disobedience (παρακοή), is also a matter of faithfulness (Christ's) and perfidy (Adam's). Indeed, so important is this point for Prof. Hays that he finds here

[7] Hays, p. 43.

[8] This essentially mirrors Hays's own discussion at the bottom of p. 40.

[9] Paul makes the same point in Rom 10:16, and repeats the phrase in 16:26.

the only real link between what Paul discusses the first four chapters of Romans and the succeeding four chapters. Only because the discussion of Adam and Christ centers in the same way on Christ's faithfulness as does Rom 3:21–26 can we find unity in Paul's argument. In that way, Romans 5:12–19 and the discussion of Christ and Adam reinforces the subjective genitive construction of Romans 3:21–26, with the latter being a further explication of the former. Yet if obedience and faith play so significant a role in Romans 5, it becomes redundant; after all, we already know all that. Thus the argument cuts both ways: if chap. 5 says the same as chap. 3, then it need not be seen in chap. 3, since it is made so plainly, and with a different vocabulary (!) in chap. 5. One must also wonder why, if this point is so critical for Paul, there is no reference to Christ's faithfulness or to Adam's faithlessness in the comparison between the two figures. We will return to this point below when we discussion questions raised for each of our authors by the other.

3.3 Any discussion of the significance of faith(fulness) for Paul must include a discussion of Abraham who had faith, and of what Paul understands him to be paradigmatic. Prof. Hays, who had earlier argued that Abraham in Galatians was exemplary not of faith but of one "in and through whom others are blessed," i.e., exemplary more of the faith of Jesus than of the faith of his followers, in this paper argues that there is a sense in which Abraham is the "prefiguration both of Christ and of those who are in Christ."[10] In Romans 4, on the other hand, where, unlike in Galatians, Paul was not forced to consider Abraham because Abraham was part of the argument of his opponents, his purpose in using Abraham was to show that his gospel does not do away with the law, and hence he needed a figure to point to the *continuity* between faith and Torah.[11] One might note that Rom 3:31 indicates that part at least of Paul's agenda includes a demonstration of the *priority* of faith, since by recalling Abraham's justification by faith, not law, Paul affirms Abraham shows the way in which the law can legitimately be understood (νόμον ἱστάνομεν), i.e., as founded on and pointing to faith (cf., e.g., Rom 10:4; Gal 3:23–24).[12] Prof. Hays concludes that Abraham in Romans is a typological prefiguration of

[10] Hays, 52.

[11] Hays, 48.

[12] The statement in Gal 3:12 (νόμος οὐκ ἔστιν ἐκ πίστεως) is conditioned by v. 10, and is determined by the opponents' claim that one could still rely on the law for righteousness with God. As Hays correctly points out, the discussion in Romans cannot presume prior acquaintance with Paul's theology, and hence must be more "self-explanatory,"(p. 40) and of course less determined by prior parameters of dispute.

Christian believers, since they, like Abraham, are to direct their faith "toward the God who raised Jesus."[13]

Prof. Dunn on the other hand argues that in both Galatians and Romans, Abraham is paradigmatic of Christian believers only. He finds a straightforward parallel in Gal 3:6, 9: Abraham was justified by (his) faith; Gentiles are justified by (their) faith.[14] In Romans, Paul attacks the traditional Jewish understanding of Abraham as a paradigm of faithfulness (i.e., his willingness to offer up Isaac) by emphasizing Abraham's "naked trust in God's promise (4:16–22)."[15] Hence, Abraham is an example of trust in the life-giving power of God (the conception of Isaac), prefiguring the Christian's similar trust in the life-giving power shown through the resurrection. Thus Prof. Dunn argues that Abraham serves Paul in the same way both in Galatians and Romans, and in neither case as a prefiguration of Jesus. One may note that Romans 4 is constructed to display a two-fold sequence: the first half argues that Abraham's righteousness is a matter of faith, not law (4:1–15); the second half shows in what that faith consists, i.e., relying in face of contrary evidence on the promise of God who brings life from the dead (4:16–22).

3.4 What is absent in both papers, not only in relation to the figure of Abraham, but also in the discussion of the phrase πίστις Χριστοῦ, is the contrast, where not explicit (e.g., Gal 2:16, Phil 3:9) surely implied (e.g., Rom 3:21–22; Gal 2:20–21), between πίστις Χριστοῦ and ἔργα νόμου. To do that surely requires some understanding of the meaning of ἔργα νόμου, and such a task is daunting enough for angels to fear to tread. The fact that I now rush in will confirm the estimate of my own intelligence demonstrated when I agreed to respond to these two papers.

I will draw here on an insight of Prof. Hays, one with which I fully agree, namely that in such matters it is well to begin with Romans, since Paul was unknown there, and hence had to write in a way less dependent on shared, and to us unknown, information and situations. Of course they shared common Christian convictions, and surely knowledge of other areas, whether of agreement or conflict, less clear to us, but nevertheless, Paul was in this letter under constraint to "set forth a relatively self-explanatory exposition of the gospel."[16]

13 Note well, not the God whose will Jesus obediently followed to the cross; this will be important below.

14 Dunn, 72. He also notes that if Gal 3:22 were to be understood as saying Christ believed as Abraham believed, Paul does not say it very clearly (71).

15 Dunn, 75. See also the discussion in Roy A. Harrisville III, *The Figure of Abraham in the Epistles of St. Paul* (Lewiston, NY: Mellen Press, 1992)

16 Hays, 40.

A key passage in understanding what Paul meant by works of the law is the sequence in Rom 3:28-29, part of Paul's conclusion to his argument begun in 3:21. 3:28 sums up his point: we reckon a person is made righteous by faith (*n.b.* πίστει, not πίστει Χριστοῦ) apart from law's works. Its meaning is the made clear by the alternative Paul poses as a question in v. 29: Or is God the God only of the Jews? The answer is clearly no; God is God also of the gentiles. Yet what prompted that question? Why would v. 28 lead one to conclude that the position opposed by Paul (i.e., justification by law's works rather than faith) would lead to the conclusion God was the God solely of the Jews? The answer: since law's works are available only to Jews (cf. 2:17-18!). Yet if, as the sequence makes clear, law's works could only be available to Jews, thus limiting God's care to them, then law's works cannot be understood metaphorically to mean human accomplishment generally. It must mean commands of the Torah, and since the Torah was given to the Jews (cf. Rom 3:2), they alone can follow it. Thus, ἔργα νόμου refers far more to "Jewish religious heritage" than to "human religious accomplishment."[17] Here, as earlier (e.g., 1:16, 3:22), Paul's point is to emphasize the universal element played by faith, opening righteousness to all, not just to the Jews, although surely also to the Jews.

Thus, in considering the meaning of πίστις Χριστοῦ, we must bear in mind the universalizing thrust displayed by its contrast with the law's works, which concern only the Jews.

Now how does that bear on the question here under consideration? Let me count (some of) the ways. First, it removes from the debate the possibility that Paul meant πίστις Χριστοῦ as a contrast to ἔργα νόμου which he understood to mean "human accomplishment". Second, it imports into this contrast the similar contrast between a universal and a limited scope of God's right-making activity. Whatever else πίστις Χριστοῦ is, it is a sign of the now-universal extent of God's saving intent embodied in Jesus Christ.

But does it help in resolving the type of genitive found in the phrase πίστις Χριστοῦ: i.e., objective or subjective? It may, but again, certain cautions must be noted. For example, one may not say the contrast is between law's works as something people do, and πίστις Χριστοῦ as something they do not, thus perhaps arguing for the subjective genitive. Standing overagainst such an understanding is not only Paul's (strange?!) phrase in 1 Thess 1:3: τὸ ἔργον τῆς πίστεως, but also the whole perspective of faith as obedience, which we discussed above. Clearly, faith does involve human activity, as of course the whole range of Pauline ethical exhortations attests.

17 That point is confirmed in the discussion in Phil 3:4–11, where it is clear that Paul understood his "conversion" as a change from reliance on his Jewish religious inheritance, which was considerable, to reliance on faith.

But does it help? Does the universal scope of God's grace implied in this contrast aid in resolving the question in Romans 3:22, where the πάντας τοὺς πιστεύοντες is made explicit? Does it help in the interpretation of Gal 2:16, where, if ἔργα νόμου refers to Jewish religious heritage, the intention of the ἐάν μή can be understood not so much in an adversative sense ("but"—had Paul meant that, why not use the perfectly acceptable ἀλλά!) as in a qualifying sense ("if not"), implying that one is not made righteous ἐξ ἔργων νόμου (thus including the Jews) unless it be also διὰ πίστεως Χριστοῦ (thus including the gentiles)?[18] Does it throw light on Phil 3:9, where the contrast between Paul's former reliance on his Jewish religious heritage for his righteousness is so clearly contrasted with his current reliance on πίστις Χριστοῦ for his righteousness? Does it throw light on the other places where the phrase in question appears, e.g., Rom 3:26; Gal 2:20; 3:22? The answer will perhaps become clearer as our discussion proceeds.

4. QUESTIONS RAISED BY HAYS AND DUNN

4. Finally, we may ask what questions the discussion contained in each paper poses for the other.

4.1 First, questions that may be directed to Prof. Dunn.

4.1.1 In his paper, Prof. Hays proposes that Gal 2:16 may well represent an objective genitive use of the phrase πίστις Χριστοῦ.[19] Is there any use of this phrase in the accepted Pauline letters that you think would be a likely candidate for a subjective genitive interpretation?

4.1.2 Prof. Hays suggests that the parallelisms between Rom 3:26 and 4:16 represent a fatal embarrassment for all attempts to find in the Ἰησοῦ of 3:26 an objective genitive.[20] Does the context of Romans 4, where Abraham is one who trusted in God, affect the importance of the linguistic parallelism, since there is no such clear parallelism in content, i.e., that Jesus is such an example of faith in 3:26 or its context?

4.1.3 Prof. Hays suggests that one of the great strengths of the subjective genitive interpretation is its ability to clarify the relationship between christology and soteriology in Paul, particularly with respect to the question "*how* the death of Jesus can be understood to be the source of salvation."[21] Lacking the subjective genitive, how would you bridge this "puzzling arbitrariness"

[18] In fact, Hays concedes here the possibility of an objective genitive (39). On that basis, this could have importance for the interpretation of other verses where this contrast is either expressed or implied.

[19] Hays, 39.

[20] Hays, 47.

[21] Hays, 55.

Prof. Hays finds in the "standard Lutheran-Reformation accounts of justification by faith"?

4.1.4 Drawing on the discussion of Adam and Christ in Romans 5 and the phrase earlier on in Romans that virtually identifies faith and obedience (Rom 1:5), Prof. Hays argues that the subjective genitive interpretation allows Romans 5 to be seen as elucidation of Rom 3:21–26, thus providing an otherwise nonexistent link between the discussions in Romans 1–4 and 5–8.[22] You have argued that the discussion in Romans 5 would more clearly support the notion of Christ's faithfulness if only Paul had cast at least part of the argument in such terms by including the contrast πίστις/ἀπιστία to go along with the contrasts of ὑπακή/παρακοή and παράπτωμα/χάρισμα. Lacking that link between Romans 1–4 and 5–8, do you concede difficulty therefore in linking those discussions?

4.2 Second, questions that may be directed to Prof. Hays.

4.2.1 Prof. Dunn notes that while faith was an important motif for Paul there is a relative absence from the undisputed Paulines of phrases other than πίστις Χριστοῦ to designate "faith in Christ;" on that basis, he argues, the view that the great preponderance of references linking Jesus and faith are to be seen as subjective genitive means that "*either* πίστις Χριστοῦ is Paul's way of speaking of 'faith in Christ,' *or* Paul for some yet to be explained reason, seems to have avoided speaking of 'faith in Christ'."[23] Did Paul avoid it?

4.2.2 Prof. Dunn argues that a prominent theme in Romans is God's faithfulness (πίστις θεοῦ) a theme to be found not only at 3:3 but also in 3:3–7, 15:8 ("truth"), and in the term ἐκ πίστεως in 1:17, possibly in 3:25, implicit in 15:11 and the whole of 9–11.[24] If Christ's faithfulness is also an important theme, why is it found only in two "grammatically ambiguous phrases," 3:22 and 26? Why is there no reference to Christ as πιστός? Would not references to *Christ's* faithfulness serve to obscure the emphasis on *God's* faithfulness, surely a central theme for any understanding of a covenantal dimension in Paul's theology?

4.2.3 You have argued that the besetting sin of the objective genitive is its emphasis on the salvific efficacy of individual faith, turning it, as it were, into a "work."[25] Yet it is also clear that the subjective genitive urges Christians to imitate the self-giving faithfulness of Christ. Why is that not also an

22 Hays, 49.
23 Dunn, 67.
24 Dunn, 76–77.
25 Hays, 55.

attempt to "cultivate the right sort of disposition"? Moreover, does the subjective genitive understanding not run the danger of seeing Christ as the bringer of faith (much as the gnostics see Christ as the bringer of knowledge) and hence as a transitory figure, no longer needed once we too have achieved such a "faith"? Is that not as dangerous as the docetic Christology to which the objective genitive seems open?

4.2.4 You have argued that one of the advantages of the subjective genitive interpretation is that it shows how the death of Jesus can be understood as a source of salvation.[26] Yet for Paul, we are saved by the death *and* resurrection of Christ (cf. Rom 4:25 with 5:21b; on the importance of the resurrection for Christian faith, see 1 Cor 15:14, 17). Christ can be obedient (faithful) "unto death" (Phil 2:9) but not "unto resurrection"; it is always God who raises him (Phil 2:9; cf. Rom 10:9b). Since the subjective genitive can point only to Jesus' death, not to his resurrection, does that not represent an intolerable short-circuiting of Paul's actual understanding of the relationship between Christology and soteriology? If the objective genitive understanding leaves too little room for emphasis on Jesus' obedience, does not the subjective genitive understanding leave too little room for emphasis on Jesus' resurrection?

5. CONCLUSIONS

As is by now apparent, I have some considerable sympathy for the positions held by both authors. I find very attractive the attempt by Prof. Hays to see Pauline theology in terms of a story with apocalyptic overtones, and to see Paul's interpretation of that story in terms of a covenantal theology in which Abraham plays a central part. I also find attractive the kind of sober exegesis carried on by Prof. Dunn in the course of looking at the passages crucial for this discussion of "genitival interpretation." I find it possible to hold to a Pauline covenantal story without the necessary support of a subjective interpretation; whether or not that is possible will be clearer, I hope, at the conclusion of our discussion.

6. AFTERWORD

The discussion of the two papers led the participants, Hays and Dunn, to certain refinements in their own arguments, but not to any significant reversals.

[26] Hays, 55.

6.1 Prof. Dunn emphasized the need to stick to the arguments of the letters in which the disputed genitival constructions appear, rather than reading them in the light of a proposed "story" which underlies, and gives coherence to, Paul's theological thought. Yet some such underlying unity must be posited if Pauline theology is not finally to be reduced to a collection of somewhat coherent, but also somewhat incoherent, attempts to resolve problems which arose as the result of his missionary efforts.

6.2 Prof. Hays emphasized the need to read Paul's language as metaphorical and multivalent. While it is true that there are cases where Paul is intentionally metaphorical, and there are cases where multivalency seems characteristic of his language, it is dangerous, in my view, to use this insight as a primary appeal in the resolution of exegetical problems. I find particularly questionable the assumption that in critical areas of argument, Paul intended to be so vague as to include a kind of "both-and" force to his language, i.e., that he intends to express himself so ambiguously that either one of two contrasting meanings can be found in his language (so Hays on Gal 3:14: the genitive is intended to convey the sense both of Christ's faithfulness and of the faith of the believer in Christ).

6.3 Finally, it was clear from the discussion that the answer to the problem of the kind of genitive use—subjective or objective—represented by χριστοῦ remains free of consensus, and will continue to occupy those who seek to understand the nuances of Paul's letters to his fellow Christians. If identifying a problem is necessary before it can be resolved, at least such identification became clearer as a result of the papers and the ensuing discussion.

Part III

Evaluating a Ten-Year Experiment

6 IN QUEST OF PAUL'S THEOLOGY

Retrospect and Prospect

James D. G. Dunn

THE QUEST FOR Paul's theology has been a frustrating experience.[1] In the earlier sessions of the quest we wrestled repeatedly with the problem of defining our subject matter. The issue was posed in the opening paper of the resultant volume by Paul Sampley: are we talking about "Paul's thought world," that is, "the fundamental frame of reference within which things made sense to Paul and out of which he operated?" Or do we mean the "communication of his thoughts in his letters to various churches?"[2] Alternatively expressed, by "Paul's theology" do we mean only the theology of each particular letter, or the theology of all the letters aggregated into a whole? Do we mean the theology of the Paul who stood behind the letters, or the theology of Paul the letter writer as such? Or as the issue was posed on several occasions do we mean Paul's theology or Paul's theologizing?[3] Or again, to adapt a distinction from current hermeneutical debate, do we mean the theology behind the letter(s), or the

1 I refer, of course, to the decade of meetings of the Pauline Theology Consultation, latterly the Pauline Theology Group, at the SBL meetings from 1986 to this its final-session in 1995. Papers from the earlier meetings (1986–88, 1989–91; 1992–1993) have been published as *Pauline Theology, Volume I: Thessalonians, Philippians, Galatians and Philemon*, ed. J. M. Bassler (Minneapolis: Fortress, 1991); *Pauline Theology, Volume II. 1 and 2 Corinthians,* ed. D. M. Hay (Minneapolis: Fortress, 1993); and *Pauline Theology, Volume III: Romans,* ed. D. M. Hay and E. E. Johnson (Minneapolis: Fortress, 1995), cited hereafter as *Pauline Theology I, Pauline Theology II,* and *Pauline Theology III*, respectively.

2 J. P. Sampley, "From Text to Thought World: The Route to Paul's Ways," *Pauline Theology I*.4–5.

3 So, e.g., V. P. Furnish: "while Paul's letters do not yield any kind of a comprehensive theological system, they introduce us to Paul the theologian, to a person engaged in earnest theological reflection. Hence, the subject of the present essay is not '*the* theology of I Corinthians,' but Paul's theological reflection as that is evident in this letter" ("Theology in I Corinthians," *Pauline Theology II*.61; see also his description of the actual task, *Pauline Theology II*.63).

theology in front of the letter(s), that is, the theological event "as it was intended and actively anticipated by Paul."[4]

The degree of confusion within the ongoing discussion is easily illustrated by noting the various working definitions used in the course of the decade of the quest.

> Bassler: "theology . . . defined as Paul's appropriation and application of scripture and Christian traditions to the specific situation of the Thessalonian community";[5]
>
> Stowers: "Theology is a method of organizing religious knowledge that arose at a particular time in the history of Christianity";[6]
>
> Wright: "Paul's theology consists precisely in the redefinition, by means of christology and pneumatology, of those two key Jewish doctrines," referring to what he has just described as "the twin heads of Jewish theology, namely, monotheism and election, God and Israel";[7]
>
> Scroggs: "Paul's theology is what he thinks about the transcendent and its intervention into immanent reality";[8]
>
> Hays: "When we seek the 'theology' of the letters . . . we are concerned neither with the performance as such nor with the competence as such, but with the ideational *mediating structures* that characterize Paul's critical selection, organization, and interpretation of the elements of the communal symbolic universe"; "the specific task of 'Pauline Theology' is to study the hermeneutical transformations that Paul performs in appropriating elements of his symbolic universe for the situation of his readers";[9]
>
> Furnish: "the presuppositions, convictions, and concerns which inform and thereby distinguish Paul's interpretation of the gospel"; or again, "critical re-

[4] J. L. Martyn, "Events in Galatia: Modified Covenantal Nomism versus God's Invasion of the Cosmos in the Singular Gospel," *Pauline Theology I*.161. In his earlier version of the paper delivered to the 1988 Chicago meeting, Martyn put the point more specifically: "it is that aural event (the Galatians' hearing Paul's letter read out to them) and its Pauline anticipation that constitute the theology of the letter" (manuscript p. 11).

[5] J. M. Bassler, "Peace in All Ways: Theology in the Thessalonian Letters," *Pauline Theology I*.71.

[6] S. K. Stowers, "Friends and Enemies in the Politics of Heaven: Reading Theology in Philippians," *Pauline Theology I*. 106. To be fair, Stowers adds that Paul "deserves to be considered at most only a precursor of Christian theology" (1.106).

[7] N. T. Wright, "Toward a Synthesis of *Pauline Theology* (1 and 2 Thessalonians, Philippians, and Philemon)," *Pauline Theology I*.184.

[8] R. Scroggs, "Salvation History: The Theological Structure of Paul's Thought (1 Thessalonians, Philippians, and Galatians)," *Pauline Theology I*.212.

[9] R. B. Hays, "Crucified with Christ: A Synthesis of the Theology of 1 and 2 Thessalonians, Philemon, Philippians, and Galatians," *Pauline Theology I*.228, 246.

flection on the beliefs, rites, and social structures in which an experience of ultimate reality has found expression";[10] and

Bassler again: "The *raw material of Paul's theology* (the kerygmatic story, scripture, traditions, etc.) passed through the *lens of Paul's experience* (his common Christian experience as well as his unique experience as one 'set apart by God for the gospel') and generated a *coherent (and characteristic) set of convictions.* These convictions were refracted through a prism, Paul's *perception of the situations that obtained in various* communities, where they were resolved into specific *words on target for those communities.*"[11]

Engberg-Pedersen suggests "that we understand Pauline theology in terms of the following two categories ... [T]he first category is that of Paul's own *variously formulated theological conceptions.* The other category is that of the 'application' of the theological conceptions to those other things" ("for example, particular moral issues, personal experiences, social conditions, and also such contingent matters as the theological conceptions of Paul's opponents").[12]

Hay: "Theology emerges as Paul listens to the doubts of others and those in his own mind, reflects on essential convictions, and ponders which warrants preserve 'the fear of the Lord' and are likely to persuade."[13]

With such a diversity in understanding of the object of the exercise and of the method of pursuing that object, it was not surprising that Steven Kraftchick's two contributions to the second volume of collected papers struck a gloomy note: "regardless of the methods of inquiry we have adopted, the full recovery of Paul's thought has remained beyond our collective grasp"; "the more a Pauline theology is predicated upon its historical and rhetorical circumstances, the more just those things recede from our grasp."[14] Kraftchick's challenge is one to which the Group has not so far responded.

Another factor contributing to what appeared to several as a steady lowering of spirits within the Group in its latter stages was the chosen way of proceed-

10 V. P. Fumish, from an unpublished paper distributed to the 1986 meeting, cited by J. M. Bassler, "Paul's Theology: Whence and Whither?" *Pauline Theology II*.7 n.16. The second quotation comes from his "Paul the Theologian," in *The Conversation Continues: Studies in Paul and John in Honor of J. Louis Martyn*, ed. R. T. Fortna and B. R. Gaventa (Nashville: Abingdon, 1990) 25, also cited by C. B. Cousar, "The Theological Task of 1 Corinthians: A Conversation with Gordon D. Fee and Victor Paul Fumish," *Pauline Theology II*.90.

11 Bassler, *Pauline Theology II*.11.

12 T. Engberg Pedersen, "Proclaiming the Lord's Death: 1 Corinthians 11:17–34 and the Forms of Paul's Theological Argument," *Pauline Theology II*.104.

13 D. M. Hay, "The Shaping of Theology in 2 Corinthians: Convictions, Doubts, and Warrants," *Pauline Theology II*.155.

14 S. J. Kraftchick, "Seeking a More Fluid Model," *Pauline Theology II*.34; also "Death in Us, Life in You: The Apostolic Medium," *Pauline Theology II*.156.

ing. By deliberate choice we have focused on each letter in turn and roughly in chronological sequence, leaving the four *Hauptbriefe* till the end. The intention was impeccable: that we should gain as clear a perception as possible of what the smaller Pauline letters contributed, individually and together, to the quest, without their contribution being determined or swamped by the impact of the *Hauptbriefe.*[15] The problems, however, have been severe. For one thing, by the time we reached the later letters the question of definition and method had largely run out of steam,[16] so that we lost the benefit which their theological weight would have brought to our discussions. Moreover, the inference that initial syntheses would somehow provide a core for subsequent syntheses, resulting in a final grand synthesis, was probably too naive from the start. Worst of all, in leaving Romans till the end, we found ourselves, with the day already far spent, confronted by the highest mountain peak of all. The initial scouting parties led by Tom Wright and Lee Keck made good progress,[17] but thereafter we were confronted by a maze of different paths and may have lost our way, at least insofar as real theological engagement was concerned, with the question of how the theology of Romans might be added into the earlier syntheses left to one side. To attempt some sort of summary, of course, is the task in hand. But experience to date in the Group will not raise expectations very high.

On the other hand, we should not allow ourselves to become unduly depressed. A careful reading of the above definitions reveals a considerable degree of consensus on the nature of what it is we are looking for—in particular, on the dynamic character of Paul's theology, that his theology was an "activity" (to use Bassler's term),[18] or, alternatively expressed, that his theology was always interactive. Even when the definition is drawn up in terms of content and its "application" (Engberg-Pedersen) there is no attempt to identify a theology which could be spoken of somehow independently of and unaffected by Paul's

15 The ground rules were not always observed, however.

16 Kraftchick had called for a moratorium on the onward procession of papers "until questions of definition and procedure are more fully agreed on" *(Pauline Theology II.*34).

17 N. T. Wright, "Romans and the Theology of Paul," *Pauline Theology III.*30–67; L. E. Keck, "What Makes Romans Tick?", *Pauline Theology III.*3–29. Keck devotes most of his paper to introductory matters, although its too brief final section is highly suggestive. Unfortunately I was unable to attend the 1992 meeting, so my impressions of the 1992 meeting are not first-hand. However, it will become apparent that my own way of modeling Paul's theology (below section II) has important points of similarity with Wright's. And Keck's conclusion—"What makes Romans tick is neither Paul's situation nor even the actual content . . . but the convictions that not only permit/require these contents to be articulated but which also allow them to be juxtaposed" (*Pauline Theology III.*21)—is similar to the perspective from which I approach particular issues in Paul's theology in section III below.

18 Bassler, *Pauline Theology II.*10–11, 16–17. See also Fumish, cited by Cousar, *Pauline Theology II.*91; Hay, *Pauline Theology II.*135–136; Kraftchick, *Pauline Theology II.*157.

addressing his churches. To put the same point another way, Paul is never simply theologian, he is always at one and the same time Paul the theologian, missionary, and pastor, or simply, Paul the apostle.[19] The main difference between the definitions is the degree of complexity of model which each has used—some content with a simple or general statement, whose complexity will become apparent in the elaboration of the theology itself, others striving for a definition which encapsulates the way Paul's theology/theologizing actually worked in practice.

Again, when we look at particular controversies which marked the different meetings of the Consultation/Group, it becomes clear that the disagreements often boiled down to points of detail and emphasis, to the effects of perspective and the degree of light and shade. In contrast, there was broad agreement on larger issues, not least on the character, focus and major themes of Paul's gospel. Indeed, part of the disappointment of the later meetings was the lack of really meaty theological disagreements to spark the passions and rekindle the enthusiasms.

The first volume of the collected papers gives a remarkable indication of consensus even in disagreement. A rereading of the papers in that volume (covering Thessalonians, Philippians, Philemon and Galatians) indicates two large measures of consensus. One was over the apocalyptic substratum of Paul's theology, early on proposed by Chris Beker in his restatement of Paul's theology (or hermeneutic) as "shaped by a complex interaction of coherence and contingency."[20] This evidently struck a chord, not only in the papers on Thessalonians,[21] but also in Martyn's strong presentation, followed by Beverly Gaventa's,[22] of the apocalyptic character of the theology of Galatians, a letter which, oddly enough, Beker had found difficult to fit into his scheme.[23] It is also to be seen in Paul Achtemeier's initial response to Beker and in the final (partial) syntheses of Tom Wright and Richard Hays.[24]

19 In earlier papers, cf. B. R. Gaventa, "Apostle and Church in 2 Corinthians," *Pauline Theology II*.193–199; R. Jewett, "Ecumenical Theology for the Sake of Mission: Romans 1:1–17 + 15:14–16:24," *Pauline Theology III*.89–108.

20 J. C. Beker, "Recasting Pauline Theology: The Coherence-Contingency Scheme as Interpretive Model," *Pauline Theology I*.15. See his earlier *Paul the Apostle: The Triumph of God in Life and Thought* (Philadelphia: Fortress, 1980).

21 By E. Krentz, "Through a Lens: Theology and Fidelity in 2 Thessalonians," *Pauline Theology I*, chap. 5; R. Jewett, "A Matrix of Grace: The Theology of 2 Thessalonians as a Pauline Letter," *Pauline Theology I*, chap. 6; Bassler, *Pauline Theology I*, chap. 7.

22 Martyn, *Pauline Theology I*, chap. 12; B. R. Gaventa, "The Singularity of the Gospel: A Reading of Galatians," *Pauline Theology I*, chap. 11.

23 Beker, *Paul*, 58.

24 P. J. Achtemeier, "Finding the Way to Paul's Theology," *Pauline Theology I*.30; Wright, *Pauline Theology I*.184, 197–201; Hays, *Pauline Theology I*.231ff.

Yet at the same time, all four of those contributing the final (partial) syntheses of the first volume were agreed that some version of "salvation history,"[25] or what Stowers calls "the grand narrative" about God, Christ, and Paul,[26] was unavoidable in speaking of a basic schema underlying Paul's theology.[27] It is true that Martyn puts himself in direct opposition to any rapprochement between the two emphases: "the singularity of the Seed spells . . . the end of *Heilsgeschichte* as a view that encompasses a linear history of a people of God prior to Christ"; "*throughout* Galatians, far from proposing a linear history that begins with Abraham, Paul stands in opposition to such a view."[28] But the double consensus shows that it is not necessary to pose the two as such sharp alternatives and antitheses: after all, Israel's own apocalyptic expectation (as indeed Paul's too) was as much of consummation and transformation as of disruption and new beginning; and the papers of Wright and Hays show clearly that it is possible to construct (or recognize) a synthesis which combines both a narrative substructure to Paul's theology and a full recognition of the apocalyptic/eschatological break-through of the cross and resurrection.[29]

To mention but one other point of consensus underlying fierce disagreement. The debate on the meaning and significance of *pistis Christou* divided the Group more or less down the middle.[30] And there seemed to be no middle ground between the alternatives: either "the faith(fulness) of Christ," or "faith in Christ."[31] What became evident in the debate on the issue, however, was that each side agreed in large measure with the theological point being claimed by the other. Those opting for the objective genitive rendering ("faith in Christ") were equally ready to accept a reading of Paul's theology in terms of Christ's obedience on the cross as an expression of God's faithfulness to his people and promises. And those who insisted on a subjective genitive reading ("the faith of Christ") certainly had no wish to deny that belief in Christ was a fundamental part of Paul's gospel. In other words, the disagreement was, in effect, only over

25 Scroggs, *Pauline Theology I*.215f, D. J. Lull, "Salvation History: Theology in 1 Thessalonians, Philemon, Philippians, and Galatians," *Pauline Theology I*, chap. 16.

26 Stowers, *Pauline Theology I*.117.

27 Wright, *Pauline Theology I*, chap. 13; Hays, *Pauline Theology I*.231ff. But note Bassler's caution (*Pauline Theology II*.8).

28 Martyn, *Pauline Theology I*.174–176.

29 Wright, *Pauline Theology I*, chap. 13; Hays, *Pauline Theology I*, chap. 15.

30 Though there will probably be different estimates of whether one side or other was in the majority, the point, for what it is worth, is difficult to determine since only a minority of those present took part in the debate.

31 The main papers in the debate were by R. B. Hays, "*Pistis* and Pauline Christology: What is at Stake?" and J. D. G. Dunn, "Once More, ΠΙΣΤΙΣ ΧΡΙΣΤΟΥ," in the present volume.

the rendering of that particular phrase—more a grammatical dispute than a theological dispute.

These illustrations probably indicate a truer picture of the debate about Paul's theology—broad consensus on fundamental structures, with vigorous disagreement on particular details of content and interaction with his audiences. So perhaps we may proceed with lighter hearts than at first seemed possible.

II

Much of the discussion on methodology and definition focused on the model by means of which we can most helpfully conceptualize Paul's theology and theologizing. We became accustomed to images like substratum, master symbolism, basic grammar, integrative metaphor, narrative structure, and so on. The most popular one, by a short head, seems to have been that of "lens," though what the lens was and what was passed through it was less agreed. For Edgar Krentz "apocalyptic was the theological lens"; for Hays our objective was "to trace the contours of the hermeneutical lens through which Paul projects the images of the community's symbolic world onto the screen of the community's life"; for Bassler, as we have already seen, the lens is Paul's experience through which the "raw material of Paul's theology" passed (*sic*).[32]

For myself I wonder if such imagery is not as much a hindrance as a help: the flash of illumination which it brings to one aspect of the process of Paul's theology can be soon lost in the qualifications and complications we have to introduce to make the image adaptable to the complex reality of that theology. Is there not a simpler and more natural model or parallel—that of our own theologizing? Perhaps it takes a European to make this point, given that theology as such continues to hold an honored place within the academic and university traditions of Europe. Is it inappropriate and unjustified to wonder out loud whether the difficulty of this forum in gaining a handle on Paul's theology may perhaps reflect what, to European eyes, appears to be an embarrassment at the enterprise of theology and loss of theological nerve in North America? Be that as it may, our best insights into the complexity of Paul's theology as activity may well come from reflection on our own activity in theologizing.

In most contemporary theologizing three phases or levels can be distinguished. The first or deepest level is that of inherited convictions or traditional life patterns. At this level we are dealing with axioms and presuppositions, often hidden or undeclared. An important part of theological education is to enable

32 Krentz, *Pauline Theology I*.52; Hays, *Pauline Theology I*.228; Bassler, *Pauline Theology II*.11.

and facilitate critical self-reflection on these presuppositions. The second is the sequence of transformative moments in the individual's (or community's) growth and development. These window opening experiences, including conversion experiences, usually generate other insights and corollaries and can shape attitudes and determine important life choices. They will be much nearer the surface of the person's theology and more obvious to the onlooker. The third level is, of course, the ongoing interaction of the presuppositions and principles of the other two levels with the questions and challenges of each day. This will be the level nearest the surface, by which I mean the level most accessible to the onlooker, which is not the same as saying it is a superficial level.

In addition we need to recall that most theologizing is undertaken within a community (and/or communities) and in relation to a community's traditions, life, needs and opportunities. This means that theology is unavoidably dialogic in character. There is something missing in a theology conceived simply as the individual wrestling with some concept or belief in some secluded academic's study. According to Paul, community grows out of shared experience (the *koinonia tou pneumatos*), and the community of Christ's body grows by the interactive sharing of the Spirit's gifts. The encounters of theological dialogue within and between communities are the life-blood of theology, and as such encounters move to and include the deeper level they can be among the richest and most challenging of theological experiences.[33]

All this is fairly basic stuff but it bears upon our concerns in several ways. First, it should reassure us that the enterprise of questing after Paul's theology is a worthwhile exercise, that our degree of failure to pin Paul down at various points should cause us no surprise. After all, we engage in lively theological discussion with our contemporaries. Yet which of us can pin down the living theology of our dialogue partners? We can encounter each other theologically at different levels of our theology, but which of us can describe with confidence more than a handful of the others' theological convictions and principles? How often have you and I mused over a colleague's position on some controversial theological point, uncertain as to where she or he finally stands? And yet we nevertheless can and do have real theological communication. And yet most theologians belong to communities of faith and worship and can even use the same creeds and liturgy. Astonishing!

Why should we expect more in our dialogue with Paul? Of course we cannot argue with and interrogate Paul as we can a contemporary. On the other

33 This movement to deeper depths of theological differences has characterized the course of the ecumenical movement's intra-traditions dialogue through the twentieth century.

hand, the variety of letters he has left us, and to a variety of situations, yet over a comparatively short period, allows us to come at Paul's theology from a variety of angles and brings us as close as we can ever get to a dialogue with a historical figure. Moreover, when we look at the theology of Paul as presented by the full range of his modern dialogue partners, what we actually find can be represented as a standard distribution curve[34]—that is, a large degree of consensus within fairly limited parameters, with increasingly divergent views gaining sharply decreasing support And why should we expect more? This simply reflects the nature of interactive theology, including our own with Paul's. When I write a theology of Paul all I can hope for is to strengthen the broad consensual positions where I also think they are correct and to help gain support towards a fresh consensus on items and details where I think the contemporary consensus has become a little lopsided.

That being said, I would have to add that the value of theologizing Paul's theology, or of theologizing in dialogue with Paul, should never be measured merely in terms of the votes of theologians. That would be wholly contrary to Paul's own theological evaluation. Consequently, my primary hope in any theology of Paul would be to re-express something of the life-shaping power which his first readers and hearers evidently experienced through his writings, to help my readers experience afresh Paul's theology as activity and event, perhaps even, dare I say it, as Word of God. However frustrating, the quest for Paul's theology is never less than rewarding, so long as it is carried through as a theological exercise.

Second, our own experience of dialogue generally (not just theological dialogue) should give us pointers on how we ourselves can hope to move between the different levels of Paul's theology. The key term here is "allusion." This is a term which Richard Hays in particular has brought into our dialogue.[35] But as Harold Bloom had already pointed out,[36] our guild as a whole has been remarkably insensitive to the reality and power of allusion within our documents. Despite our best efforts we have on the whole been content to stand outside the communities of discourse within which our documents emerged and flourished and to which they give expression. We have been like people trying to listen in to other peoples' conversation, a conversation with which we were ourselves too

34 Properly speaking, of course, the standard distribution curve should be four-dimensional (including movement through time), but that would simply make the model so complex as to lose its heuristic value.

35 R. B. Hays, *Echoes of Scripture in the Letters of Paul* (New Haven:Yale University Press, 1989).

36 H. Bloom in *Poetics of Influence*, ed. J. Hollander (New Haven: Henry R. Schwab, 1988) 387–424: "New Testament scholarship manifests a very impoverished notion as to what literary allusion is or can be" (392). I owe the reference to my doctoral postgraduate Stephen Wright.

little conversant, and indeed sometimes unsympathetic. That so much of their conversation consequently passes us by should cause us no surprise.

Which of us is not aware of the character of community discourse, and particularly of the bonding power of allusion within that discourse? It is the shared experiences and convictions which can be taken for granted which bond a community together. It is the shared experiences and convictions to which an allusion is sufficient to evoke a corporate sense of belonging and well-being which tell you most about the character of a community. Which of us has not been a guest at some celebration or gathering where in-jokes and allusions function almost tangibly to bond the community together, while also making the guests aware that they are outsiders? Which of us has not had the experience of joining with a different faith community, perhaps in another country, and stumbling repeatedly at the taken-for-granteds and allusions which we do not recognize?

The importance of this observation for our quest of Paul's theology is that it undermines the strategy which the Consultation/Group adopted. That is to say, it becomes virtually impossible, or at least unrealistic, to try to confine our dialogue with Paul's theology to a single letter. For each letter is itself part and expression of the larger community of discourse within which Paul and his churches were caught up. Each letter, therefore, contains taken-for-granteds and allusions which we will be unable to elucidate from that letter alone (if at all); we will always find ourselves as strangers at some other community's meal table, missing and misunderstanding more than we can grasp. We need the other parts of the dialogue available to us, which are Paul's other letters, if we are to have any hope of penetrating to any degree at all below the surface of any single letter. And we need the corpus of Paul's letters set against the background of other NT writings and other Jewish and Hellenistic writings of the period if we are to have any hope of catching the allusions which must, a priori, have been part of the discourse of Jewish and Hellenistic Christian assemblies.[37] In short, even if we want to stick at the level of the individual letter, the letter itself, with its varied more and less obvious allusions, forbids us to do so.

This line of reflection leads to a third observation. The model thus far sketched out, the model of contemporary theological dialogue, with its communal dimension and therefore also its frequently allusive character, might seem to leave all in a state of flux. Certainly at the most surface level of the letters, Paul's own stated strategy of "all things to all" (1 Cor 9:19–22) suggests a pragmatism and flexibility whose integrity we at our distance might not be able

37 I have developed the point in my SNTS paper, "Prolegomena to a Theology of Paul," *NTS* 40 (1994) 407–432.

fully to comprehend.[38] And when we switch attention to the deeper level of underlying convictions and paradigms, the degree to which we are forced to depend on hearing allusions correctly or appropriately again makes the enterprise more hazardous.[39] The disagreement between Krentz and Jewett on whether "grace" in 2 Thessalonians is merely part of a "stock formula" (Krentz) or "the underlying theological matrix of the letter" (Jewett)[40] is a small reminder of just how difficult it is to locate oneself within a discourse with whose terms one is not wholly familiar. And the danger of our last observation (no letter is an island!) is that we might find ourselves going round in circles, always having to refer elsewhere to illuminate any individual text, caught in another version of the hermeneutical circles, or, alternatively expressed, in the exegetical equivalent of an infinite regress.

Here again, however, there is some ground for hope. For there is one letter of Paul's which is less caught in the flux and developing discourse of Paul's churches than the others. And that is Romans. In the movement and dialogue of Paul's theology, his letter to the Romans is a relatively (I stress, relatively) fixed point. It was written to a church which was not his own founding. It was not so much occasioned by circumstances and his own personal involvement. It was written at the end of a (or better, the) major phase of Paul's missionary work which included (almost) all the other undisputed letters. It was written under probably the most congenial circumstances of his mission, with time for careful reflection and composition. And above all, it was written to set out his own understanding of the gospel as he had thus far proclaimed it, and as he hoped to commend it both in Jerusalem and beyond Rome to Spain. In short, it is the most sustained and reflective statement of Paul's own theology by Paul himself.

This suggests to me that the most obvious place to locate oneself within the dialogue of Paul's theology is in Romans itself. That is to say, not to attempt to describe simply the theology of Romans as the theology of Paul. But rather to view Paul's theology from the perspective given by Romans, to use Romans as the relatively fixed point in the flow and development of Paul's theologizing and to compare other formulations with that in Romans. This will mean look-

38 As I believe to be demonstrated by the theses regarding the self-contradictions within Paul's writings associated particularly with the names of E. P. Sanders, *Paul, the Law, and the Jewish People* (Philadelphia: Fortress, 1983) and H. Räisänen, *Paul and the Law* (Tübingen: Mohr, 1983). Not to mention the debate as to how principled and how pragmatic was Paul's advice regarding the role of women within worship and ministry.

39 As Wright's grand narrative thesis warns us *(Pauline Theology I,* chap. 13; also "Romans," e.g., 211).

40 Krentz, *Pauline Theology I*.59; Jewett, *Pauline Theology I*.65.

ing backwards to earlier formulations, to see how Paul had varied and developed them. It will also mean looking forward, to see how Pauline theology continued to develop, on the assumption that the tail of the comet can tell us something about the comet itself. But the main hope and effect of a Romans-centered theology of Paul will be to recognize the living and dynamic character of Paul's theology as a faith- and religion-shaping activity.

In short, the model of our own theologizing has highlighted three useful pointers in the quest for Paul's theology. One is the recognition of different levels—the inherited, axiomatic level of taken-for-granted presuppositions, the transformative moments of personal insight and development, and the interaction with diverse situations and issues. It will not be merely coincidental that these three levels are particularly evident in Paul's theology. I have elsewhere already described these as, first, the elements of his faith inherited from his ancestral religion ("the story of Israel"), second, the impact of his conversion in particular ("the revelation of Christ") but also of further interaction with pre-Pauline Christian tradition and crises in his mission to the Gentiles prior to his letter writing, and third the interaction of the letters themselves.[41] The second pointer is the importance of being sensitive to allusions as a way of recognizing dimensions of Paul's theology not immediately evident on the page in front of us and as a way of discerning the relative weight to be given on the one hand to the understated taken-for-granted, and on the other to the particular formulation intended for the situation actually being addressed. The third pointer is the advisability of taking Romans as providing the relatively most stable framework on which we should be able to reconstruct a theology of Paul which Paul himself might have owned.

III

In what follows, we have time to give only an outline of what such a theology of Paul might look like. Even so it will have to be a selective outline, seeking chiefly to provide a few illustrations which might help shed light on some of the still contentious issues within the continuing debate on Paul's theology. That the outline will look somewhat like older-fashioned theologies should neither surprise us nor cause us to shy away from such an outline. On the contrary, these older theologies simply demonstrate the influence of Romans in their construction—and quite properly so, as I have just argued. Indeed, our

41 "Prolegomena," 427–31, where for sake of fuller analysis I distinguished two levels within the present second level.

contemporary attempt to distance ourselves from the model of such older theologies may have been a factor in feeding our own frustrations, since in spurning them we have too readily spurned Romans as the model, making our task immeasurably more difficult rather than more modern.

1. A theology of Paul really does have to begin with Paul's *theology of God*. God is the greatest of all taken-for-granteds in Paul's writings, despite the fact that *theos* occurs nearly 550 times in the Pauline corpus, as against nearly 380 occurrences of *Christos* and 275 occurrences of *kyrios*. Given these figures we should perhaps rephrase our point, that God is not so much taken for granted in Paul's theology as taken for granted in our dialogue with and attempts to describe Paul's theology. As Nils Dahl pointed out twenty years ago, "the understanding of God has been the neglected factor in the study of NT theology as a whole."[42]

The reason for the neglect is obvious. God was not a point of theology at issue, save where Paul made it so; Paul did not have to argue for belief in God. God was common ground between Paul and the recipients of his letters. Even former polytheists did not have to be re-persuaded with regard to the one God of Israel and Father of the Lord Jesus Christ (cf. particularly 1 Thess 1:9–10). And so, the unemphasized too easily became the overlooked. In other words, theology in the narrow sense, belonged to the theology and faith which Paul inherited as a Jewish boy and from which he never shifted. And even with his Gentile converts, the transformative moment of their conversion had evidently become so axiomatic as to require no further exposition. But simply because Paul does not treat of God as subject matter of his particular theologizing, in the way he does subjects like justification and the church, should not be an excuse for us to ignore this dimension of his theology or to assume in effect that it was not a vital and fundamental factor in the theologizing as well as worship of his churches.

Here is where Romans provides an important guideline. For its exposition of Paul's gospel begins at once with a threefold statement about God's power, God's righteousness and God's wrath (Rom 1:16–18). And its now generally recognized climax is Paul's defense of God's faithfulness and mercy (Rom 9–11; 15:7–13). It is precisely the strength and to the credit of Beker that he brought this neglected dimension so much center stage in his own theology of Paul.[43] And earlier papers of the present Consultation/Group are to be commended

[42] N. A. Dahl, "The Neglected Factor in New Testament Theology," *Reflection* 73 (1975) 5–8, cited by L E. Keck, "Toward the Renewal of New Testament Christology," *NTS* 32 (1986) 363.

[43] Beker, *Paul*, particularly 355–367.

likewise.[44] Nevertheless the full significance of this axiomatic feature of Paul's theology still needs to sink in. Not least the fact that Paul retained his fundamental belief in God as one (Rom 3:29; 1 Cor 8:6; 15:28). At no point does he give any hint or suggestion that he thought he was abandoning or calling into question that foundational credo. On the contrary, this evidently continued to be the framework within which Paul developed and expressed his christology (not least 1 Cor 8:6), and the recognition of this fact simply has to be a constraining factor in our interpretation of the great christological passages like Phil 2:6–11. As Kraftchick justifiably observed, "part of Paul's task as a 'theologian' was to create contexts that narrowed the possible avenues of interpretation to those consonant with other aspects of the gospel."[45] In this case, the context of Paul's christology was Paul's continuing monotheism which narrows the possible avenues of interpreting Paul's christology.[46]

2. A second fundamental strand of Paul's theology, in the light of Romans, has to be *the framework of Israel's story.* This is not to downplay the universal perspective which also shapes Paul's theology—God as Creator (Rom 1:19ff.), who will have mercy on all (11:32). It is rather to draw attention to the degree in which Paul interweaves Israel's story within this larger indictment and hope. It is well known, for example, that the indictment of human failure and idolatry in 1:23ff. echoes the Psalmist's own condemnation of *Israel's* fall in the idolatry of the golden calf (Ps 106:20).[47] Nor is it accidental that the main thrust in the second half of the indictment in Rom 1:18–3:20 is clearly directed against Israel (2:lff.), with 3:19a deliberately underlining the point.[48] So the fact that 11:32 ("God has confined all in disobedience in order that he might have mercy on

44 See E. Richard, "Early Pauline Thought: An Analysis of 1 Thessalonians," *Pauline Theology I.*43; Krentz, *Pauline Theology I.*57–9; Gaventa, *Pauline Theology I* 1.150; Wright, *Pauline Theology I.*184; Lull, *Pauline Theology I.*250; G. D. Fee, "Toward a Theology of I Corinthians," *Pauline Theology II.*40–43; Furnish, *Pauline Theology II.*67–69, 79–80; C. J. Roetzel, "The Grammar of Election in Four Pauline Letters," *Pauline Theology II*, chap. 11; A. T. Lincoln, "From Wrath to Justification: Tradition, Gospel and Audience in the Theology of Romans 1:18–4:25," *Pauline Theology III.*130–159.

45 Kraftchick, *Pauline Theology II.*180.

46 See further L. W. Hurtado, *One God. One Lord. Early Christian Devotion and Ancient Jewish Monotheism* (Philadelphia: Fortress/London: SCM, 1988); J. D. G. Dunn, "Christology as an Aspect of Theology," in *The Future of Christology: Essays in Honor of Leander E. Keck,* ed. A. J. Malherbe and W. A. Meeks (Minneapolis: Fortress, 1993) 202–212.

47 See, e.g., my *Romans* (WBC 38; Dallas: Word, 1988) 61. I am more open than I was in *Romans*, 383 to the likelihood that Rom 7:9–11 includes an allusion to Israel's own fall into sin and death as well as that of humankind at large; see particularly F. Thielman, "The Story of Israel and the Theology of Romans 5–8," *Pauline Theology III.*169–195.

48 Similarly, Lincoln, *Pauline Theology III.*145–146.

all") comes as the climax to Paul's attempt to resolve the problem of Israel and of God's faithfulness to Israel should occasion no surprise.

There are several points of contemporary importance which follow from this. One is the point that Paul's doctrine of justification arose within this framework, the framework of presupposition that the one God was the God of Israel, that God was thus committed to Israel as over against the (other) nations, and that God's righteousness was to be understood in terms of this commitment. That is to say, in Stendahl's terms, the doctrine of justification as we find it in Paul arose precisely as an attempt to resolve the problem of how the other nations can after all be acceptable to God.[49] This was a point made occasionally in the past,[50] but it was largely lost to sight in the dominant tendency to focus the theology of justification in the individual's finding peace with God.[51] And though this nationalistic dimension is now more widely heard and recognized, an adequate integration of these different dimensions has yet to be achieved.

Another point which has exercised me greatly in recent years is what this continuing framework of Paul's theology says about Christianity's own identity, particularly insofar as it allows Paul to be a shaping force in defining that identity.[52] For if Paul is right, if the story of Israel is still fundamental to a Pauline shaped Christian theology, then what should that say to Christianity's understanding of its relationship not simply with historic Judaism but with the other main religion which has grown from the same root, and which, on the face of it at least, has more claim to the scriptures of Israel than Christians have? If, alternatively, Paul's understanding of his mission to the Gentiles as a fulfillment of Israel's responsibility to be a light to the nations is a properly Jewish interpretation of the Abrahamic promise, then what does that factor add to contemporary Jewish/Christian dialogue? The debate about Paul as apostle or apostate is still only in its early stages.[53]

3. A third element in the outline has, of course, to be *the Christ focus of Paul's theology.* This is the theme to which Paul turns at once having completed his indictment in Rom 3:20. What is striking in this case, however, is that Paul

49 K. Stendahl, *Paul Among Jews and Gentiles* (Philadelphia: Fortress/London: SCM, 1977) 1–2.

50 Particularly W. Wrede, *Paul* (London: Philip Green, 1907) 122–128.

51 See further my "The Justice of God: A Renewed Perspective on Justification by Faith," *JTS* 43 (1992) 1–22.

52 I may refer here simply to my *The Partings of the Ways between Christianity and Judaism and their Significance for the Character of Christianity* (London: SCM/Philadelphia: TPI, 1991), which one or two Jewish scholars saw as an expression of some kind of Christian triumphalism, failing to recognize that the critique and challenge was directed primarily to Christian self-definition (as the last part of the title indicates). Further papers on the theme are in press.

53 The echo of A. F. Segal, *Paul the Convert: The Apostolate and Apostasy of Saul the Pharisee* (New Haven: Yale University Press, 1990) is deliberate.

spends so few verses expounding his christology: a mere six verses (3:21–26) answers to an indictment of some sixty-four verses (1:18–3:20). Evidently this too belongs to a deeper level of Paul's theology, what I have described as the second level, the impact of the revelation of Christ on Paul. In this case it largely consists of what is usually recognized to be an earlier kerygmatic formulation (3:24–26),[54] what Paul had learned from others or had himself formulated at an earlier period. At any rate the fact that it can be simply cited rather than argued for presumably means that Paul could assume it was common ground with his Roman audiences. This is the level, we might say, where the matter is not so much taken-for-granted, as not-requiring-to-be-elaborated since it was part of the common stock of Christian tradition shared among the churches. I have elsewhere reflected on the fact that so much of Paul's christology seems to share this same character and how surprisingly uncontroversial so much of his christology seems to have been, among his own churches at any rate.[55] But I still await fuller engagement on the point from those who I know disagree.

Since so much has been said on this subject, a natural focus for Christian engagement with Paul's theology, as reflected not least in the papers of the Consultation/Group, I need add little more in this particular exercise. We should recall, however, the tension referred to above, between an apocalyptic christology and a climax-of-salvation-history christology, which remained unsolved from the discussion of the theology of Galatians.[56] I have already re-indicated my own conviction that this conflict should surely be resolvable since Paul seems to speak in both sets of terms. But perhaps the model developed in the meantime strengthens that case. For what we have here, surely, is a clash between two levels of Paul's theology, or, as we might say, two of his constitutive narratives. The one, Israel's story, which, as Romans indicates, Paul thought was still to reach its climax. The other, Christ's story, whose shattering impact on Paul on the Damascus road gave it a lastingly and definitively apocalyptic character. Paul continued to tell—and to live—both stories. Alternatively, could we not say that Paul's theology focused round two dominant integrative metaphors? And, as is the case when several metaphors are in use, the metaphors did not jell entirely. But that is the nature of metaphors, and the impulse to make them jell or to subordinate one to the other is actually a failure to respect their metaphorical character, an attempt to turn them into propositions which can be measured for consistency. At any rate, the debate should not be left in its present unsatisfactory, unresolved condition.

54 See, e.g., the brief discussion and those cited in my *Romans*, 163–164.

55 J. D. G. Dunn, "How Controversial was Paul's Christology?" in *From Jesus to Paul: Essays on Jesus and New Testament Christology in Honour of Marinus de Jonge* (ed. M. C. de Boer; JSNTS 84; Sheffield: Academic Press, 1993) 148–67.

56 See above (section 1) and *Pauline Theology I*, Parts IV and V.

4. A fourth foundational strand in Paul's theology is his emphasis on faith as the appropriate human response to divine grace. I have little need to restate here the central role of faith in Romans, as elsewhere in Paul. We may think, for example, of its place in Paul's self-definition of his apostolic task (Rom 1:5), of its role in the thematic statement of the letter (1:16–17), and of its focal significance in the crucial passage 3:21 to the end of chap. 4. Particularly important is the latter part of Romans 4 where Paul states more clearly than anywhere else what he understands "faith" to be and involve—an unconditional trust and reliance on God alone, on God's promise and power and on nothing of human capacity or ability (4:18–21). Also to be noted in the same passage is the way Paul portrays this faith as the trust and reliance of the creature on the Creator and integrates acknowledgment of (old) creation with hope of new: the faith is in God "who gives life to the dead and calls things which have no existence into existence" (4:17). Such trustful reliance is obviously the reversal of humankind's initial failure to glorify and give thanks to God (1:21).[57]

This line of theological reflection raises one of the perennial issues of Pauline theology which, despite that, still receives too little attention. I refer to the tension between the christocentric faith for which Paul's gospel calls and the fact that he is able to document, define and justify that faith from OT precedents and texts (Gen 15:6 and Hab 2:4). Putting the point bluntly, if it is faith like that of Abraham which is called for, why need it be specifically faith in Christ? Paul's answer would presumably be that God's eschatological purpose so focused in Christ that faith in Christ is now the eschatological equivalent of Abraham's faith. But the answer raises the further question, whether the focus of God's grace is now so exclusively in Christ that there can no longer be faith in God (like that of Abraham) unless it is faith in Christ. That seems a harsh corollary to draw, only validated by 9:32–33 in relation to Israel, and even so put in some question by his understanding of faith in terms elsewhere applied to universal wisdom in 10:6–9, 18.[58]

It is not unimportant to appreciate that this is another example of the tension between the different levels of Paul's theology. For the tension is that between Paul's continuing faith in God and his new, eschatological faith in Christ. In fact it is another way of posing the tension already observed between some form of *Heilsgeschichte* and the apocalyptic dimension in Paul's theology, between the continuity and discontinuity of Paul's gospel with the preceding story of God's of Israel. Once again we have to insist that Paul did hold both together in his theology. But now we also have to say in addition that it is constitutive of Paul's understanding of faith that the two be held together: to put too much weight

57 Hence the significance of both eaters and non-eaters being able to "give thanks" in 14:6.

58 For details of the argument behind this assertion see my *Romans,* 602–5.

on the one would make Paul's christology redundant; whereas to put too much weight on the other would be to separate Paul's christology from his theology of God. This latter, it seems to me, is the ultimate danger of the emphasis of Martyn and Gaventa, that they open the door to a kind of Marcionism.

Here too it may be appropriate to add a further thought on my own dispute with Hays on *pistis Christou*.[59] For if *pistis Christou* does denote "the faith (fulness) of Christ" (Hays), then that would put it more on the side of continuity with the divine purpose as laid out in the OT. At the center of Paul's gospel would be the claim that Jesus himself was faithful, very much, indeed, as Abraham had been found faithful in his readiness to offer up Isaac (1 Macc 2:52; Jas 2:21–23)—or so Paul's assertion would surely have been heard—faithfulness being understood as an expression of the divine faithfulness (cf. Rom 3:25 and 8:32).[60] My problem with such an exposition is that it would make the *pistis Christou* phrase in effect continuous and consistent with Jewish (= Abraham's) faithfulness in doing what the law requires ("the works of the law") (in contrast to Rom 4:2). And yet Paul seems to set the two concepts (covenant faithfulness and *pistis Christou)* in antithesis, not least in Gal 2:16, with *pistis Christou* more on the side of "the revelation (apocalypse) of Christ" (1:12, 16) than of continuity with older understandings.

Moreover, quite how this faithfulness of Christ would count as decisive in exempting Gentile Christians from showing an equivalent faithfulness is a logic which proponents of the *pistis Christou* = "the faith of Christ" thesis need to explain. On the contrary, a *pistis Christou* = "the faith of Christ" thesis makes better sense of *Peter's* position in the Antioch confrontation (Gal 2:11–14), a Christ whose faithfulness justified faithful Jewish believers in refusing to eat with Gentile believers. Whereas Paul's position makes better sense if *pistis Christou* denotes the faith in Christ which called in question the need for the faithfulness more likely practiced by Peter and the other Jewish Christians. In short, it seems me that at this point *pistis Christou* should be reckoned more on the apocalyptic rather than the *Heilsgeschichte* side of the tension in Paul's understanding of faith. If Martyn pushes too hard in one direction, on this point Hays pushes too hard in the other. Neither succeeds in getting the balance quite right between these two fundamental levels of Paul's theology.

5. Time and space permit only one other example of how a theology of Paul might proceed using the model of our own theologizing. The illustration I choose is Paul's understanding of and attitude to *the law.* It has been a surprising feature of the Group's debates that this subject has not come to the fore in more

59 See above, n. 31.

60 So in effect Wright, *Pauline Theology III*.39.

explicit terms. And yet it has been one of the most burning issues in recent literature on Pauline theology. In preparation for an international symposium on "Paul and the Law" in Durham in September 1994 I found no difficulty in amassing some 150 recent titles (essays and monographs) on the subject, well over half of them with "law" or "Torah" in the title.[61] In contrast, our own relative lack of interest in this subject in the Pauline Theology Group probably provides a further indication of a regrettable and growing divergence between the concerns of North American NT scholarship and those of Europe, with a warning to us lest, despite the vitality and rich diversity of North American scholarship, we (I speak as a member of the Group) are in danger of becoming somewhat parochial.

Of course, there are obvious reasons for the divergence of concerns at this point. For one thing, the impact of Sanders's work has been more immediate and far-reaching in North America, whereas German scholarship in particular is only beginning to come to terms with it. And for another, the reason why there has been relatively little debate on the issue among ourselves is presumably that there is a broader consensus on "the new perspective on Paul" in North America than in Europe, which could be a cause for some gratification. And yet the European debate has brought to the fore some fundamental theological issues in the exegesis and interpretation of Paul and the law which a *Pauline Theology* Group cannot ignore.

Perhaps the most important of these has been the question whether Paul's critique of the law had to do more with the relationships between Jew and Gentile in the Christian churches or with the standing of the human being before God. As hinted earlier, there has been a measure of agreement in the new perspective debate that justification by faith arises as an issue in Paul's letters within the context of his mission to the Gentiles. But the dispute continues as to whether Rom 4:4–5 exposes a deeper issue and constitutes a critique of a contemporary Jewish belief that acceptance by God could be and was to be earned by works.[62] Here again, however, it may well be that the solution lies in

61 The relative silence of the Group on the subject is all the more surprising since the three most recent full studies on the theme all come from North America: S. Westerholm, *Israel's Law and the Church's Faith: Paul and his Recent Interpreters* (Grand Rapids: Eerdmans, 1988); T. R. Schreiner, *The Law and its Fulfillment: A Pauline Theology of Law* (Grand Rapids: Baker, 1993); F. Thielman, *Paul and the Law: A Contextual Approach* (Downers Grove, Ill.: Intervarsity, 1994). The papers of the Durham Symposium are published under the title *Paul and the Mosaic Law,* ed. J. D. G. Dunn (WUNT 89; Tübingen: Mohr-Siebeck, 1996).

62 See particularly Westerholm's *Israel's Law,* which has caught well the concerns of many European, particularly Lutheran *Neutestamentlers*. In contrast, the papers on Romans 1–4 seemed content to stay rather more at the level of the surface issue: C. H. Cosgrove, "The Justification of the

a confusion of the different levels of Paul's. theology. For my own part, the most obvious exegesis of Rom 4:4–5 sees it not as a critique of a current Jewish attitude, but as an appeal to a generally accepted Jewish theologoumenon. No Jew nurtured in the story of Abraham's call by God or in the theology of Deuteronomy would readily conclude that divine choice and acceptance was based on human achievement. The fundamental axiom of human dependence on divine initiative is common ground between Paul and characteristic Jewish theology. The dispute arose rather over how this axiom applied to Gentiles, particularly Gentiles in relation to an Israel already chosen by God and in covenant relation with God.

In other words, the clash over the law between Paul and his fellow Christian Jews was most probably between two levels of Paul's theology, or between the fundamental level of his inherited theology, and the level determined for him by the revelation of Christ. The fundamental level of justification by grace was a point of consensus between them. That is why Paul could refer to divine grace and faithfulness so briefly, as to an accepted axiom; there was no need to explain or defend it, in contrast to the meaning of "faith." The technique is similar to that used in the preceding paragraph, where appeal was made to the common credo that God is one, as something none of the disputants would question. In both cases mere reference to the underlying agreement enables Paul to focus the argument on the actual issue between him and his critics: how this common theologoumenon speaks to the issue of Gentile acceptance before God and to the role of "works of the law" in the process.

This distinction between the levels on which Paul's theology (here of the law) functions should help to ease if not resolve the most important standing problem in modern perception of Paul's attitude to the law. For if the law is at the heart of a fundamentally mistaken understanding of how humans may be accepted by God (as though acceptance had to be earned by good works), then it should follow that Paul rejected the law entirely and broke with the law completely. And so most who read Rom 4:4–5 in that way want to read Paul. The problem is, however, that Paul seems to want to continue attributing a very positive role to the law (Rom 2:13; 3:31; 8:3–4; 13:8–10). If, on the other hand, Paul's critique of the law has in focus particularly Jewish unwillingness to accept Gentiles as full members of the same faith community, then a better balance between Paul's negative and positive treatments of the law can be achieved.

Other: An Interpretation of Rom. 1:18–4:25," *Society of Biblical Literature 1992 Seminar Papers (*ed. E. H. Lovering; Atlanta: Scholars, 1992) 613–634; Lincoln, *Pauline Theology III.*130–159.

There is, of course, more to be said,[63] but at least the model of different levels in Paul's theology points a hopeful way out of the impasse on this particular question.

IV

There are many other themes which a theology of Paul needs to tackle, but I hope the above examples have dealt with at least some of the most important and deeply felt issues. It would also be my hope that the examples illustrate a larger continuity and consensus between Paul and his Jewish heritage than has often been recognized, and that in consequence a larger degree of consensus might be seen to be possible among present-day students of Paul's theology.

63 See further my "Was Paul Against the Law? The Law in Galatians and Romans: A Test-Case of Text in Context," in *Text and Context. Biblical Texts in Their Textual and Situational Contexts: in Honor of Lars Hartman*, ed. T. Fornberg and D. Hellholm (Oslo: Scandinavian University Press, 1995) 455–475; and "In Search of Common Ground," *Paul and the Mosaic Law* (see above, n. 61).

7 AN ASYMPTOTIC RESPONSE TO DUNN'S RETROSPECTIVE AND PROPOSALS

Steven J. Kraftchick

"WHEN I WRITE a theology of Paul all I can hope for is to strengthen the broad consensual positions where I also think they are correct and to help gain support toward a fresh consensus on items and details where I think the contemporary consensus has become a little lopsided." (J. D. G. Dunn)[1]

"One tends to forget that at times it is much easier to agree on what a text says than on how to understand what the text says or how to understand how one can agree or disagree on what the text says." (Hans Frei)[2]

"The chance is high that the truth lies in the fashionable direction. But on the off chance that it is in another direction—a direction obvious from an unfashionable view of field theory—who will find it? Only someone who has sacrificed himself by teaching himself quantum electrodynamics from a peculiar and unfashionable point of view; one that he may have to invent for himself." (Richard Feynman)[3]

I. INTRODUCTION

From its early stages three traits have characterized Professor Dunn's work: industry, consistency, and a willingness to engage the larger and harder concerns of New Testament criticism. Not all of his answers have found acceptance, but there is little debate that he has addressed the important questions and issues. Dunn's present paper reflects those same traits and scope. It is fair, if not sur-

1 James D. G. Dunn, "In Quest of Paul's Theology: Retrospect and Prospect," 103.

2 Hans Frei, *Types of Christian Theology (*ed. George Hunsinger and William Placher; New Haven: Yale University Press, 1992) 56.

3 "The Development of the Space-Time View of Quantum Electrodynamics." A talk at CERN Geneva, quoted by James Gleick in *Genius* (New York: Pantheon Books, 1992) 380.

prising, consistent with his previous work, and it shows a willingness for a long-term engagement with some crucial topics in Pauline exegesis. Whatever other interpreters might ultimately conclude about his proposal as a course for determining a Pauline theology, the present paper will allow them to explore the issues involved more fully. All of this is to Dunn's credit and I hope that this response reflects respect for his efforts. This is especially so, since, in the end, I will disagree with Professor Dunn's understanding of the task of theology, his conception of the critical task, and with his proposed course for constructively analyzing Paul's work.

By way of preface let me say that there are areas where Professor Dunn and I agree. For instance, I think that Dunn's choice of Romans and the topics he has selected to explore within that letter need continued investigation, so he has provided important starting points in this proposal. My question is: Can they serve the purpose that he suggests, namely to frame discussions of Paul's thought? It is not clear to me that Dunn's selections are the necessary or even the sufficient choices to do so.

I also think that Dunn's demonstration of the need for cogent exegetical procedure and execution is well taken and needs to be heeded. The attempt to secure his analysis of Pauline thought to a particular form of theological construction also makes sense. At these levels, then, the disagreements we will have are not harsh or heated, but they are fundamental. What for Dunn are shared commonplaces and matters of consensus within scholarship (i.e., the role of Romans and the nature of theology) are for me precisely the matters that are or ought to be open to debate. At the heart of the matter lie different understandings of what claims about theology and about Romans can be accepted as givens and how those claims can be justified.

In my experience, Professor Dunn has been a fair and amenable commentator, still this response is written with two small notes of trepidation. First, no one disagrees with a sturdy and consistent interpreter without some hesitancy. Dunn's exegetical acumen is strong and I am sure that in such a debate I would look the poorer. Second, in this paper Dunn suggests that my own contributions to the seminar have struck "a gloomy note." Since I am again in the position of saying "Fair enough, but, . . ." it is possible that I will once again be tagged with that moniker. If I were Danish this would not be so terrible, for then I could claim Kierkegaardian precedent. But, alas, I am of Polish descent and the best I can do is call on ancestors such as Nicholas Copernicus, Baal Shem Tov, and Alfred Tarski. Unfortunately, none of them was known for a lighthearted countenance either.[4]

4 All three, however, allow me to express the nature of my reservations about Dunn's proposals. Copernicus, because it was through his radical break with the received consensus that a funda-

II. PROCEDURE

In his paper Dunn focuses attention on the Pauline Theology Group's work over the last few years. While he is appreciative of its efforts and some of its findings, ultimately he finds the work lacking for two reasons. First, the proposals for models of Pauline theology, though necessary, have proved too cumbersome for Dunn's tastes. He prefers "simpler and more natural models" and offers one here. Second, Dunn believes that the decision to postpone Romans until the final stages of the seminar's work was a mistake. In his essay he suggests why that course was in error and offers a sketch of how work in Pauline theology would look if Romans were given privilege of place. The paper concludes with abstracts of themes and concepts that Dunn considers were essential for Paul.

One form of response to Dunn would be to offer questions about the choice and explication of these essentials. I trust that other critics will not hesitate to enter into the fray over Dunn's depiction of God as purposeful, the relationship of *Heilsgeschichte* to apocalyptic disruption both in and for Paul's understanding of Israel and christology, and the position Dunn outlines on the role of faith and faithfulness as necessary human responses.[5] Those who do so will likely agree with Dunn's overall conception but will differ with him over the particular choices and readings he has offered in and about Romans, or at least differ over the weight each one has received. They might ask questions like: Was Romans written for the purposes Dunn suggests? Are the topics within Romans that Dunn has chosen sufficient to explain Paul's thinking? or, Is Dunn's explanation of those topics sufficiently justified by his exegesis?

---

mentally new insight and conception of the universe occurred; Shem Tov, because as a founder of Hasidism he exemplifies how different communities of belief produce radically different perspectives on God even when sharing common texts.

I assume that the names of Copernicus and Shem Tov are close enough to our experience so as not to require further statements. This is probably not so with respect to Tarski. A mathematician and logician, he turned his attention to truth theories early in his career. Tarski's work in logic demonstrates the need for justification of truth claims and causes us to recognize that even a theological statement's truth value requires some form of correspondence to the world in which it is uttered. His theory/conception of semantic truth is nicely discussed by Richard L. Kirkham, *Theories of Truth: A Critical Introduction* (Cambridge: MIT Press, 1995) 141–173. See also Donald Davidson, "The Method of Truth in Metaphysics," in *Inquiries into Truth and Interpretation* (New York: Oxford University Press, 1984) 199–214.

5 These encompass the five elements of a Pauline theology which Dunn suggests have been ignored or need further attention. He lists and discusses Paul's convictions about God, the framework of Israel's story, Paul's Christ focus, faith as a human response, and the Pauline conceptions of the Torah (107–115).

However, as I read him, the main argument of Dunn's proposal stands or falls with his understandings of the theological enterprise and the nature of the letter to the Romans. As that is the case, a second form of response could be offered. Those choosing this avenue would focus their remarks on these foundational aspects of the proposal. The procedure would be to inquire into the acceptability of Dunn's two major tenets, and then to test their coherency by explaining the logic implied by them.

For this second group, who conceive of the task of theology differently, the choices and topics from Romans, while interesting in their own right, will require another form of justification before they can be accepted as the essential parts of Pauline thought. They too may have exegetical disagreements with Dunn, but this group's initial questions will focus on other aspects of the proposal. They will want first more reflection on matters like the different venues for the theological enterprise, the relationship of critical inquiry to those venues, and how the hermeneutical commitments of interpreters play a role in determining how texts are appropriated and understood. Essentially they would be asking if (as Dunn argues) our own understandings of and methods for doing theology are sufficiently close enough to Paul's to serve as analogies or heuristic models.

Members of this second group will grant the importance of the exegetical conversations but they will also admit to their embedded nature. Such exegetical arguments, they would suggest, presuppose other commitments and it is good to examine them in order to understand the role played by the exegesis. On their view, without this conversation a form of exegetical gridlock results that keeps us from the level of understanding of Paul that both Dunn and they think is necessary and important.[6] To use Dunn's own schema, the differences in exegesis would not always happen at the level of surface expressions but could reflect deeper levels of difference about the nature of the actual enterprise. To analyze that dynamic it would be necessary to move away from particular exegetical arguments to the evaluations which suggest them.[7]

6 In discussing the opaque nature of Paul's theology Dunn points to the types of conversations that occur between biblical critics. There he points out that although we engage in "lively theological discussion with our contemporaries...[we rarely] pin down the living theology of our dialogue partners" (102). I am not trying to pin Dunn's theology down but I do think that considering how we enter the discussions and explicating what goals we have in mind for them will get us closer to the understanding Dunn obviously desires with this statement.

7 The idea is that many of Dunn's stated exegetical decisions, especially where there appears to be no headway in changing others' positions (e.g., the debate between Martyn and Dunn or between Hays and Dunn), are best approached on a formal level rather than offering further exegetical arguments. These would simply be countered by other pieces of exegetical data with no

I belong to this second group and that influences the disposition of this response. I do not think that my response will cause some form of major reversal since the differences are at a formal rather than material level, but I do hope that by differentiating the types of questions we will arrive at clearer perspectives on the tasks we define as necessary. In doing so, perhaps we can clarify why certain agreements and disagreements have recurred in the course of our corporate deliberations.

III. DUNN'S PROPOSAL

Professor Dunn's paper is broken into four sections, but contains three major parts. In Section I Dunn provides an overview of the seminar's work and assesses its strengths and weaknesses. Section II contains Dunn's proposals for constructing Pauline theology, and Section III is an outline of the shape of a Pauline theology based on Dunn's understanding of Romans. Section IV contains an apology for the brevity of treatment of the major topics broached in Section III and a wish for a larger consensus among students of Paul. While Section IV expresses a noble and high hope, it is best seen as an eschatological benediction. Since we are, at this juncture, still in the "not-yet" interim, it is better if we concentrate on the first three sections.

A. Section I: Retrospect

Dunn's review and appraisal of the seminar begins by noting the divergent discussions of method and definitions of theology, a factor that resulted from and, in some cases, created a frustrating experience. Dunn suggests that these method discussions and the procession from smaller to larger epistles, reserv-

resolution in sight. There is here a quasi-form of Kurt Gödel's arguments that there are sentences and expressions within any formal system of thought that cannot be adjudicated as true or false within that system. As a result one must move to another class of expressions to make a decision. Gödel's Incompleteness Theorem entitled "On Formally Undecidable Propositions of *Principia Mathematica* and Related Systems" relates to the fundamental undecidedness of even the most basic number systems. The implications of Gödel's arguments about the incompleteness of mathematical systems have been extended into the fields of humanities, music, and art in the popular book by Douglas Hofstadtler, *Gödel, Escher, Bach: An Eternal Golden Braid* (New York: Random House, 1979). For more formal discussions of how Gödel's work relates to fields other than math theory see Hao Wang, *Reflections on Kurt Gödel* (Cambridge: MIT Press, 1987) 187–230. Unfortunately Gödel, born in Brno, Moravia was not Polish, but his incompleteness argument incorporates the use of the Liar's Paradox that is found in Titus 1:12, sometimes attributed to Paul.

ing Romans until the end of the discussions, contributed to a "steady lowering of spirits within the Group" (Dunn, 97). Dunn realizes that these were initial elements in the seminar's experiment and that part of the goal was to discover how the conscious and unconscious effects of Romans had determined earlier syntheses of Paul's thought; he nevertheless thinks that the decision resulted in severe problems. First, although some of the attempts at synthesis and reading Romans were of help, for the most part with these results, "we were confronted by a maze of different paths and may have lost our way, at least insofar as real theological engagement was concerned" (Dunn, 98). Second, Dunn suggests that the arduous nature of analyzing Romans caused the group's work on that letter to suffer because the energy left was not sufficient to the task. As he describes it, "in leaving Romans till the end, we found ourselves, with the day already far spent, confronted by the highest peak of all" (Dunn, 98).

Dunn does point to a few factors which could mitigate this inchoate group depression. First, although the different proposed models for Pauline theology were complex, a "considerable degree of consensus" was reached on the nature of Paul's theology as an activity, that is, theology as a dynamic and fluid rather than static and fixed mode of thinking and discourse. Second, eventually a broad agreement on the major themes of Paul's theology (which include the apocalyptic substratum, some version of a narrative schema, and the significance of πίστις Χριστοῦ) was reached.[8] Thus, despite the arduous sojourn through method and the detour through the earlier and shorter letters which resulted in the lack of trenchant readings of Romans, Dunn concludes that these two general agreements should "indicate a truer picture of the debate about Paul's theology—broad consensus on fundamental structures, with vigorous disagreement on particular details of content and interaction with his audiences" (Dunn, 101). Since that is the case, he suggests that "perhaps we may proceed with lighter hearts than at first seemed possible" (Dunn, 101).

8 In the cases of the role of apocalyptic thinking and narrative schemas Dunn recognizes some significant disagreement, but in a move that foreshadows other aspects of his proposal he proposes that one need not pose the alternatives as sharply as some critics have suggested. Thus, in the case of the discontinuity created by the apocalyptic Christ event for Israel's "salvation historical" narrative Dunn suggests that the papers of Hays and Wright show that a synthesis between the two can be created. And, in the case of the slippery genitive Dunn suggests that this disagreement was "in effect, only over the rendering of that particular phrase [*pistis Christou*]—more a grammatical dispute than a theological dispute" (Dunn, 100–101). Likewise, Dunn suggests that the purpose of Romans is a composite of concerns that others have considered separately and the relationship of Paul to the Law is similarly solved by a consensus approach (Dunn, 105, 113–14).

As a short digression it is probable that just this form of synthesis is at issue for many members of the seminar. As Bassler pointed out in her critique of Hays, the fact that such a synthetic narrative can be offered only points out the difficulty in Paul's letters more clearly. First, it is not that a

B. Section II: Prospect

Dunn's review in the first section presents two problems with the legacy left by the seminar: the mode of theology used to interpret Paul and the position of Romans in the discussion of his composite thought. In Section II Dunn returns to the proposed models and notes that despite an heuristic value they are hampered by their complexity. The result is that the models are "as much a hindrance as a help" because "the flash of illumination which it [the imagery of a given model] brings to one aspect of the process of Paul's theology can be soon lost in the qualifications and complications we have to introduce to make the image adaptable to the complex reality of that theology" (Dunn, 101). To avoid this, Dunn offers a solution based on an understanding of theology drawn from his own experiences. The value of this model, according to Dunn, is that it is "simpler and more natural" than the models thus far proposed (Dunn, 101). It can suffice to explicate Paul without succumbing to the complexity and qualifications that have plagued the other models. Since Dunn's model works from contemporary forms of theological discussion to that of Paul himself, he suggests further that this conception of theology can help with the imprecise and allusive nature of Paul's thought. On Dunn's reading, because similar forms of imprecision and blurriness characterize contemporary theology (Dunn, 102–105), we can anticipate as much from Paul. That is, if we take the present forms of theological discussions as analogies to Paul then it would be odd to expect any more coherency from him than we do from ourselves.

---

synthesis can be composed but whether such a synthesis is Paul's or not. Second, even if it did exist for Paul, the concern is how he made use of the narrative. At stake is not whether a narrative existed, but how it was appropriated by Paul because the visible appropriation in his letters shows a greater discontinuity than the syntheses of either Hays or Wright (or in this case Dunn) can accommodate.

With respect to πίστις Χριστοῦ/Ἰησοῦ I think that the argument is much more than grammatical. In fact, the choice made results in (or from) different conceptions of the human/God roles in salvation as much as or more than the rules of Greek grammar. (Such a recognition of the theological ramifications is found in Luke T. Johnson, "Romans 3:21–26 and the Faith of Jesus," *CBQ* 44 [1982] 77–90.) More to the point it suggests different emphases on conceptions of the activity and function of Christ and God. In the first instance—a subjective genitive—the focus is on Christ as an active agent through whom God's objectives are met. In the second—the objective genitive—the Christ is more functional as a means by which God performs particular activity. Granting that Paul has both the foci of God and Christ in mind, the decision about the genitive does play a heavy role in which focal point is granted priority. In other words, the understanding of both Paul's christology and theology is affected. That the matter is not simply grammatical but indicative of competing understandings of Pauline thought is also demonstrated by Hendrikus Boers in "'We Who Are by Inheritance Jews; Not from the Gentiles, Sinners,'" *JBL* 111 (1992) 273–281.

According to Dunn's model, theological activity occurs between the interaction of expressions from three levels of cognition: Level One, the deepest level, contains the "inherited convictions and traditional life patterns" of a given individual. At this level a researcher would find a collection of axioms and presuppositions often hidden or undeclared by an author or speaker. Among these Dunn includes Paul's belief in God and his inherited understanding of Israel (Dunn, 107–109).[9] Level Two is created from "the sequence of transformative moments in the individual's (or community's) growth and development" (Dunn, 102). Here one would include Paul's conversion experiences and particular significant life-shaping choices and happenstances such as his revelation of Christ (Dunn, 110). These experiences are nearer to the surface of the individual expressions found in the letters, but not necessarily equivalent to them. At Level Three one finds the "ongoing interaction of the presuppositions and principles of the other two levels with the questions and challenges of each day." Or, following the lead of other interpreters, the third level illustrates the interaction of situation with convictions and previous experience (Dunn, 102).

Having sketched this model for analyzing Paul, Dunn turns to the second problem—the one created by the group's decision to postpone work on the larger epistles until the end of its work. Dunn acknowledges that his own model might, because of the nature of Paul's letters, "leave all in a state of flux" (Dunn, 104). Fortunately the interpreter is not completely at sea because there is one letter among the collection that is not so inherently metamorphic—Romans. According to Dunn, in comparison to the other Pauline letters, Romans is "relatively fixed." This is a crucial part of Dunn's argument, so I quote it in full.

> In the movement and dialogue of Paul's theology, his letter to the Romans is a relatively (I stress, relatively) fixed point. It was written to a church which was not his own founding. It was not so much occasioned by circumstances and his own personal involvement. It was written at the end of a (or better,

[9] It appears that there is some unclarity about the referents for the terms "hidden" and "undeclared." In some sense the model suggests that they refer to the individual author rather than her or his audience. At this depth level it would seem that "hidden" would be in reference to the individual but that does not help with "undeclared." Some term could be available to the speaker's conscious thought but left undeclared. A case in point: in Section III Dunn argues that Paul's "theology of God" is part of the undeclared level (pp. 107–108). But the discussion of the material suggests that, while it may be axiomatic for Paul and undeclared, it is not unknown by him. That is the "theology of God" is undeclared by Paul but it is not hidden to him. The result is that there is an ambiguity created by the description of the model in Section II and its application in section III. If "hidden" and "undeclared" refer to the audience rather than the writer or speaker, then the different levels Dunn proposes become confused. More specificity of the terms is needed here in order to understand what level of non-disclosure Dunn has in mind.

> the) major phase of Paul's missionary work which included (almost) all the other undisputed letters. It was written under probably the most congenial circumstances of his mission, with time for careful reflection and composition. And above all, it was written to set out his own understanding of the gospel as he had thus far proclaimed it, and as he hoped to commend it both in Jerusalem and beyond Rome to Spain. In short, it is the most sustained and reflective statement of Paul's own theology by Paul himself" (Dunn, 105).

In other words, although Dunn earlier commends Beker's conclusions about the always and everywhere contingent nature of Paul's thought and expressions, he suggests that Romans is the "most obvious place to locate oneself within the dialogue of Paul's theology" (Dunn, 105) because it displays the least amount of contingent effect. This choice of Romans means for Dunn that the interpreter of Paul can now not only describe the theology of Romans, but, since Romans functions as the relatively fixed point by which Paul's other expressions are evaluated and understood, its theology can also be used to understand the theology of the other letters (Dunn, 105–106). In the final analysis, Romans ought to have priority because: 1) it contains the best and most readily available formulations of Paul's complex thought and 2) the other letters contain theological expressions that are explicated or understood by the light it sheds. Thus, since Romans can provide this heuristic key to Paul, dealing with the other letters first would be to ill spend the seminar's (or an individual's) energy.

These two suggestions comprise Dunn's attempt to slip the double Gordian knot left by the group's prior work. To summarize: he suggests that a simpler model for analyzing Paul's work is available to us, namely "our own activity in theologizing." Second, Dunn thinks that Romans could and should provide the starting point for producing a theology of Paul. These two points form the foundation of Dunn's prospect for doing a Pauline theology and so merit particular attention.

C. Section III: Romans as a Source

Section III is comprised of short sketches of the issues in Romans that serve as the key components of a Pauline theology. Dunn offers five points that provide a basis for a critical analysis of Pauline thought. First he notes Paul's unspoken understanding of God. Paul's theology (in the specific sense of "God-talk" proper) is the unspoken element in his theology (in the broad sense of all ruminations about God talk, christology, ecclesiology, etc.) since "God was not a point of theology at issue, save where Paul made it so; Paul did not have to argue for belief in God" (Dunn, 107). In this specific case Romans serves as an important guideline because "its exposition of Paul's gospel begins at once with a threefold statement about God's power, God's righteousness, and God's wrath (Romans 1:16–18). And its now generally recognized climax is Paul's defense of God's faithfulness and mercy (Romans 9–11; 15:7–13)" (Dunn, 107). This unspoken belief in God as actor is part of Paul's axiomatic convictions, foundational and non-negotiable. More to the point it is a presumed given and is not taken as a problematic.

The second strand is provided by the framework of Israel's story (Dunn, 108) which allows Dunn to locate discussions of "Paul's doctrine of justification" that arose as an attempt to explain the inclusion of other nations under God's good graces.[10] The story is part of Paul's inherited understandings and so is located at the deeper level of his thinking. This framework also provides room for contemporary reflection on "Christianity's own identity," especially in present-day dialogues with other faith communities. This leads to the third fundamental strand in Paul's thought, the Christ focus of his theology, which belongs to the second level in Dunn's theological model. This Pauline focal point is produced by a combination of the personal Christ's own story and the function of that Christ within Israel's story. The two stories do not match completely but Paul continued to tell both.

A fourth foundational strand is provided by Paul's emphasis on faith as the appropriate human response to divine grace, for in Romans, as elsewhere, faith plays a central role. Here Dunn returns to the issue of the faith(fulness) of Christ and to other models of faith found in Romans (Dunn, 112). He also raises this as an instance of the *Heilsgeschichte* debate that was and remains an issue for Martyn and Gaventa. Finally, Dunn allows that Paul's understanding of the role of the Law provides a fifth interpretive strand. Here he notes that there are diverse perspectives on that role, especially on the scope of Paul's arguments (specific or universal). Dunn then attempts to show by means of his tri-level model how and why the dispute between Paul and his fellow Jewish Christians arose (Dunn, 113–114).

All of this is necessarily dealt with summarily and Dunn has treated them all more fully elsewhere.[11] His desire here was only to illustrate the effectiveness of using Romans as a source for Paul's theology and the efficacy of his three-level

10 The nature and scope of this story is, I presume, more recognized by Paul than by other interpreters. Part of the problem is in understanding what Paul would take as the story, the other part is how contemporary interpreters reconstruct it since unfortunately Paul has not left a complete version. Here Dunn sides, more or less, with Hays and Wright.

11 The present paper is related to a similar proposal that Dunn made at the Chicago meeting of the SNTS. In that paper some of these positions are more fully explicated. See J. D. G. Dunn, "Prolegomena to a Theology of Paul," *NTS* 40 (1994) 407–32.

model. Dunn realizes that all of the strands are more or less loci of controversy, but his point is that all are found in Romans and, indeed, found in their most robust form. The combination of content and form once more suggests Romans as the most fertile field for those wishing to do Pauline theology.

IV. RESPONDING TO THE PROSPECTUS

A. Pillar I: The Logic of the Consensus Approach

All of these proposals will prompt questions; here I raise just three: the logic implied by Dunn's commitment to scholarly consensus, the nature of Romans as "a relatively fixed . . . and congenial letter," and the competency of the proposed model for theology to serve as an analogy to Paul's theological activity. I will return to some conceptual forms of the latter two topics but I give here an example of a general logical difficulty that Dunn's proposal's face.

In the second section of his paper Dunn expresses his understanding of the scope and practice of theology. From Dunn's perspective when we engage in this form of investigation we hope to achieve a two-part result: balance within scholarly consensus and re-expression of first-century reading experiences. In Dunn's opinion the review of theology, or exegesis for that matter, finds a typical distribution curve. For any given arena of inquiry there is a large degree of scholarly consent on broad issues and an increasingly divergent set of findings about particulars. Hence, when Dunn desires to write a theology of Paul all he "can hope for is to strengthen the broad consensual positions where [he] think[s] they are also correct and to help gain support towards a fresh consensus on items and details where [he] think[s] the contemporary consensus has become a little lopsided" (Dunn, 103). Secondly, when Dunn has honed this consensus about Pauline theology and provided his own version of that theology he voices another hope: "to re-express something of the life power which his first-century readers and hearers evidently experienced through the reading of his writings, to help my readers experience afresh Paul's theology as activity and event. However frustrating, the quest for Paul's theology is never less than rewarding, so long as it is carried through as a theological exercise."[12] In other

[12] By this I take it Dunn's reference is to an application or contemporary interpretation. Further, it appears that such an application has its locale and audience among others who grant Paul the authority that Dunn does. This seems to narrow the goal of the analysis to contemporary application. Otherwise one would end up with something less than rewarding. Could it not be that one might find it rewarding to show that Paul's thought did not or even could not produce such results today? This appears to be, at least theoretically, a genuine possibility. I think that those in-

words, according to Dunn, the role of the interpreter is to strengthen broad consensual positions or correct a contemporary consensus when it has become lopsided. Then the interpreter is to present that consensus in ways that recreate for the contemporary reader the "life power" Paul's initial readers experienced.

Let us consider first Dunn's idea about the relationship of a given critic to the scholarly consensus. In Dunn's view, an interpreter has two options: either to refine a "lopsided" consensus or to maintain an established equilibrium. Within Dunn's model, however, there are no explicit instructions for those who differ significantly with the consensus. Presumably as points located under the thin sides of the bell curve they are to adjust their respective positions. The implied onus for such interpreters is to justify their aberrant stances. They may be able to do so, but the consensus provides the mode of argumentation and how they are to mount a substantive case remains unclear. On Dunn's suggested approach one receives the consensus and shapes it further, but the consensus sets the agenda by which one proceeds. The process is one of refinement rather than discovery. At least on initial approach it appears that the novel has a hard time breaking through.

With this in mind let us next consider these remarks of Stan Stowers, offered as a preface to his analysis of Romans 3:21–31. "Rare are the occasions when the weight of scholarly argument on a subject shifts decisively and probatively. But recently such a shift has taken place in the understanding of the word *pistis* (faith, faithfulness) in Paul's letters. In particular, the evidence and arguments for reading *pistis Iesou* as the 'faith' or 'faithfulness of Jesus' rather than as 'faith in Jesus' have proven decisive."[13] This shift in scholarly consensus along with the understanding that *dikaiosyne tou theou* means God's own righteousness causes "a dramatic change in the way one reads 3:21–26, Romans as a whole, and the entire Pauline corpus."[14]

According to Stowers, a new consensus has replaced an old one. The weight of arguments about *pistis Iesou* has meant a shift from the objective genitive reading to the subjective genitive one. Moreover such a shift is significant enough to require complete re-readings of a passage, a letter, and even the entire Pauline corpus. According to Dunn's understanding of the relationship of a scholar to the consensus, one would expect him to follow the new consensus and change his position on *pistis Christou*, since this follows logically from his own plan. If Stowers is accurate, a new consensus has corrected the lopsided old consensus,

---

terested in Paul who are not willing to grant this ecclesial authority for Pauline texts might quarrel with Dunn's evaluation of the efforts. There appears in this formulation of Dunn's a confusion of a hermeneutical goal with an historical one.

13 Stanley K. Stowers, *A Rereading of Romans* (New Haven: Yale University Press, 1994) 194.

14 Stowers, 194.

hence this should result in Dunn's adopting the new position. In fact, according to Stowers it should require Dunn to reassess his positions on Romans 3 and the letter as a whole. But according to Dunn's remarks on that matter (on page 100), he maintains his former position on the objective genitive. Here Dunn's conception of the scholar's role is of little help. Without a critical assessment of why the consensus exists, including institutional reasons, it appears that Dunn is bound logically to release his position on the genitive, even if it is only a grammatical dispute (or at least to admit that it is only his position).

At times, then, Dunn argues that he adopts the consensus but here is an instance where he does not. One asks then what is the role of consensus in the scheme of Dunn's arguments. Obviously Dunn could and would offer arguments for his positions. That I grant and happily so. Probably Dunn would argue that Stowers is incorrect, hence he has not violated his position. But on what grounds? Certainly not the one of consensus, for that is the matter under debate. This leads us to a further question: What happens when two different perspectives on consensus arise as here? How are we to adjudicate this difference? Dunn provides no guidance. But if he did, he would be moving in the direction of the complexity of the other models, a direction which he has determined is not too helpful.

The example is not to argue that Stowers or Dunn is correct about the consensus, only to suggest that it is not very helpful in determining the position a scholar should adopt. There does not seem to be a place for such forms of argument in Dunn's model. To make Dunn's position tenable there needs to be room in his understanding of the scholar's role for questions such as: What are the warrants for the differences in positions? Why are some choices acceptable and not others? Here, in other words, are the questions that one needs to ask in order to understand what expressions represent. This is true for both modern interpreters and for the expressions of Paul, but in Dunn's proposal these sort of questions are not raised, at least not explicitly.

B. Pillar II: The Role and Nature of Theology

As I noted in the summation of Dunn's proposal, the model for theological reflection is based on our "own activity in theologizing." That is, the interpreter begins with his or her own forms of theological activity and then applies that template to Paul's theological activity. Leaving aside the complexity of assigning elements to the various levels of Dunn's model and the notorious issue of how the different levels interact, significant problems arise along the direction Dunn suggests we proceed.

For purposes of reference, here again is Dunn's goal for doing a Pauline theology: "my primary hope in any theology of Paul would be to re-express something of the life-shaping power which his first readers and hearers evidently experienced through his writings, to help my readers experience afresh Paul's theology as activity and event, perhaps even, dare I say it, as Word of God" (Dunn, 103). First, it is not at all apparent that one can read Paul's letters in the same way that first-century readers did, and thus achieve the same experience they achieved. The centuries-long reliance on Paul's letters as authoritative in the church makes it nearly impossible for us to read them as first-century readers did. This is true on the level of both Paul's acceptance and his rejection by audiences. Indeed, when one considers the apparent difficulties Paul had in appealing to the Corinthians it is hard to conclude that those first-century readers experienced Paul's letters as "life power."

Second, when one considers Dunn's statement that he wants his readers to experience this power afresh, it appears that the venue of theology is among like-minded readers, that is, those who accept Paul as an authority and his letters as "word of God." Significant difficulties present themselves here. First, it is a particularly Protestant perspective, but it also neglects other manners in which the "experience" could occur, including worship and prayer, both of which Paul is more concerned to mention than he is his own letters. Simply put, if one takes Dunn at his word that the most natural model for doing Pauline theology is our own, then we should ask why "Word of God" is privileged when it is not shared by all members of the conversation as the only mode of theological reflection? And if this is true, then why talk of "our own" reflection as if that were a given?

Second, the audience Dunn suggests already grants Paul an authority that I do not think is necessary if one is to do a theology. One could, it appears to me, reject Paul's perspectives and still do a superb job of understanding his thought. To give an example of what I have in mind, let us suppose that we were to analyze the writings of Ignatius in order to explore the three levels of his thought expressions. Would it be necessary to make the modern application in order to produce a theology? Could we not come to a point of understanding Ignatius and still also disagree with his positions? Could we not adequately explain the nature of his thought without accepting it? I think that Dunn would agree to this. But if that is so for a theology of Ignatius, why is it not so for a theology of Paul? Consider an alternative reason for producing a theology of Paul, one suggested by the remarks of Jeffrey Stout.

> Philosophical and literary texts often enter the humanistic canon because they provide uniquely valuable occasions for normative reflection. We lavish great

> interpretative care upon them, but not always in order 'to get them right.' Getting them right sometimes ceases to matter. We sometimes want our interpretations to teach us something new, not so much about the text itself, its author, or its effective history as about ourselves, our forms of life, our problems.
>
> Why do philosophers who are not historians of philosophy go on reading and assigning Plato? Not because they want to know what Plato was doing under his circumstances, for they show little interest in finding out enough about his circumstances to situate him. And not because they agree with very much of what their interpretations make him seem to be saying, for they don't. They do it for other reasons: because Plato's Socrates (interpreted in a certain way) has an enduring allure for the moral imagination; because the dialogues throw up hundreds of enthymemes worth mapping onto formulae in symbolic logic and criticizing; because students who have grappled with Plato seem less shallow than the ones who haven't; or because Plato's sentences suggest a picture that holds us captive. The interpretations that count as good in this context will be the ones that lead us to a new moral insight, the discovery of a fallacy, deepened habits of thought, or the sense that we can cease doing philosophy when we want to. Getting Plato right, historians' objections notwithstanding, isn't always germane.[15]

To coin a phrase, wherever Stout writes Plato, read Paul. Certainly those who hold Christian beliefs, including the acceptance of Paul's letters as some form of contemporary authority, could agree with Dunn's statement about the goal of theology. However, it also seems perfectly clear that others might interpret Paul and do so without accepting him as authoritative or even correct. They might suppose that Paul is worthwhile for other reasons like those Stout suggests for reading Plato.

Still others, pure historians, might simply want to know how Paul's thinking was constructed without ever arguing that it would be necessary to adopt that thinking as their own. One might reasonably and legitimately offer compelling analyses of how Paul thought and never argue that contemporary citizens need adopt such thinking today. Thus, it is not clear why the writing of an accurate and convincing theology of Paul would require contemporary experience of Paul as authoritative or even motivating, for either the interpreter or the reader. It might be preferable, but it is not necessary. Any number of reasons for constructing a theology of Paul might contribute to the frustration involved in that construction, not just the reason Dunn suggests.

Here is a clear point for the discussion. What is the goal of the enterprise? Is it necessary to conduct the quest as a theological exercise? I take it Dunn means something in terms of application. I do not deny him the right to be a

15 Jeffrey Stout, "The Relativity of Interpretation," *The Monist* 69 (1986) 111–112.

churchman or even the position that theology be done for the church, nor that the Pauline texts be taken as canonical, but I do not think that these are necessary requirements for doing justice to Paul's thought. To focus the point, it seems that Dunn collapses the hermeneutical application of Pauline thought with an historical and structural investigation of that thought as found in the letters. Again, this is Dunn's preference and he is certainly within his rights to choose it, but once more this shows that the contemporary forms of theology are not particularly simple or obvious. If then, there is multiplicity of contemporary procedures for producing theology both in form and goal, which is to be taken as the "our own" model for analyzing Paul?

Third, the audiences Paul wrote to are not those that the contemporary theologian or exegete addresses. Paul can avoid the question of justifying his discourse at the bar of contemporary understandings of truth. In contemporary discussions of "theology" this cannot be done, especially within the arena of the university. Here the matter of theology as a critical enterprise arises and this does not appear to be something that Paul bothered about.

The point is not that theology cannot be discussed today, but rather that it is not an accepted given in any ongoing cultural dialogue, including those of the university. Unlike the discourse in Paul's letters a contemporary discussion of theology includes some obligation to provide reasons for its inclusion as a part of the conversation. This can be illustrated in two ways: by considering the comments of two recent critics and by observing the nature of "God talk" by two theologians involved with the problems of contemporary address.

This is underscored by the remarks of Jon Levenson with reference to the increasing difficulty academicians have making arguments for the inclusion of biblical studies within university faculties. Levenson notes:

> That the cultures of the Jews and of the Christians have been enormously influenced, indeed shaped, by the Bible for the past two millennia (more in the case of the Jews) cannot be gainsaid. But why should the history of those two very different but related cultures be privileged over the Indian, Chinese, or, for that matter, African-American culture? And why, a dean might justly ask (and some doubtless do), should we devote a second appointment to the history of the Bible as scripture when we lack even one appointment in the history of the scriptures and the classics of most of the world's other religious traditions? To answer with the claim that the Bible is a foundational document of *our* culture is to imply more cultural homogeneity that many believe to be warranted.[16]

16 Jon Levenson, "Historical Criticism and the Fate of the Enlightenment Project," in *The Hebrew Bible, the Old Testament, and Historical Criticism* (Louisville, Kentucky: Westminster/John Knox, 1993) 109.

Perhaps in countries where the state supports the inclusion of theological faculties within the university hesitation to use the term is not typical, but where the term is disputed such hesitancy is at least understandable. But perhaps even in those countries where theology is part of the university a hesitancy at using the term might be observed.

At an earlier stage in his essay Dunn gently chides his North American counterparts for not using the term theology very freely. He suggests that this failing occurs frequently and that as a European he can see it better than his North American friends can. This embarrassment and loss of nerve, he suggests, is not so apparent in Europe (Dunn, 101). This is somewhat surprising to hear since part of the hesitancy in the Americas arises because of the fallout from debates that took place in Berlin, Germany in the early 1800's. The situation there Hans Frei takes as an ideal type of an argument that has continued within the academy and the church. Frei notes in his historical account of that period:

> Whether on the basis of Christian faith as a form of action, as inward experience of religious meaningfulness or salvation from sin and evil, or as doctrine of belief embodying the true knowledge of God, there were Christians deeply skeptical for religious and conceptual Christian reasons that a university dedicated to the ideal of *Wissenschaft* could provide training appropriate to the exercise of ministry in the Christian Church.
>
> The same doubt had been expressed with at least equal force by the academics. In the traditional view, Christian theology was regarded as simply incompatible with instruction in a university dedicated to the ideal of *Wissenschaft*.[17]

Again, the venue of theological discussion influences both the use of the term and the actual productions of theology in ways that make it suspect as a tool for analyzing Paul's mode of thinking.

When we turn to the matter of God-talk, another difference between Paul and the contemporary theologian comes to the surface. In his recent attempt to produce a constructive theology, Peter Hodgson begins with this note: "All the crises of late modernity have contributed in one way or another to the experience of the absence of God. This is the primary theological signification of our cultural passage."[18] In this same context Hodgson's quotations from Sallie McFague and Mark K. Taylor suggest that he is not alone in his understanding of contemporary experience of God. Note his summary comment: "The chal-

17 Frei, *Types of Christian Theology*, 104.

18 Peter C. Hodgson, *Winds of the Spirit: A Constructive Christian Theology* (Louisville: Westminster John Knox, 1994) 61.

lenge of post-modernity, I contend, is to 'speak meaningfully' of God's presence and action in the world. The presence of God may indeed be a function of our ability to speak meaningfully of God."[19] Obviously, from Hodgson's perspective "God" is not an axiomatic given but rather the seat of the critical problem. Rather than something one can assume, it must first be argued for in a cogent and persuasive manner. Hodgson's remarks are made emphatic by those of Gordon Kaufman, who begins his own theology with an even more acute statement of the difficulty in using God language. He argues:

> The question about God is the question whether there is some extra-human reality in relationship to which human existence gains its being and its fulfillment, some ultimate point of reference in terms of which our human life and its problems and possibilities must be understood.
>
> We do not know how to answer this question. Our symbol "God," heavy with the mythic overtones of our religious traditions, suggests a kind of being—an all powerful sovereign, creator, and king of the universe—which no longer seems intelligible in our world, and which, moreover, may today offend our moral sensibilities. To worship such a God, or to attempt to understand human existence in relationship to such a God, may thus seem to require a fundamental compromise of our moral and intellectual integrity (if we do not close our eyes to the self-deception in which we are engaged)."[20]

It is difficult, in light of such comments by practicing theologians, to follow Dunn's suggestion that contemporary theological discussions form an analogy for understanding Paul's. In Dunn's model God-talk is part of Paul's first axiomatic level. It is, according to Dunn, not a problem except where Paul chooses to make it so (Dunn, 107). In other words, for neither Paul nor his audience was the understanding of God as an actor in the world a problem. On the other hand, such a term and understanding is deeply difficult within the contemporary culture and theology. Whatever else we may do to produce a theology, on Hodgson and Kaufman's account, we must reckon with this. In other words, what Paul could take as a given is in the present setting a matter of dispute.

All of these suggest that the idea of taking "our own theologizing" as the model for analyzing Paul's thought presents us with a multitude of difficulties. In the end the proposal is fraught with more problems than Dunn's paper suggests.

19 Hodgson, 65.

20 Gordon D. Kaufman, *In Face of Mystery: A Constructive Theology* (Cambridge: Harvard University Press, 1993) 4.

C. Pillar III: The Relatively Neutral Nature of Romans

A final objection to Dunn's proposal will arise when one focuses on his acceptance of Romans as "relatively neutral." One of the aspects of the seminar has been its disagreements over the audience and purpose of Romans.[21] Since Dunn's characterization of the nature and audience of Romans is offered without argument it appears that he views these descriptions as representative of a consensus. At the least, they would appear to be reflections of the consensus or minor refinements of it. Leaving aside the arguments that arose in the seminar's own work in this area, when one looks at only a few recent commentators' work on the epistle such a consensus appears suspect. Dunn's conclusion that Romans is the letter "which is less caught up in the flux and developing discourse of Paul's churches" appears to be his position but not necessarily one shared by others.

What follow are three descriptions of the purpose and purview of Romans recently put forth by A. J. M. Wedderburn, Robert Morgan, and Stanley Stowers. In using them I am not suggesting that their perspectives on Romans are exhaustive, nor am I arguing for the correctness of any one of the positions. My purpose is only to illustrate that the idea is mistaken that Romans is more or less a peaceful territory in which to explore Paul's thought because its circumstances are generally neutral and its thought is less in flux than the other letters.

In his own commentary on the letter Dunn locates Romans within a critical argument about the self-understanding of Jews and Judaism in the first century.[22] According to Dunn, the church in Rome is composed of gentiles who had been God-fearers or proselytes schooled in Jewish thought and writings (*Romans*, l). Eventually, Dunn surmises, Paul writes to Rome with missionary, apologetic, and pastoral purposes. As the apostle to the gentiles, Paul writes a "careful statement of his gospel and faith" for the Romans and others that he uses to set out a "more general statement of his missionary purpose"(*Romans*, lv). This statement also serves as a general defense against "actual misunderstandings of his gospel" (*Romans*, lvi) and to gain backing from the congregations in Rome for his upcoming trip to Jerusalem. Finally, Paul seeks with this same statement to address divisions in Rome between "gentile believers and less liberated Jewish believers" (*Romans*, lvii) in order to provide counsel on how "gentile and Jewish Christians should perceive their relationship to each other" (*Romans*, xlv). In the final analysis, "all three of these main emphases and pur-

21 See the papers in *Pauline Theology: Volume III: Romans*, ed. David M. Hay and E. Elizabeth Johnson (Minneapolis: Fortress, 1995).

22 James D. G. Dunn, *Romans 1–8* (WBC 38a; Dallas: Word, 1988).

poses hang together and indeed reinforce each other when taken as a whole" (*Romans*, lviii).

A. J. M. Wedderburn begins *The Reasons for Romans* by providing a general review of the different positions taken on the circumstances of the Roman church and the objectives Paul had for writing the epistle. Wedderburn openly admits that "Why Paul wrote Romans is still something of an enigma."[23] Wedderburn notes that the arguments have been chronicled before (by Karl Donfried and Dieter Zeller) and that those collective essays demonstrate a significant disagreement over the purpose of Romans within the scholarly community. Wedderburn, like Dunn, recognizes the strength of Beker's articulation of the role of the contingent, thus he suggests, "it follows that to understand what Paul is saying in any of his writings one needs to know as much as possible what that 'specific situation' and that 'need' were. But it is precisely the answers to those questions which are disputed in the case of Romans."[24] Like Dunn, Wedderburn concludes that Romans was written for a number of reasons. First, Paul addressed an audience "divided along a line marked out by the conflicting attitudes of those in it towards Paul's Law-free mission to the gentiles."[25] Paul's argument thus was "an attempt to maintain that the preaching of his gospel does reveal God's righteousness, which his Judaizing critics doubted. At the same time the follower of the Law-free gospel needed to be reminded both that that gospel does still call for righteousness, and that they could not shake themselves loose from the Jewishness of the faith which they had received."[26] Second, again like Dunn, Wedderburn suggests that the letter was an attempt to gain the support of the various congregations for future missionary tours. Unlike Dunn, Wedderburn ties this directly to the request for monetary support.

Most significantly, though Wedderburn shares many of Dunn's perspectives about the goal of Romans, he is less sanguine about taking Romans to be a result of Paul's relatively stress-free thinking. On the contrary, in Wedderburn's view, a large part of Paul's reason for writing to Rome is to gain encouragement and welcome from this church and to secure a support that he had not found from Jerusalem. Thus Wedderburn considers the letter to be written in response to a conflicted situation in Rome but related to Paul's own difficulties derived from the mission to the East.[27] In opposition to Dunn, Wedderburn does not

23 A. J. M. Wedderburn, *The Reasons for Romans* (Edinburgh: T. & T. Clark, 1988) 1.

24 Wedderburn, 3.

25 Wedderburn, 140.

26 Wedderburn, 141.

27 Wedderburn, 41–43.

view Romans as a letter relatively unaffected by Paul's external purposes. It is as contingent as all of his other letters, perhaps more so.

Robert Morgan also argues that Paul's purpose for Romans is conjoined with his personal situation. Noting the indirect nature of Paul's arguments and the caution he employs, Morgan notes:

> We can explain his silence about the actual situation in Rome as tact (1.12; 15.14). Even his praise can be read as courtesy. But the indirectness of his argument may be a sign of something else, and the "Roman situation" explanation does not do full justice to the indications that Paul is having to defend his own position (3.8; perhaps 9.1; 10.1). Even if we give priority to the supposed situation in Rome, as many [sic] now do, this may not be a sufficient explanation. The sinister tone of 15.30–32 coupled with our partial knowledge (from Acts 21) of the outcome suggests that the epistle needs to be related to Paul's immediate concerns as well as his plans.[28]

Here Morgan depicts the thought of Romans as deeply conditioned both in its explicit statements and in its overall mode of argument. To Morgan, Paul is not neutral but cautious, even circumspect, and Paul's perception of the situation at Rome deeply affects both his choice of topics and his manner of discussion. Here the letter is clearly taken to be constrained by Paul's sense of the congregation.

Morgan concludes: "We can make no claim to detailed knowledge of Paul's mind, but can only select what seems to throw most light on the text itself. The difficulties in making historical inferences on the basis of this epistle can best be explained on the supposition that Paul was playing a delicate hand, half concealing his main concern, which was highly controversial (especially among Jewish Christians), behind his main theme of God's present activity which (among believers) was not."[29]

Both Wedderburn and Morgan claim the letter has multiple purposes, as does Dunn; the difference among them is the degree to which Paul himself is affected in his letter writing. For Dunn the degree is small, for Morgan and Wedderburn it is far greater. Dunn might argue, however, that although Morgan and Wedderburn vary from his consideration they do not do so to disturb the notion of a consensus.

Stan Stowers, on the other hand, differs with Dunn decisively. After a careful account of Dunn's own understanding of the audience in Rome he notes:

> As a further warrant for this procedure of reconstructing the empirical audience in Paul's mind when he wrote, Dunn says that Paul was obviously

28 Robert Morgan, *Romans* (Sheffield: Sheffield Academic Press, 1995) 65.

29 Morgan, 76–77.

> writing to gentiles. Here he follows scholarship of the past forty years that has, often grudgingly, come to acknowledge the letter's explicitness about its gentile audience. Amazingly, however, Dunn reimports Jewish Christians into the letter in the second half of the same paragraph when he explains that "Paul was aware of the ethnic composition of Christian groups in Rome" and that the letter provides counsel on "how gentile and Jewish Christians should perceive their relationship to each other."[30]

Stowers continues with his critique and concludes that the traditional readings (among which he includes Dunn's) erase the gentile audience to replace it with one composed of "Christians, both gentiles and Jews."

> The erasure is a hermeneutical move that facilitates reading the letter as canonical scripture of the orthodox catholic church. This move is analogous to the ancient church's theory that the letters of Paul, being a perfect seven in number, represent the whole church to which they are truly addressed and to the editions of Paul's letters that have removed references to particular churches and addressees.[31]

Stowers is convinced that the only viable reading of Romans focuses on the gentile audience being addressed. The importation of Jewish Christians confuses the explicit and encoded audience with a speculative reconstruction of an empirical audience.[32] Stowers insists, then, that Paul's audience is a gentile one and that the letter's references to law, *et al.*, must be read in light of that. In his criticism Stowers suggests both that Romans is not read as its first-century audience read it and that its initial audience was composed in a manner utterly unlike that proposed by Dunn.

30 Stowers, 23.

31 Stowers, 33. This characterization of Pauline scholarship may not be wholly accurate, but it is not far from Dunn's own assessment of the enduring role of Romans in Western thought. Note Dunn's prefatory remarks: "We see in Romans Paul operating at the interface between Pharisaic Judaism and Christianity, and the transition from the one to the other in process of being worked out. That, I would suggest, is why the letter has always struck a chord in those of subsequent generations conscious of a similar tension, caught at a similar point in time when long established traditions came under question from their own insight and experience, when well entrenched institutions and ideologies ceased to provide an answer to the sharpest of the new questions. That is probably why it exerted such a powerful influence on such as Augustine, Luther and Barth. Not for its literary or aesthetic appeal; not because they saw it as some dogmatic treatise; but because they too were at similar transition points in history (the disintegration of the western Roman Empire, the breakdown of medieval Christendom, the profound shock of the 1914–18 war on the old European empires and on the hitherto dominant liberal optimism). And in the Paul of Romans they recognized a kindred spirit whose wrestling with the tensions between his tradition and his experience spoke with word-of-God power to their own situation" (Dunn, *Romans*, xvi.).

32 Stowers, 30.

More extreme suggestions about the purpose of Romans and the nature of Paul's arguments could be offered. These are fairly moderate but again the point of rehearsing these views has not been to argue that Stowers or Morgan or Wedderburn is correct in his individual interpretation of the letter's mode and audience, but rather to suggest once more that the consensus on which Dunn depends for his proposal does not appear to exist. In their approaches none of these scholars is far from the center Dunn speaks of earlier in his essay, but all demonstrate the variation in conceptions of Romans that continues to exist. Based on these different understandings of Romans and of Paul's expression within the letter we should reasonably conclude that Romans is neither as neutral as Dunn suggests nor is its context as clear as he implies. Its expressions, like those found in Paul's other letters, are deeply affected by context and purpose. Unfortunately those two features of the letter are some of the most contested and this creates significant problems for Dunn's proposal that Romans establishes the equilibrium the other letters fail to provide. Here, as in his positions on the scholar's arguments and the role of contemporary theology Dunn needed more justification of his arguments.

V. CONCLUSION

Even if there were no problems with Dunn's conception of theology or there existed the consensus about the nature and audience of Romans he suggests, it is probable that important questions would still arise. We would need to do much work to clarify the relationship of similar themes between letters (as for example between Romans 11–14 and 1 Corinthians 8–10). Likewise we would need to explain why important issues in Romans do not arise in other letters and why other topics crucial to Paul (e.g., the death of Christ) are only obliquely raised in the letter to Rome. Dunn is, I am sure, prepared to enter into those discussions and to offer important suggestions for answering the questions. But if he does and if we join him, we will be suggesting that Romans is more like the other letters than is suggested in this proposal.

Dunn's retrospective began by noting a lowered spirit within the seminar, a tide he was keen to stem. Hence, to produce more optimism, he worked hard to find moments of consensus and to propose an avenue to reach more of the same. However, if optimism is a function of these findings, based on this consensus, it may be a fleeting disposition. The consensus that Dunn finds and depends on here leaves too many troubling details to the side. Whether in the choice of Romans or in the individual features of that letter which Dunn chose to emphasize his suggestions supposed a common departure point. By now it is clear that we have not agreed on that point, nor on his use of modern theological discussion as a model for analyzing Paul's ancient letters.

At its heart, Dunn's essay takes as given precisely those things that I think require arguments of warrant. A closer look at the different forms of consensus which Dunn accepts turns out to show significant fissures in the details. And in the final analysis, it is those details which determine the thrust of the work. As much as I admire Dunn's desire for simplicity and stability I think they have been purchased at a cost of the close analysis of the material under discussion. Perhaps, in the end, this is a function of different understandings of the role of theology, as I have suggested above. If that is true, however, it shows that, despite the intention of Dunn's essay, we will have to return to the matters of complex models and particular letters, for that is the nature of what we have.

I hope that I have shown that Dunn's own model grows ever more complex as it is asked to provide explanations for its choices. As that is the case, Dunn's model becomes more like those he had earlier rejected. I also hope that the degree of disagreement and the length of engagement shows how seriously I have taken Dunn's proposal. Unfortunately, in the end it does not appear that the pillars of his argument can support the thesis. Both contemporary theology and Romans are complex, as Dunn would agree, and as admirable a goal as simple elegance might be, Paul's work (for better or for worse) does not seem to yield to it.

8 PAULINE THEOLOGY

A Proposal for a Pause in Its Pursuit

Paul W. Meyer

THE MATERIAL produced by the Pauline Theology Group since 1985 attests to an immense amount of diligent analysis of Pauline texts, careful methodological reflection, and lively and earnest debate.[1] Nonetheless, in the Prefaces to each of the earlier volumes of *Pauline Theology,* the editors call attention to the great diversity that has resulted both in the approaches taken by the essays that follow and in the interpretations of Paul's theology at which they arrive. A retrospective survey of what is here presented is thus an enlightening experience, but also a chastening one. On the one hand, the diversity of material shows that the task of understanding the apostle's theology remains unfinished, so that the termination of the Group's existence can provide at best only a pause in its pursuit. On the other hand, that same wealth of material calls for taking such a pause as a fresh opportunity for reflection and appraisal. Not the least of the questions still open for discussion is the very central one: just what do we mean by "Pauline theology"?

If there is no consensus at the end of this stage of the inquiry, there is one conspicuous thread that has run through the discussion; namely, the repeated

1 Most of this material is preserved and accessible in the *SBL Seminar Papers* of these years, but especially in selected and revised form in the three volumes: Jouette M. Bassler, ed., *Pauline Theology, Volume I: Thessalonians, Philippians, Galatians, Philemon* (Minneapolis: Fortress, 1991), hereafter simply *Pauline Theology I;* David M. Hay, ed., *Pauline Theology, Volume II: 1 and 2 Corinthians* (Minneapolis: Fortress, 1993), hereafter *Pauline Theology II;* and David M. Hay and E. Elizabeth Johnson, eds., *Pauline Theology, Volume III: Romans* (Minneapolis: Fortress, 1995), hereafter *Pauline Theology III.* In addition, at least three important articles, written independently by members of the Group but with explicit reference to its work, should be mentioned: Victor P. Furnish, "Paul the Theologian," *The Conversation Continues: Studies in Paul and John in Honor of J. Louis Martyn* (ed. Robert T. Fortna and Beverly R. Gaventa; Nashville: Abingdon, 1990) 19–34; idem, "On Putting Paul in His Place" (the 1993 SBL Presidential Address), *JBL* 113 (1994) 3–17; and Leander E. Keck, "Paul as Thinker," *Int* 47 (1993) 27–38.

use, in one way or another, of the uncommonly suggestive pair of terms, "coherence" and "contingency," that J. Christiaan Beker brought into play early on.[2] Beker's own first definition, before the work of this Group began, was:

> Paul's hermeneutic cannot be divorced from the content of his thought, because he relates *the universal truth claim of the gospel* directly to *the particular situation to which it is addressed*. His hermeneutic consists in the constant interaction between the *coherent center* of the gospel and its *contingent interpretation*.[3]

For some, the polarity of this language will recall issues that exercised New Testament interpretation at an earlier time under such rubrics as the universality and particularity of the gospel, revelation and history, and even, from longer ago, "the necessary truths of reason" and "the accidental truths of history."[4] Others may balk at even suggesting such a connection. Our subject, after all, is Pauline *theology*. What can the rational opposites of coherence and incoherence, of consistency and confusion in theology, have to do with the metaphysical difference between the transcendent and history? Furthermore, times have changed. One goal in the use of this "coherence-contingency scheme" is to try to get beyond some of those older antitheses and polarities. But that is just the point; it may be worth asking whether we have succeeded.

One may perhaps begin with *contingency* and with a brief historical reminder. Robert Morgan has written about a major turn in New Testament theology that took place about the time of the first World War.[5] The historical criticism of the closing 19th century had so driven home the contingency of early Christian history and its documents that all previous sense of divine transcendence had been rather thoroughly wrung out of it. The New Testament had become the merely human sediment left by a multiplicity of first-century developments in religion. The result was the loss not only of a sense of the unity of the New Testament but also of the very category of revelation. It was only the neo-Reformation "theology of the word" after the War that was able to recover the latter, and then only by relocating revelation in proclamation.

> Revelation occurs in the act of proclamation when the message is "got across" and a hearer "gets the message" and acknowledges Jesus as his Lord in faith. It

2 "Recasting Pauline Theology: The Coherence-Contingency Scheme as Interpretive Model," *Pauline Theology I*, 15–24.

3 *Paul the Apostle: The Triumph of God in Life and Thought* (Philadelphia: Fortress, 1980) 11; emphasis added. The book's discussion after this opening definition should not be read without consulting Beker's own corrective and refining reflections in the article cited in the preceding note.

4 Gotthold Lessing, "On the Proof of the Spirit and of Power," *Lessing's Theological Writings* (trans. and ed. Henry Chadwick; Stanford: Stanford University Press, 1957) 53.

5 Robert Morgan, "Introduction: The Nature of New Testament Theology," *The Nature of New Testament Theology: The Contribution of William Wrede and Adolf Schlatter* (ed. Robert Morgan; SBT 2/25; Naperville, Ill.: Alec R. Allenson, 1973) 33–35.

> is therefore no longer located in the documents (or tradition), nor in the history, but in the event in which, on the basis of the tradition, the Christ (who touches history only as a tangent touches a circle) is represented. This event is not within human control but the human activity of proclamation sets the stage for it. God will enter the stage or speak to the hearer, evoking faith or rejection, where and when he wills.[6]

Such a relocation opened up some distinct advantages, the foremost one being the complete freedom with which the true historical contingency of all New Testament documents could now be acknowledged. One did not have to compromise historical evidence and findings about their provenance, date, authorship, literary character or integrity, or suppress the discovery of real historical diversity or variation (including outright "contradictions") for the sake of preserving the gospel "message." Of that freedom we have all been beneficiaries.

Other effects were less benign. The relocation itself can be regarded as an attempt to rescue Christian faith and the idea of revelation from the tyranny of the contingent. Separated from the particular historical occurrence of the life of Jesus of Nazareth and (to focus now more closely on the Pauline letters) his crucifixion, the revelatory event of proclamation was movable, and its relationship to the theology contained in the New Testament writings could vary. That act of proclamation, as the point at which human activity could become transparent to, and transmissive of, God's challenging presence and life-giving power, that founding *kerygma* that elicits and validates human believing, could be understood as coming *before* the written gospels and Pauline letters. This was the case in the generally more historical perspective of a Rudolf Bultmann, for whom "the kerygma of Jesus as Messiah is the basic and primary thing which gives everything else—the ancient tradition and Jesus' message—its special character."[7] What one finds in Paul's letters, then, are "theological thoughts" that "are the unfolding of faith itself growing out of that new understanding of God, the world, and man which is conferred in and by faith" (understood as "faith in the kerygma").[8] Here the revelatory event calls forth and shapes theology. Still, kerygma, as the event of the gospel's encounter, and theology, as its subsequent and derivative elaboration and elucidation, however important the living connection between them, are kept distinct in both function and form.[9] This does justice to the event-character of the gospel—"For Paul, the gospel is first and fundamentally *an event,* not a message"[10]—but it draws a fairly sharp

6 Ibid., 34–35.

7 Rudolf Bultmann, *Theology of the New Testament* (2 vols.; trans. Kendrick Grobel; New York: Scribner's, 1951 and 1955) 1.42.

8 Ibid., 2.239.

9 So Furnish, "Paul the Theologian," 27.

10 Ibid., 26; emphasis original.

line between preaching and theology, a line that may be self-evident in later church life but is much harder to locate exegetically in Paul's letters.[11]

Or that founding act of proclamation could be understood as coming *after* the written gospels and Pauline letters. This was the case in the generally more systematic and ecclesiological perspective of a Karl Barth and rather specifically in the words of Robert Morgan cited above; this is proclamation in the ongoing life of the church throughout its history. What one sees in Paul's letters from this point of view is the historically contingent "raw material" of early Christian tradition that is interpreted in the direct address of the sermon and only there becomes "gospel." Here the relationship between Paul's theology and preaching is reversed. Paul's letters are more like proclamation in form, which, even though now relegated to a past that has become distant and exotic, still provides both standard and example to the present; and their theological content, as tradition, shapes and norms contemporary proclamation. Still, the distance between the "event" of the preached gospel and the historical event of the cross has become even greater.

In either case, no matter where the founding act of proclamation is understood to be located, the relationship of that proclamatory event to the preceding history that calls it forth and validates it, remains in some doubt, and so then does also the theological importance of that history. The historical contingency of the cross has been escaped or overcome or transcended. In the first instance this has been done by resort to an indefinable kerygma in which the historical Jesus of Nazareth *becomes* the Christ. This kerygma presupposes faith, so that the truly founding event is the rise of Easter faith. In the second instance, it has been done by shifting the crucial occurrence to the epistemological event, the "aural event,"[12] in which the hearer "gets the message." Either way, to the historical contingency of the cross there has now been added the existential or epistemological contingency of human believing. The attempt to rescue the Christian faith and revelation from the supposed and feared tyranny of the contingent has ended in the doubling of that tyranny.

Let us leave "contingency" and turn to "*coherence*." In our discussions there have been many attempts to define and locate it, starting with Beker himself,

11 Furnish ("Paul the Theologian," 33, n. 70) tries to preserve this line when he questions Lou Martyn's language about a "theological event" Paul was confident God intended to occur at the reading of his letter in the Galatian congregation (see J. Louis Martyn, "Events in Galatia: Modified Covenantal Nomism versus God's Invasion of the Cosmos in the Singular Gospel: A Response to J. D. G. Dunn and B. R. Gaventa," *Pauline Theology I* [160–179] 161, the revised version of the paper to which Furnish refers). But he implicitly concedes how hard this is when he remarks, "Paul's apostolic service, which includes but is by no means restricted to his preaching . . . , bears witness to this event [of the gospel] and is thus in its own way *eventful*" (ibid., 26; emphasis added).

12 The term is used by Martyn, "Events in Galatia," 161.

the person responsible for putting it in the forefront of our vocabulary.[13] There has been widespread agreement with Beker concerning the occasional and situationally diverse character of Paul's letters, coming to a head in the discussion of Romans and the rejection of Melanchthon's now notorious assessment of it as a compendium of Christian doctrine. But, beginning with Beker's own initial juxtaposition of these two key terms, there has persisted a powerful tendency to use "coherence" as the *opposite* of contingency, to direct the search for it toward various strategies for *transcending* or even suppressing the historical and the contingent, and so to escape the supposed tyranny of the latter in still another way.

This search can take various forms. One is to look for coherence in a belief system that is assumed to be the single source behind all the variety of what Paul writes. N. T. Wright's very definition of "Pauline theology" has it "refer to that *integrated* set of beliefs which may be supposed to inform and undergird Paul's life, mission, and writing, coming to expression in varied ways throughout all three."[14]

> It is not enough, however, merely to consider the specific topics treated by Paul at this or that point in his letters. It is also important to ask questions about the underlying structure of his belief system. . . . Here we have to do with issues too large to be seen frequently on the surface: questions of monism and dualism; of paganism, pantheism, and polytheism; of monotheism, its alternatives and its implications. It is my conviction that if we are really studying Pauline theology these issues must at least be on the table, if we are not to condemn ourselves ultimately to *shallowness.* Ultimately, *theology is all about the great wholes,* the single worldviews that determine and dominate the day-to-day handling of various issues. Most, perhaps all, *great thinkers and writers* can in the last resort be studied at this level.[15]

It is no surprise that immediately following these words, Wright devotes a rather full (and not uninstructive) discussion to such "worrying things" as "contradictions, tensions, inconsistencies, and antinomies." There is more than a hint here that greatness and substance and profundity in theology, as well as coherence, is to be found only beyond and behind the contingencies of history. Yet in the same context Wright says of Paul's theology that it "consists precisely in the redefinition, by means of christology and pneumatology, of those two key Jewish doctrines [sc. monotheism and election],"[16] suggesting on the contrary

13 See especially his "Recasting Pauline Theology," 15–18.

14 "Putting Paul Together Again: Toward a Synthesis of Pauline Theology (1 and 2 Thessalonians, Philippians, and Philemon)," *Pauline Theology I* (183–211) 184; emphasis added.

15 Ibid., 186; emphasis added.

16 Ibid., 184.

that Paul's theology is after all deeply imbedded in significant historical change. Part of what Wright is after is to counter "aggressively deconstructive analyses such as Heikki Räisänen's,"[17] and to make sure that we do not reduce Pauline theology "on the one hand to a mere function of social forces or rhetorical conventions nor subsume it on the other hand under the traditional loci of a different age."[18] So the search for coherence is motivated at least in part by the desire to respect Paul's integrity as a thinker. But that is not all.

Richard Hays looks for coherence in the "symbolic world" shared by Paul and other early Christians, including his readers, and shaped by tradition. He finds Noam Chomsky's model useful:

> Paul's particular statements, which are contingent pastoral responses to specific historical situations, are to be read as performances of a competence supplied by this larger communal symbol system; the symbol system is a language, and Paul's letters are utterances within the language.[19]

Pauline theology does not reside in this symbolic world, but consists of the "characteristic patterns of critical reflection" that recur as Paul "attempts to persuade his readers to interpret the practical consequences of *foundational assumptions* (*axioms*) that they putatively share with him in the light of his convictions."[20] Though such foundational assumptions still seem to be the origin of coherence, Hays is more ready to concede that "ideational coherence" is the product or *our* own constructive efforts "to make sense of Paul's writings by rearticulating their message in a form different from the form that Paul himself employed."[21] Why are such synthetic reconstructions important? They "hope to generate imaginative accounts of Pauline theology that have the power to *elicit consent* from the community of putatively competent readers"; they are our attempts by trial and error to reach a level of understanding that will strike informed readers as a satisfying account of the texts.[22] Coherence is here much more closely linked to the hermeneutic process of interpreting Paul's letters in the modern world, and Hays's essay in synthesis ends with a very useful summary of the unresolved issues with which anyone is left who attempts to interpret the five Pauline letters covered in *Pauline Theology I.* In the end, however, Hays returns to Paul's own thinking rather than that of his interpreters;

17 The words are those of Richard Hays, "Crucified with Christ: A Synthesis of the Theology of 1 and 2 Thessalonians, Philemon, Philippians, and Galatians," *Pauline Theology I* (227–246) 229.

18 Wright, "Putting Paul Together Again," 196–7.

19 Hays, "Crucified with Christ," 228.

20 Ibid., 228–9; emphasis added.

21 Ibid., 230.

22 Ibid., 230–31; emphasis added.

he finds "the *ground of coherence* in Paul's thought" to lie in "the narrative framework of the symbolic world presupposed by that theology," which has its heart in "the kerygmatic story of God's action through Jesus Christ."[23]

This turn to narrative has two consequences. One is that it encourages the idea of "the history of salvation" as the place to look for coherence in Paul's theology, thus renewing a debate that remains unresolved in our discussions. The suggestion is adopted and developed by David Lull and Robin Scroggs.[24] Hays himself, after making the suggestion that it is the narrative dimension of Paul's theology that supplies its coherence, raises the most serious problem with it:

> In other words, Paul does not interpret the foundational story as a simple linear *Heilsgeschichte* from Abraham to the present moment. Rather, for Paul, Christ's death has introduced a surprising discontinuity in Israel's history, simultaneously necessitating and enabling a new reading of scripture that discloses its witness to the gospel.[25]

The second consequence of Hays's move, and the net result, is this pointer to "God's action through Jesus Christ" as the root and fount of theological coherence in Paul. This is fruitful and promising, for it moves the discussion of coherence to another level since Jesus Christ (or Christology) is also for Paul the point at which ultimate theological meaning is most intimately linked to the contingency of a very particular historical event. We shall return to this point. For the moment, one further observation on the search for coherence may still be in order.

The question persists: what accounts for the urgency and drive behind this search? There can be little doubt that human understanding, by its very nature, reaches for inclusiveness and universality. There is always a touch of human hybris in that, but also of the human freedom that includes the impulse toward systematization. The inductive reasoning that shapes our work as historians aims at comprehensive conclusions, for what cannot be accounted for lives on to threaten the plausibility of every explanation. So, for example, as Victor Furnish reports, Joseph Fitzmyer does not hesitate to provide "a systematization of the Apostle's thought in a form in which he himself did not present it" since it

23 Ibid., 231–2; emphasis added.

24 David J. Lull, "Salvation History: Theology in 1 Thessalonians, Philemon, Philippians, and Galatians: A Response to N. T. Wright, R. B. Hays, and R. Scroggs," *Pauline Theology I,* 247–265; Robin Scroggs, "Salvation History: The Theological Structure of Paul's Thought (1 Thessalonians, Philippians, and Galatians)," *Pauline Theology I,* 212–226. For two vigorous rejections of "salvation history" as the solution to the problem of coherence in Paul's theology, see Martyn, "Events in Galatia," 172–174, and Keck, "Paul as Thinker," 33–34.

25 Hays, "Crucified with Christ," 237.

is the task of the biblical theologian "to express the *total* Pauline message, which *transcends the contextual situation* and embraces also the relational meaning of the Pauline utterances."[26] We may protest that the total Pauline message is beyond our reach, if for no other reason than the limitations of our sources. But even if we should narrow the theological interpreter's task within these limits to its more descriptive dimensions and eschew such systematization, and even when we have become less sanguine about the search for a "center" to Paul's thinking, there still remains that strong desire to find what it takes to integrate the apostle's thinking into a coherent whole, or to find, in the very expressive words of Jouette Bassler,

> a pattern, a center, a commitment, a conviction, a vision, an underlying structure, a core communication, a set of beliefs, a narrative, a coherence—*something*—in Paul's thoughts or behind them that dispels any abiding sense of mere opportunism or intellectual chaos on the part of the apostle. Yet nowhere, it seems, does this core, center, vision, etc. come to expression in a noncontingent way.[27]

Another clue to the pathos behind this search for an inclusive coherence appears in an observation made early in the Group's discussions by Paul Achtemeier, who formulated the search for the coherence of Paul's gospel as a question; namely,

> how to isolate from the welter of situation-conditioned material present in Paul's letter[s] that material which represents *positions or expressions which themselves do not depend on a given contingent situation for their validity.*[28]

This suggests that what is at stake is to identify not only what controls or shapes the apostle's argument at any given moment but also what can so transcend the limitations of historical contingency as to supply warrant for its truth and reliability. That adds another dimension to the search. But it also raises a new set of questions. If we are dependent for that kind of warrant on a "coherence" that exacts from us the price of suppressing the historical and contingent, does that not disclose a new tyranny, this time of "coherence"? Can coherence supply what is here being asked of it? Is that the source, the originating fountain, the authenticating signature of "the truth of the gospel" for Paul?

Are we then torn between a tyranny of contingence and one of coherence? The material produced by this Group is permeated with intimations that this

26 Joseph Fitzmyer, *Paul and His Theology: A Brief Sketch* (2nd ed.; Englewood Cliffs, N.J.: Prentice-Hall, 1989) 38, as quoted by Furnish, "Paul the Theologian," 22; emphases added.

27 "Paul's Theology: Whence and Whither?" *Pauline Theology II* (3–17) 6; emphasis added.

28 "Finding the Way to Paul's Theology: A Response to J. Christiaan Beker and J. Paul Sampley," *Pauline Theology I*, 25–26; emphasis added.

polarity, useful as it has proven to be as a heuristic device, cannot provide the key to understanding Paul's theology. One may begin with Achtemeier again, who stresses the dynamic quality not only of Paul's thought but also of Paul's particular and occasional reactions to the various situations he addresses.[29] Of special importance are the many scattered observations that recognize the contingent character of Paul's *theology* and his "core convictions." "We do not have a non-contingent expression of what Paul felt represented the coherent center of the faith."[30] We have seen that Bultmann already spoke of Paul's theology as an "unfolding" process. In offering retrospective modifications of his book *Paul the Apostle,* Beker speaks more and more of a hermeneutical process characterized by "the reciprocal and circular interaction of coherence and contingency."[31] Bassler prefers to speak of Paul's theology as an "activity"[32] and she is vigorously seconded in this by Steven Kraftchick, who develops the thought in his own way.[33] Furnish portrays the apostle's theology as a continuous working out of an understanding of the gospel, not merely the application to a "target" situation of a gospel already formulated.[34] In his earlier article, both the title and the concluding sentence imply that the search is not so much for Paul's theology as it is for "Paul the Theologian."[35]

These intimations have deeply colored our discussions of Paul with the twofold benefit that his theology is conceived in a much more flexible and dynamic way, and the rigid polarization of "coherence" and "contingency" has broken down to the point where it no longer confronts us as an inescapable alternative. Nevertheless, these advances notwithstanding, something of the inherited model of "theology" still clings to many of our formulations. This is the assumption that Paul's relatively coherent thought world (rightly recognized to be highly complex and syncretistic) is always the starting-point, the storehouse, the repertoire, the competence *out of which* Paul addresses each of the particular crises he confronts. This can be illustrated from Beker's own uncommonly suggestive, and for our discussions seminal, essay. A major step forward is taken when Beker identifies Paul's theology with his "interpretive activity." But then in the next breath "coherence" is located in the "convictional basis" from which Paul's activity moves, "the truth of the gospel" (Gal 2:5, 14).[36] Even if "coher-

29 Ibid., 33–34.

30 Ibid., 32.

31 Beker, "Recasting Pauline Theology," 24.

32 "Paul's Theology: Whence and Whither?" 10–12.

33 "Seeking a More Fluid Model: A Response to Jouette M. Bassler," *Pauline Theology II* (18–34) 30–33.

34 "On Putting Paul in His Place," 12–17.

35 "Paul the Theologian," 30.

36 "Recasting Pauline Theology," 15.

ence" refers to something "fluid and flexible," it "nourishes" Paul's thought.[37] It is "the *abiding solution* to Paul's private contingency (in *answering* the crisis of his personal life) but also the *abiding solution* to the various *problems* of his churches (in *answering* their several crises)."[38] It does not matter how flexibly "coherence" is defined; if "the truth of the gospel" is understood as the "answer" to various problems, we are still stuck in the image of Paul as a problem-solver in the churches that came to him for "answers" and of the gospel as a resource in the tool-bag of this "fixer." The English word "answer" does not function here as "Antwort" (a response in a process of dialogue) but as "Lösung" (a solution to a puzzle). But the underlying conception of theology, not to mention this image of Paul, ill fits either the apostle's argument or Beker's. In both verses in Galatians 2, "the truth of the gospel" is used teleologically; it is not something ready-made and given but is at risk and has to survive (διαμεῖναι, v. 5, a punctiliar aorist) or be attained (πρός and acc., v. 14). In the very same sentence, Beker himself also identifies "the truth of the gospel" as "the apocalyptic interpretation of the cross and resurrection of Christ." That is a powerful move in a different direction in which cross and resurrection are the "given," the precipitating occasion is the crisis confronting Paul, but the "theology" is the "Antwort," the response, the *resulting outcome* of the process of interpretation. (If theological "content" is to be located anywhere, it is here; "content" and "process" may be a useful distinction but in the end it is a false alternative for defining Paul's "theology".)

It is the conception of "theology" operative here that is the issue. Once again, there have appeared, scattered throughout the Group's materials, many pointers in this alternative direction. Andrew Lincoln's very careful and instructive analysis of the interplay among tradition, gospel and audience in Rom 1:18–4:25 offers repeatedly a close-up look at Paul's argument as a theology in the making, though he stops short of calling it that.[39] "These insights [in Rom 2:17–27] *produce* finally a whole new perspective on who is a Jew."[40] "The early chapters of Romans show Paul *forging a theology* based on his gospel through *creative* interpretation of Jewish and Jewish Christian tradition."[41] Beker suggests that "a disclosure theory of truth" might prove to be more compatible with Paul's hermeneutic than "a coherence theory of truth," though he does not pursue the question of what the former might look like.[42] Troels Engberg-

37 Ibid., 16–17.

38 Ibid., 17; emphases added.

39 "From Wrath to Justification: Tradition, Gospel and Audience in the Theology of Romans 1:18–4:25," *Pauline Theology III,* 130–159.

40 Ibid., 144; emphasis added.

41 Ibid., 157; emphasis added.

42 "Recasting Pauline Theology," 20.

Pedersen writes: "All this tends to emphasize the dynamic and open-ended character of Paul's theologizing. What we see in the letters is a symbolic universe *in the making,* not a fully worked out, static, and final one."[43] This series of quotations may be ended with the arresting, and I believe correct, observation of Steven Kraftchick: "Sometimes Paul discovered where he wanted to go during the act of composition rather than prior to it."[44]

In view of such suggestions, *the proposal being made here* is simply this: Instead of assuming most of the time that Paul's "theology" or "convictions" are the *resource* or starting-point *from* which he addresses the issues placed before him, may one rather, as a kind of "experiment in thought," think of them more consistently as the end-product and result, the *outcome to* which he arrives in the process of his argument, his "hermeneutic," or his "theologizing"? Many features of Paul's letters that have come under scrutiny in the course of these discussions recommend such a shift.

(1) The later letters, most conspicuously of course Romans, incorporate the experiences and the theological formulations of earlier crises. It is not just the case that we find blocks of text in Romans that look like sermonic materials or arguments used on previous occasions. New contingencies produce new coherences in formulation; the process of reflection yields new theological affirmation, less inchoate, more pregnant. Can anyone deny the sense of progression in the work of this Group as it has moved from 1 Thessalonians to Romans? Has this been only a progression in the scope and range of Pauline texts under review, or has it not also been a progression in the *emergence* of the "Pauline theology/theologies" we have been seeking, at a new level of coherence just because of the new diversity? If so, then the "coherence" of Pauline theology is itself the product of historical process, i.e., it is itself "contingent"—as is demonstrated in the sometimes painful awareness that the end result of one line of "theologizing" on one occasion is not in all respects logically compatible with that of another and cannot be made to be so. Then one would no longer be able to speak of "the non-contingent bedrock of Pauline theological convictions."[45]

(2) Romans 9–11 may well serve as Exhibit No. 1. This is a matter of much dispute and hangs on the detailed exegesis of these chapters, about which there

43 "Proclaiming the Lord's Death: 1 Corinthians 11:17–34 and the Forms of Paul's Theological Argument," *Pauline Theology II* (103–132) 106; emphasis original.

44 "Seeking a More Fluid Model," 24. This observation recalls the striking declaration attributed to Daniel J. Boorstin, one-time Distinguished Service Professor of American History at the University of Chicago, Librarian of Congress, Pulitzer Prize recipient, and author, among many other books, of *The Discoverers* (New York: Random House, 1983): "I write to discover what I think."

45 Achtemeier, "Finding the Way to Paul's Theology," 31.

is important debate within the Group.[46] But a not unpersuasive case has been made out by Nikolaus Walter for the view that Paul himself did not clearly see, when he wrote Rom 9:1, where chap. 11 would end, and "that we actually share in a mental struggle here, the outcome of which was not already settled with the first sentences of chap. 9."[47] Despite wildly differing conclusions about where Paul comes out, many interpreters seem willing to agree on the highly contingent nature of Paul's "theologizing" here. The main disagreements over the "coherence" that does or does not emerge from Paul's "mental struggle" in these chapters boil down, it seems to me, to what Hays has called "vicarious inclusion in corporate salvation," the second of the three unmet "hermeneutical challenges" with which he ends his partial synthesis of the shorter letters.[48] But that is another matter that cannot be pursued here.

(3) Galatians may provide an example on which we agree more quickly. Lou Martyn has observed, "Had the Teachers not had such extraordinary success with their Abraham sermons, we would probably know nothing of Paul's interpretation of the patriarch, for Romans 4 is clearly a reworking of Galatians 3."[49] Perhaps even more significant is the lesson he credits to E. Grässer and approvingly passes on,

> that the term "covenant" does not itself point to a fundamental element of Paul's theology. With few exceptions, Paul employs the term only when one of his churches has become enamored of the use being made of it by traveling evangelists who stand in opposition to his mission (Galatians 3–4; 2 Corinthians 3).[50]

It is actually a confirmation of this point when Richard Hays points out that "righteousness/justification language . . . appears only in the letters where the question of covenant membership for Gentile Christians is a disputed matter" (for the debated "covenant membership" one may substitute the more Pauline "standing in God's grace" [e.g. Rom 5:21] and the point still stands).[51] Despite the argument between Martyn and Dunn over whether "covenantal nomism" best characterizes Paul's theology or that of the Teachers he is opposing, they seem to agree "that the Antioch incident was a decisive factor in *the development*

46 E. Elizabeth Johnson, "Romans 9–11: The Faithfulness and Impartiality of God," *Pauline Theology III,* 211–239, and Douglas Moo, "The Theology of Romans 9–11: A Response to E. Elizabeth Johnson," *Pauline Theology III,* 240–258.

47 "Zur Interpretation von Römer 9–11," *ZTK* 81 (1984)(172–195) 176; my translation.

48 "Crucified with Christ," 246.

49 "Events in Galatia," 166–7, n. 15.

50 Ibid., 171, n. 26.

51 "Crucified with Christ," 237.

of Paul's understanding of the gospel."[52] The question whether the situational demands in Galatians *suppress* the coherent "core" of Paul's theology or rather *elicit* it and bring it into full view,[53] has proven to be a fruitful test case for examining the validity of any definition of "coherence," but either outcome to that debate will serve as a powerful support for the contention that "coherence" (and in its wake Pauline "theology") is the result of Paul's "theologizing" and not its presupposition.

(4) Paul's use of scripture seems also to justify this proposal. It turns out on closer observation that scriptural citations are in most cases not a starting-point of Paul's "theologizing" but are drawn into the argument as a kind of ladder by which to reach a new level of meaning and coherence—a ladder on which Paul knows he can rely but one that he redesigns as he uses it. He has a certain confidence that scripture can help him reach a goal that is not yet in his grasp. The resulting pattern comes close to showing that "theology" is something one "does" or produces rather than "has," and that Paul's theology in particular is not the *father* of his "theologizing" but its *child*. Much remains yet to be done in any analysis of Paul's use of scripture from this perspective; "interpretation of Israel's scripture" is another of Hays's unmet "hermeneutical challenges."[54]

(5) In the early discussions of method in this Group, Paul Sampley formulated a series of "specific procedures" for moving upstream, so to speak, "from text to thought world" in Paul's letters.[55] Although Sampley stresses "pervasive flexibility" and adaptability as characteristic of Paul's letters and the degree to which their agendas are "fundamentally set by his perception of the needs and struggles of a given community,"[56] these procedures were nevertheless formulated with an eye to moving backward "to the thought world from which his thoughts gain expression," in order from there to facilitate a "reconstruction of what we might call a theology of Paul"; this "will always be a modern abstraction, a distillation that we gain from his thought world."[57] What is being proposed here on the contrary is in many ways a reversal of direction in this

52 James D. G. Dunn, "The Theology of Galatians: The Issue of Covenantal Nomism," *Pauline Theology I* (125–146) 144; emphasis added. Cf. Martyn, "Events in Galatia," 164–5 and *passim*.

53 In the context of Beker's claim that apocalyptic is the heart of Paul's gospel, this question has taken the specific form of a debate over whether Galatians is devoid of apocalyptic or "is fully as apocalyptic as are the other Paulines" (Martyn); see Beker, *Paul the Apostle,* 58, and Martyn, "Apocalyptic Antinomies in Paul's Letter to the Galatians," *NTS* 31 (1985) (410–424) 410–12 and 420–21.

54 "Crucified with Christ," 246.

55 "From Text to Thought World: The Route to Paul's Ways," *Pauline Theology I* (3–14) 9–14.

56 Ibid., 5.

57 Ibid., 3.

procedure, in which "Pauline theology" would be less an "abstraction" or "distillation" on our part and more closely identified with the actual conclusions reached in Paul's arguments. But the point to be made now is that many of the procedures Sampley recommends turn out to be just as serviceable if one is asking where Paul's theology "comes out." They include, for example, asking: "Where does Paul self-correct?"; "What matters are treated as indifferent?"; and especially "What shall we make of the frequency with which Paul mentions goals in his letters?"[58] Again, we cannot pursue that matter further here.

These may be some of the reasons encouraging one to experiment with a different way of conceiving "Pauline theology." But the proposal implies some correlates and raises some questions to which we need to turn.

In the first place, a word about "argument." Lou Martyn is not happy with a "definition of the theology of Galatians as a responsive argument" and proposes that the theology of the letter is much more closely connected with "the letter's work" and that Paul "*does* theology [here] by writing in such a way as to *anticipate* a theological *event,*" an "aural event" in which "God will re-preach his gospel to the Galatians."[59] But as Martyn's own case unfolds, it becomes clear that the real issue at stake is not whether Paul's letter contains an argument that "responds" to the situation in that congregation or intends a certain result, but rather what the strategy of Paul's argumentation is and on whose terms and within whose frame of reference it is carried through.[60] Martyn's answers to those critical questions and the suggestion that they display Paul's way of "doing" theology seem to demonstrate that no clear line can be drawn in Paul's letters between argument, rhetoric (the art of persuasion, the producing of an effect!) and theology, and even to raise doubts about how far we can go with the relatively useful but ultimately only heuristic distinction between proclamation and theology *in Paul's letters.*[61]

58 Ibid., 10 and 13.

59 Martyn, "Events in Galatia," 160–61; emphases added.

60 Ibid., 162–3.

61 The distinction is energetically defended by Furnish, "Paul the Theologian," 27. One may readily grant that the distinction is clear and even essential in the contemporary ecclesiastical and academic context. A flaw in Furnish's exceptionally clear and instructive article is that he first establishes a useful but modern definition of "Christian theology" independently of Paul and then asks whether Paul may be regarded as a theologian who fits it (ibid., 25–26). An alternative is to begin with an analysis of what the apostle does and then ask whether the umbrella of "theology" can be extended to cover that. Thus William S. Campbell: "It is a body of tradition rather than a system of theology with which Paul interacts. But if the creative reformulating and transforming of inherited images and metaphors are what constitutes doing theology, then Paul is certainly a theologian par excellence" ("The Contribution of Traditions to Paul's Theology: A Response to C. J. Roetzel," *Pauline Theology II* [234–254] 254).

A more important point is that since Paul's theology has been so frequently spoken of in our discussions in terms of his "foundational convictions," the present proposal might be construed to imply that Paul had no convictions before engaging in this activity and brought none to the writing of his letters. The absurdity of that implication might then count as a decisive reason for rejecting the proposal. This requires some discussion. Much depends, of course, on the definitions with which one starts. Bassler finds Daniel Patte's definition helpful: "A conviction is a self-evident truth." The way to locate convictions in theological argument is then to identify what in it is "established as self-evidently good and desirable."[62] Convictions remain here clearly within the realm of that *from* which Paul argues. Yet Kraftchick points out that conviction statements function in different ways in Paul's letters and for that reason should not be identified as the foundation of Paul's theologizing but as its "presuppositions or products," part of Paul's "raw data."[63] Sometimes Paul's argument is directed at *changing* his readers' presuppositions about what is good and desirable, real or illusory, so that the conviction is something arrived at in a particular setting and occasion, not only by his readers but also, as we have suggested, even by Paul himself.

To propose that one should at least experiment with an understanding of Pauline theology as the product and outcome of Paul's various concrete and contingent acts of "doing theology" does not in any way call into question the importance of convictions that Paul brings to these enterprises. But "convictions" will now carry a somewhat different meaning. If anything comes close to being self-evident, it is that not only Paul but also his readers carry to the writing and the reading respectively of those letters a large freight of pre-understandings, assumptions, opinions, beliefs and even convictions. Some are held in common; some are not. Some are silently taken for granted; some are named and drawn upon in argument. Some have been previously planted by Paul, wittingly or unwittingly; some have been planted by his opponents. Some Paul attempts to encourage and reinforce; some he aims to question and to change. This freight includes what some writers of our papers have referred to as "world view" and others as "symbolic world"; certainly we should think as well of scripture and even of pre-Pauline Christian traditions. For purposes of reflecting on Pauline theology, we may embrace most of this under the heading of (religious) "tradition." Paul, after all, was not the first to read his Hebrew scriptures or to speak of God, of God's presence and action (even in Jesus of

62 Bassler, "Paul's Theology: Whence and Whither?" 12, citing Daniel Patte, *Paul's Faith and the Power of the Gospel: A Structural Introduction to the Pauline Letters* (Philadelphia: Fortress, 1983) 11 and 17.

63 "Seeking a More Fluid Model," 28–29.

Nazareth), God's freedom and faithfulness, God's mercy and judgment, or of love, righteousness, sin, suffering, or of life and death. At this point Andrew Lincoln's careful analysis of Rom 1:18–4:25 is helpful. He has

> traced three main coordinates in the theology of Rom 1:18–4:25—*tradition,* which provides most of the symbol system within which the argument takes place; *gospel,* which supplies the convictions by which the symbols are re-aligned and reshaped; and *audience,* whose needs influence the argument but are interpreted in the light of the gospel,[64]

and he has summed it all up in one of the best one-liners of our material: "tradition, gospel and audience abide, these three; and the greatest of these is gospel."[65]

Clearly it is the "gospel" that ultimately controls the process of Paul's "the-ologizing"; on that there seems to be wide agreement. Leander Keck ended his major essay on Romans for the Group, "What Makes Romans Tick?," with the statement:

> Romans ticks because Paul did not allow his immediate situation to govern completely what he had to say, but allowed the inner logic of his gospel to assert itself even if that meant subjecting his first readers to a certain amount of theological overkill.[66]

But now, just what is that "gospel" and what its "inner logic" that not only gives coherence to this multi-faceted body of Pauline literature but also tran-scends the contextual situation of that literature so that it still calls for a hearing today? What is it that "realigns" and "reshapes" the symbols of Paul's tradition so that a distinctive "Pauline theology" that is also a *Christian* theology emerges? Lincoln still refers to "convictions" that the gospel supplies; but he has made the important step of making "convictions" depend upon and derive from this "gospel" instead of standing for its substance. Picking up Sampley's point that one clue to "coherence" in Paul is provided by basic points from which he argues,[67] Achtemeier focusses on "those generative statements or beliefs that seem to underlie larger developments in Paul's letters," and lists as one of these the resurrection. It is "a non-contingent component of valid Christian faith," which is affirmed as an act of God in the confessional formula of Rom 10:9b and which, as Achtemeier goes on to elaborate, can be shown to be not only

64 "From Wrath to Justification," 159; emphasis added.

65 Ibid.

66 "What Makes Romans Tick?" *Pauline Theology III* (3–29) 29.

67 "From Text to Thought World," 11.

central for Paul but also "generative of other beliefs and to that extent foundational for Paul's gospel."[68]

Here we have come, I believe, very close to our answer. But we have not quite reached it yet. In a crucial observation, Calvin Roetzel has remarked, "it is simply inadequate to say the cross is foundational without noting the way the interpretation of the cross is changed by its context and then bends back onto the context to shape that as well."[69] That is to say, every reference to the cross and resurrection in Paul's letters, every "affirmation," "conviction," or "belief," even every pre-Pauline confessional formula, every human statement of it as "gospel" is shaped by historical, cultural, and personal circumstances and context and so is imbedded in historical contingency. There *is* no "noncontingent bedrock of Pauline theological convictions."[70]

Here, as often in the past, Leander Keck has come to our aid, in an article written to honor Achtemeier.[71] "Paul," he writes,

> was an ex post facto thinker. Ex post facto thinking occurs not only after an event but because of it, and with continual reference, explicit or implicit, to it. The event's very "happenedness" requires thinking. . . . For Paul, this given, this event, this compelling datum that evoked his ex post facto thinking was the resurrection of the crucified Jesus.[72]

This is helpful for three reasons, which we may discuss briefly in turn in conclusion.

(1) In the first place, these words help locate more precisely that "bedrock" of Pauline theological convictions. They remind us of the crucial distinction that must be drawn between human believing, confession, affirmation, and conviction on the one hand and the "event" on the other, the "compelling datum" that calls forth these human responses. In words now widely familiar, Nils Dahl has identified what can be called the "foundational conviction," from both a material and an historical perspective, of all New Testament theology:

> The central task of early Christian theology was to come to terms with the crucifixion of Jesus. The conviction that the crucified "King of the Jews" was right and had been vindicated by God, who raised him from the dead, forms the basis of the theology of the New Testament in all its varieties.[73]

68 "Finding the Way to Paul's Theology," 35.

69 "The Grammar of Election in Four Pauline Letters," *Pauline Theology II* (211–233) 228.

70 Achtemeier, "Finding the Way to Paul's Theology," 31.

71 "Paul as Thinker," 27–38.

72 Ibid., 29–30.

73 Nils Alstrup Dahl, "The Neglected Factor in New Testament Theology," *Jesus the Christ: The Historical Origins of Christological Doctrine* (Minneapolis: Fortress, 1991) 157–58. It should not be forgotten that Dahl played a significant role in the early formation of the Pauline Theology Group.

Obviously, this "conviction" as such is part of early Christian theology. But just as clearly, the essential ingredient in this conviction is the certainty that it is not self-generating, that it has been called into being and derives its warrant and authorization from something God has done. As God's act, this is the "bedrock" that elicits and shapes "convictions" but is not itself a "conviction"—not the Easter faith of the early church or its proclamation, not some indefinable cipher labelled "kerygma" behind all the contingent theological formulations of the New Testament, not the apostolic act of preaching Jesus *as* the Christ, but God's act of confirming and vindicating the crucified Jesus.[74] To locate the "bedrock" in this way does more than define the basic content of the conviction. It points the way to a solution to that other dimension as well of the search for what controls and shapes the apostle's argument; namely, the quest for what can so transcend the contingencies of human believing as to supply warrant for its truth and reliability. It is God's raising of the crucified Jesus that provides for Paul the authenticating signature for "the truth of the gospel" and for his own apostleship in its service as well.

(2) In the second place, Keck's words open the way to a more satisfying formulation of the relationship between "contingency" and "coherence." The crucifixion of Jesus is a contingent historical event in the full sense of the word. It is a public event, fully open to historical explanation and description (knowledge of which is subject to the same limitations of accessibility, information, and evidence as any other event of the past), but also fully susceptible to contradictory human responses and evaluations. In itself, its meaning remains open and uncertain. Yet its concrete givenness is remarkably fixed, even inescapable. Nothing in the entire Bible is so certain historically or so secure from historical doubting as that Jesus did not die from so-called "natural" causes at the end of a successful career as a popular teacher but that his life was taken from him. Moreover, the *way* it was certainly taken from him constituted from the start a devastating threat to the meaning of his life and teaching, and especially to the coherence of all early Christian claims connecting him with God's purposes.[75]

74 Cf. Hans Küng, *On Being a Christian* (Garden City, N.Y.: Doubleday, 1976) 352: "The Easter faith is not a function of the disciples' faith. . . . Even according to Bultmann, the formula 'Jesus is risen into the kerygma (proclamation)' [R. Bultmann, *Das Verhältnis der urchristlichen Christusbotschaft zum historischen Jesus* (SHAW 60/3; 2d ed.; Heidelberg: Carl Winter Universitätsverlag, 1965) 27; ET (from the 3d German edition): "The Primitive Christian Kerygma and the Historical Jesus," *The Historical Jesus and the Kerygmatic Christ: Essays on the New Quest of the Historical Jesus* (trans. and ed. Carl E. Braaten and Roy A. Harrisville; New York: Abingdon, 1964)(15–42) 42] is liable to be misunderstood. Even according to Bultmann, it does not mean that Jesus lives because he is proclaimed: he is proclaimed because he lives."

75 For the factors that shaped the public meaning of this form of execution in the Greco-Roman world, cf. M. Hengel, *Crucifixion* (Philadelphia: Fortress, 1977).

That is why Dahl has identified that "central task of early Christian theology" to be "to come to terms with the crucifixion of Jesus." Because of this threat, the necessary condition for receiving and understanding his death as a benevolent and salutary "divine act" was that certainty that God had identified himself with this Crucified One and so confirmed and vindicated him. Apart from God's act, Jesus' death would remain devoid of special meaning, another merely historical and starkly contingent human defeat. The resurrection does not wipe out the death of Jesus or undo its contingent historical reality. Rather, as divine vindication, it *makes* the death of Jesus an "apocalyptic event," and Paul uses apocalyptic categories and traditions to make clear what God's raising of this Jesus makes this *death* mean: "The very structure of reality is transformed."[76] So much so is this the case that the death of Jesus plays a surprisingly more conspicuous role in Paul's letters than even the resurrection as such.

Now of course the resurrection too is received and pictured and transmitted, in narratives of appearances, in empty tomb stories, in hymnic and creedal formulas—all historically contingent ways that can be traced by the historian as diverse and developing traditions.[77] The earliest affirmations of its reality are confessional in nature. Yet, just because such confession included the realization that faith is not self-generating but has been called into being ex post facto, and because the reality being confessed cannot be reduced to or exhausted in the confessing and believing it elicits, these confessional utterances take the form of historical statements about a particular event of the past that parallel references to the contingent event of Jesus' crucifixion: "God has raised him from the dead" (Rom 10:9). But this does not mean that the resurrection itself is a contingent historical event of the same order as the crucifixion.[78] It cannot be. It has *God* as its actor. It has no eyewitness. It is not subject to historical verification or falsification. It has no content for unbelief; for belief, its "content" is the freshly disclosed status and identity of the previously known particular historical figure of the Crucified. Those twin confessional statements of Rom 10:9, "Jesus is Lord" and "God has raised him from the dead," are equivalent and

76 Hays, "Crucified with Christ," 239.

77 For the complexities of "resurrection symbolism" at the primary exegetical level and beyond, one may consult Pheme Perkins, *Resurrection: New Testament Witness and Contemporary Reflection* (Garden City, N.Y.: Doubleday, 1984). For the historical development of the diverse resurrection traditions as well as for the understanding of resurrection in Paul in particular, and as representative of a much larger literature, see Ulrich Wilckens, *Resurrection. Biblical Testimony to the Resurrection: An Historical Examination and Explanation* (Louisville: John Knox, 1978).

78 For further discussion of the question whether the resurrection may be spoken of as an "event," historical or eschatological or otherwise, cf. Küng, *On Being a Christian,* 348–356, and Perkins, *Resurrection,* 28–30.

interpret each other: to say the second *is* to confess the first. Yet it is this resurrection that makes all the difference in authorizing an understanding of Jesus' death as itself a divine act, more than a merely contingent historical event.

To return to our pair of troublesome and yet illuminating terms, we may thus suggest that Paul sees this contingently historical event of the crucifixion not only to have been made normative by God's action, but to have been made the point where human believing and knowing may genuinely transcend the contingent and find an authentic coherence to life and thought. It has become the eternally reliable clue and criterion for discerning God's true nature, presence, and intention, and thus the historical locus of "revelation." This "accidental truth of history" has been made the disclosure point for the eternally valid and "necessary" "inner logic" of the gospel.

(3) How does this work itself out in Paul's theology? This brings us to our third point, and to what is in the end the final and most telling argument for the proposal to conceive of Paul's theology as the resulting outcome rather than as the starting-point of his theological activity. In the article referred to earlier, Keck also wrote,

> Paul had no Christian teacher. He was nobody's pupil, but was an *autodidact,* that is, a self-taught thinker who, while indebted to traditions, *never appealed to an authoritative teacher.* Nor did Paul's thinking develop in a collegial context as Johannine theology did, assuming that this tradition was formed in a school.[79]

This emphasis on the creative singularity of Paul and his position at the fountainhead of Christian theology (though he is not alone there) is, I think, extremely important—something lost in the "history of religions school" with its over-emphasis on *pre*-Pauline Hellenistic Christianity. It is important because in Paul's theology (*in* his letters) we have ringside seats to watch what happens when the fully historical impact of the crucifixion, made the defining event by God's raising Jesus from the dead, *forces* the revision and recasting of all the traditional language, concepts, convictions and categories, including the reading of scripture: God,[80] God's "anointed" ("Christ"), God's righteousness, mercy, calling, etc.—not to mention the coloring and reconstruction of all the memories of the Jewish teacher of Nazareth. This may not be God's "invasion of the cosmos," but it is an invasion of the "world" of human religious thinking, speaking, and believing. It is a thoroughly historical process. This is how a "reve-

79 "Paul as Thinker," 80; emphasis added.

80 Küng, *On Being a Christian,* 361: "'He who raised Jesus from the dead' becomes practically the designation of the Christian God."

lation" that is not only existential but also historical takes place. God is not understood to act here for the first time, or for the last; he does not stop acting. But his acting can never again be perceived or understood in the same way as before. This *process of revision*, this "creative reformulating of inherited images and metaphors,"[81] this ferment that has been set in motion by this "compelling datum" and produces what can first be called by the historian distinctively *Christian* ways of speaking about God, about righteousness, sin, mercy, God's people, etc., does not all take place at one point in Paul. It *keeps* happening, in historically contingent ways: one way here in Galatians where the Teachers introduce Abraham into the discourse, another way in 1 and 2 Corinthians, another way in Romans. Thus Paul himself says that *God* is at work in the process ("event") of human persuasion and confessing. In an important sense, Paul is not an "autodidact"; he is a θεοδίδακτος ("God-taught") and he calls his converts θεοδίδακτοι because God has been present and active in their learning what it really means to love one another (1 Thess 4:9). How has God been present? Through the preaching of Christ crucified/risen, which is not unrelated to "the spirit of Christ" (= "the Spirit of him who raised Jesus from the dead" = "Christ in you," Rom 8:11).

Pauline theology, I have tried to suggest, is what emerged in these successive contingent "persuasion-events," not above or behind historical contingency but in *each act* of αἰχμαλωτίζειν πᾶν νόημα εἰς τὴν ὑπακοὴν τοῦ Χριστοῦ (2 Cor 10:5). This phrase is not unlike that other one that has caused so much discussion: ἡ πίστις τοῦ Χριστοῦ ("the faith of Christ"), and may be rendered, "taking captive every thought, concept, category and conviction to the obedience *of Christ*/to obedience *to Christ*/to *Christian* obedience." It is the resulting outcome, which can only set the pattern for subsequent generations but remains before us for our continuing profit and reflection, that is "Pauline Theology."

[81] Campbell, "The Contribution of Traditions to Paul's Theology," 254.

9 WHERE IS "THE TRUTH" IN PAUL'S GOSPEL?

A Response to Paul W. Meyer

Victor Paul Furnish
Perkins School of Theology
Southern Methodist University

IN HIS APPRAISAL of the ten-year project represented by the essays in this and three previous volumes,[1] Paul Meyer, rather like his namesake, the apostle himself, encourages us to be less concerned about celebrating the distance we have come than about pressing on toward the goal that lies ahead.[2] But what exactly is the goal? That is, in what respect, if at all, may we appropriately speak of anything like "Pauline theology"? And how, if at all, is it possible to relate the historically contingent aspects, both of the apostle's letters and of his gospel, to the coherence toward which any quest for "the truth" of his gospel would seem to be aiming?

It is primarily and properly to these two critical questions that Meyer's essay is devoted. In addressing them he ends up making not just one but two important proposals about Paul's theology. Stated briefly, and only in a preliminary way, these are, first, that we should think of Paul's theology as the "result" of his theologizing, not as a resource; and second, that what "controls" his theologizing is finally the gospel, which involves the certainty that God has acted to vindicate the crucified Jesus. By way of response I should like, first, to affirm and emphasize several of Meyer's major observations about the course and results of our decade-long discussion; second, to identify and comment on what I take to be the salient points of his two major proposals; and third, moving on from those but not leaving them behind, to offer a few suggestions of my own about the character of Paul's thought.

1 *Pauline Theology,* vols. I–III. Minneapolis: Fortress, 1991–95.

2 "Pauline Theology: A Proposal for a Pause in Its Pursuit" (chapter 8 in this volume).

I

After situating the quest for Pauline theology within the broader context of 19th and 20th-century New Testament interpretation, Paul Meyer proceeds to express some important, and I believe fully warranted, concerns about the way we have been pursuing this goal. Three of these, especially, deserve to be highlighted.

First, in so far as we have tended to think of "coherence" as the opposite of "contingency" we have been attempting in our own way to transcend or even to suppress "the supposed and feared tyranny" of the historically contingent.[3] As Meyer suggests, we are doing this whenever we seek to identify Paul's theology with some particular "belief system," set of "convictions," or "kerygmatic story." In each of these cases, as I see it, one is involved in a process that is hardly different from the process by which Paul's letters have long been mined for teachings that can be somehow fitted into the doctrinal categories which have prevailed since the time of the scholastic theologians. Whether the search is for a belief system, "bedrock" convictions, or a foundational story, one has to end up extracting selected elements and putting them together, often according to criteria that are not entirely clear or compelling. Then, in a rather awesome move, the resultant construct is said either to underlie or to transcend the particularities of Paul's letters, and, indeed, of his ministry.

Second, it is no doubt true that sometimes the search for Pauline theology has been not only for "what controls or shapes the apostle's argument" in given instances, but also for a "coherence" that will somehow validate his argument, or even his gospel as a whole. Meyer appropriately asks whether such a coherence, which necessarily "exacts from us the price of suppressing the historical and contingent," could even provide the sort of verification that is sought.[4] Indeed, is it not the case that Paul himself regards the gospel as something other than merely the sum of his statements about it, or his argument on its behalf? If so, then "the truth of the gospel" cannot be established merely by ascertaining that his representation of it is in itself "coherent."

Third, despite repeated calls to appreciate the fluid and dynamic character of the apostle's thought, we have continued to operate, by and large, with an essentially static model of Paul's theology. Looking back, it is apparent that our project as originally conceived simply presupposed a static model. To be sure, the plan to move through the letters chronologically toward a final, grand "synthesis" of the results was meant to keep us attentive to the contingent situations

[3] Ibid., 143.
[4] Ibid., 147.

reflected in the letters, and to the theological distinctiveness of each. But had this worked (and it didn't take us long to see that it wasn't going to work), we would have ended up with just one more static summary of "Pauline theology," distinctive mainly for having been formed incrementally.[5] Along the way we have sensed this and worried some about it. Nevertheless, we have been reluctant to give up the static model—perhaps, however unwittingly, yearning for the security that comes with being able to say, "*This* is Paul's theology, and *that* is not." In particular, as Paul Meyer observes, we have tended to think of the apostle's theology as "the starting-point, the storehouse, the repertoire, the competence *out of which*" he drew resources for resolving particular crises.[6] When we do, I would add, we both misunderstand the character of Pauline theology and verge, once more, on identifying the apostle's theological statements with the gospel itself.

Despite these three major concerns, Meyer's assessment is not entirely gloomy, even if its brighter side is rather like Mark Twain's opinion of the music of Richard Wagner, that "it's better than it sounds." What makes our work better than it reads are those moments, some of them more sustained than others, when we have been able to operate with less rigid construals of the coherence-contingency polarity and with less static models of Pauline theology, conceiving it (one might say) as a work in progress. Meyer observes that there have been suggestions about the "interaction of coherence and contingency" (Beker), and various proposals to understand Paul's theology in more dynamic terms, as the "activity" of a "thinker" who was continuously working out an understanding of the gospel.[7] His own basic proposal embraces these more fluid and flexible conceptions of Pauline theology, and leads him, in addition, to consider the "inner logic" of the gospel that finds expression in it.

II

Here I will comment, in turn, on the two major points that I understand Meyer to be making in his essay.

Paul's Theology as "Result"

First, challenging the assumption "that Paul's 'theology' or 'convictions' are the *resource* or starting-point *from* which he addresses the issues placed before

5 See Jouette M. Bassler's remarks in *Pauline Theology* I, ix–x.

6 "Pauline Theology," 148.

7 Ibid.

him," Meyer suggests that one "think of them . . . as the end-product and result, the *outcome to* which [Paul] arrives in the process of his argument, his 'hermeneutic,' or his 'theologizing.'"[8] On the one hand, I agree without reservation that Paul's theology should not be thought of as a "resource." To do so risks confusing his explication of the gospel with the gospel itself—although it would also be quite wrong to think of the *gospel* as merely a "starting-point" or "resource." On the other hand, while words like "end-product" and "result" are appropriate in one sense, in other ways they, too, fail to do justice to Paul's theology, perhaps even as Meyer himself proposes that we think of it. I begin, therefore, with some comments about several key terms, and the suggestion that we need to be clearer and more precise than we often are in the way we employ and distinguish them; for, indeed, "much depends on the definitions with which one starts."[9]

First, words like "end-product," "result," and "outcome" do not do justice to Meyer's own characterization of Pauline theology. He does not seem to mean that Paul ever arrived at or could have arrived at a completed "theology." His point is that Paul's thought was always itself contingent, with "new contingencies" giving rise to "new coherences in formulation," that it was always in the process of formation and re-formation, and that "the 'end result' of one line of 'theologizing' on one occasion is not in all respects logically compatible with that of another and cannot be made to be so."[10] Thus, within the developing argument of each letter or section of a letter (e.g., Romans 9–11) and also over the course of his letters (reading in chronological order from 1 Thessalonians to Romans), one may discern Paul's reflection yielding "new theological affirmation, less inchoate, more pregnant," and attaining, Meyer suggests, "a new level of coherence *just because* of the new diversity."[11]

These are key points, well supported by the exemplary instances that are offered, e.g., from Galatians and Romans. But in my view they also suggest that we should be very cautious about identifying "the actual conclusions reached in Paul's arguments"[12] as "end-products." If we apply this term at all, it must be in a significantly qualified sense. The apostle's conclusions reached in a given argument were doubtless end-products for the particular situation within which that argument was developed. However, we should not regard them as end-products in a larger sense, as elements of a (potentially) coherent entity that might be called "Paul's theology," unless we can demonstrate their recurrent use or in-

8 Ibid., 150.

9 Ibid., 154.

10 Ibid., 150.

11 Ibid. (emphasis added).

12 Ibid., 153.

fluence in arguments that he developed within and for other particular situations. Even then, and precisely as Meyer encourages us to think of them, these "results" would seem to be and remain inherently unstable. They may serve as catalysts leading to further results, including further levels of coherence *or diversity*; but they are hardly the kind of building blocks with which one constructs a theological system.

Second, any quest for Paul's theology has to proceed with a preliminary notion of what is being sought, and with some confidence that there is a reasonable chance for success; apple pickers must have some idea of what apples look like, especially when they are ready to be picked, and they will not hunt for them in a peach orchard. In stating his basic proposal Meyer buffers the words "theology" and "convictions" with quotation marks, perhaps to suggest that these terms have been quite variously employed in our discussions, as indeed they have, and therefore call for closer definition, as indeed they do. His own use of them will receive attention in due course. Meanwhile, and to prepare for that, a few preliminary observations are in order.

Although the word "theology" (θεολογία) does not appear in any surviving Pauline letter, in its basic and broadest sense—thought or speech about the gods [or God][13]—it can and indeed *must* be used of Paul's thought as it has come down to us. His letters not only provide evidence that there were occasions on which he thought or spoke about God; they are *themselves* theological in the broad sense, precisely because they are instrumental to the discharge of his apostolic commission to proclaim the gospel of God. It is not as if we had only ledgers documenting his work as a tentmaker! Of course, in so far as the term has also come to be used of theological *systems* in the scholastic sense, and of *critical* theological reflection in the Enlightenment sense, it is anachronistic as applied to Paul. This does not mean, however, that the apostle's discourse about God was *hierophantic*, a setting-forth of sacred mysteries. In 1 Corinthians, for special reasons, he does refer to the "mystery" (or "mysteries") with which he is entrusted (2:1, 7; 4:1; 15:51). But in these instances he means nothing else than the gospel, which, notwithstanding its divine origin (Gal 1:11–12) and its being "the word of God" (e.g., 1 Thess 2:13), he never conveys as a ἱερὸς λόγος ("sacred word"), but always simply as [ὁ] λόγος ("word," "speech"). Indeed, Paul generally formulates his discourse about God with some care, and characteristically presents and defends it with rational arguments.[14] Moreover, like the

13 E.g., in Plato's *Republic* (Book II, 379A) where Adeimantus asks: οἱ τύποι περὶ θεολογίας τίνες ἂν εἶεν; ("The patterns of discourse about God, what would they be?").

14 Günther Bornkamm, "Faith and Reason in Paul," *Early Christian Experience* (New York and Evanston: Harper & Row, 1969) 29–46.

prophetic speech he writes about in 1 Corinthians 14, because it is meant to be understood and persuasive it is also subject to evaluation (e.g., 1 Cor 15:14–15; 2 Cor 4:2). For this reason it is completely appropriate to inquire whether Paul's thinking about God is coherent, even though it is completely inappropriate to try to analyze, assess, or organize his thinking according to the traditional categories of systematic theology.

The word "conviction[s]" is much more difficult to pin down, even though in this instance there are some New Testament terms that appear to be roughly equivalent. The Greek ἔλεγχος and its cognates span a similar semantic range ("reproof," 1 Cor 14:24; John 8:46; "proof" or "assurance," Heb 11:1), and in some instances the rather late and rare words, πληροφορία and πληροφορεῖσθαι, are used of a confidence that amounts to certitude (e.g., Col 4:12; Heb 6:11; 10:22).[15] There are two or three pertinent instances of the latter in Paul's letters, all in passages where faith/believing is a prominent theme. Whether 1 Thess 1:5 should be included among these is debatable. Although the NRSV translates, "our message of the gospel came to you not in word only, but also in power and in the Holy Spirit and with full conviction [ἐν πληροφορίᾳ πολλῇ]," the last phrase could well mean, rather, "with great fullness of divine working."[16] Moreover, even if the NRSV is correct it is unclear whether the "conviction" was Paul's in *preaching* the gospel or his hearers' in *receiving* it, and whether it was a matter of being fully *convinced*, as by persuasive argument, that the gospel's message (e.g., 1:9–10) is true, or of experiencing an inner *assurance* of its truth, perhaps engendered by the Holy Spirit. There are two clearer cases in Romans, and in each of them a noetic element is certainly involved. Thus, Rom 14:5: "Let all be fully convinced in their own minds [ἐν τῷ ἰδίῳ νοΐ πληροφορείσθω]"; and of special interest for our topic, Rom 4:19–21, where Paul remarks on Abraham's faith:

> He did not weaken in faith [μὴ ἀσθενήσας τῇ πίστει] when he considered [κατενόησεν] his own body, which was already as good as dead . . . , or when he considered the barrenness of Sarah's womb. No distrust made him waver

15 Whether also the word πίστις ("faith") in Rom 14:22 should come in for consideration here is much less clear. Paraphrasing, the NRSV translators have changed the more literal RSV, "The faith that you have, keep between yourself and God," to "The faith that you have, have as your own conviction before God." This approximates the view of C.E.B. Cranfield (*A Critical and Exegetical Commentary on the Epistle to the Romans*, vol. 2 [ICC; Edinburgh: Clark, 1979] 726), who argues that in this instance Paul has used πίστις "in its special sense of confidence that one's faith allows one to do a particular thing" (e.g., to eat anything, 14:1, 2); but J.D.G. Dunn (*Romans* [WBC 38; Dallas: Word, 1988] 2.827) argues for the usual Pauline meaning. In Acts 17:31 πίστις means "proof."

16 See Gerhard Delling, *TDNT* 6.311.

> [οὐ διεκρίθη τῇ ἀπιστίᾳ] concerning the promise of God, but he grew strong in his faith [ἐνεδυναμώθη τῇ πίστει] as he gave glory to God, being fully convinced that God was able to do what he had promised [πληροφορηθεὶς ὅτι ὃ ἐπήγγελται δυνατός ἐστιν καὶ ποιῆσαι].

Although at least the passages from Romans suggest that some notion of "conviction[s]" is not entirely alien to Paul's thought, they also show that it is not a developed concept, and that it surfaces mainly in association with comments about faith and believing. We should therefore be very cautious about adding the word "conviction[s]" to the vocabulary of our discussions of Paul's theology. Where it may be able to serve a heuristic purpose, fine, but it is doubtful whether it corresponds to any important constituent of the apostle's own thought beyond what is contained in the terms "faith" and "believing."[17]

If it is right to say, as I have, that every theological conclusion one finds in Paul's letters is *inherently unstable*, then two factors conspire to make this so. First, every such conclusion is no less historically contingent than the argument it "concludes" and the letter in which the argument is developed. Meyer has said essentially the same, at least about statements concerning the cross and resurrection.[18] Thus, any conclusion isolated from its original rhetorical and situational contexts is at risk, if not of "self-destructing," at least of being divested of its power to illumine or persuade. This is why we have failed in our efforts to create a synthesis of Paul's theology by combining elements which, in their own contexts, seemed perfectly stable. Traditional presentations of Pauline theology have not faced this problem, at least to the same extent, because they have generally paid less or no attention to the contingent aspects of Paul's thought. But we have learned that these must be respected, and that when they are the apostle's theological conclusions are revealed to be stubbornly resistant to synthesizing or systematizing.

The second and more fundamental reason for this situation involves us with another term that must be employed with the greatest of care. All of Paul's theological conclusions—indeed, all of his theological statements and arguments—

17 Hence, despite the instructive things that Daniel Patte has to say about "convictions" and "convictional patterns" (e.g., from the standpoint of the phenomenology of religion), one has to ask whether we are any better off with the sort of static model reflected in phrases like "the convictional pattern characteristic of Paul's faith" (27), and "[the apostle's] own system of convictions" (28)—to which faith "holds" or by which it is "held" (11)—than by any other static model; see *Paul's Faith and the Power of the Gospel. A Structural Introduction to the Pauline Letters* (Philadelphia: Fortress, 1983) 9–30.

18 "Pauline Theology," 156, developing a point made in a statement he quotes from Calvin Roetzel.

are, by reason of their function, expressions of his understanding of *the gospel*; and it is the gospel itself that renders every one of them inherently unstable. They are unstable even when left *in situ* where they were first formulated for or incorporated into Paul's letters, because even as an *apostle's* formulations they remain historically contingent and always express a particular *understanding* of the gospel. For Paul, the gospel is not just statements about God, or even about God's "acting," e.g., in the cross and resurrection (these are still only "theology"). Rather, Paul understands the gospel to be the actual, eventful working of God's own saving power (Rom 1:16; see already 1 Thess 1:5; 1 Cor 1: 17–18), and as such to have an eschatological "content" that no statements about it can adequately disclose and that no argument can ever validate.[19] This means, as Paul insists to the Corinthians (especially in 1 Cor 1:18–25), that the gospel constantly calls to account each and every theological statement, including those about the gospel itself.[20] Whether he saw that this applied no less to his own theological statements than to those of, say, his opponents, is unclear. It is also beside the point, however, both because the principle is clear enough and because the letters show that his thinking about the gospel was constantly in flux.

Paul Meyer argues a similar point in the last paragraphs of his essay, where he observes that "the fully historical impact of the crucifixion, made the defining event by God's raising Jesus from the dead, *forces*" Paul to a constant revising and recasting of traditional religious ways of "thinking, speaking, and believing."[21] What this "forcing" implies—and here I am putting the matter more sharply than Meyer has, or perhaps would—is that the gospel is constantly *calling into question and placing under judgment* all theological statements and arguments, including every putative "end-product" and "result."

Crucifixion and Vindication

Having argued that Paul's theology is not something that nourishes and guides the apostle's theologizing but emerges from it, Meyer devotes the remainder of his essay to examining what it is about the gospel that both gives coherence to the apostle's theologizing and transcends the contextual situations

19 The NRSV misleads when it translates τὸ εὐαγγέλιον in 1 Thess 1:5 and 2:4 as "*the message of* the gospel."

20 Compare Peter Lampe's comment, made with special reference to 1 Cor 1:18–25: "The word about the cross proclaims that God is absolute and sovereign over human theology; it bursts open human theological expectations" ("Theological Wisdom and the 'Word About the Cross,'" *Int* 44 [1990] 117–31, here 125).

21 "Pauline Theology," 159 (emphasis original).

of his letters where one sees that taking place.[22] Because he has chosen to work out his answer to this in a series of moves which critically develop and join certain suggestions made by others, I am going to risk summarizing for him, in something like a logical sequence, what I understand to be the key elements of his own position. My intention is to affirm, at least in general, what I understand Meyer to be arguing, but also to lay the groundwork for raising two questions with him; or, as it may be, for suggesting that two points already implicit in his proposal be registered more clearly and emphatically. If I am correct, this is where his discussion ends up:

1. The historical event of Jesus' crucifixion presented a crisis of meaning for those who had found significance in his life and teaching, and who had made claims connecting Jesus to God's purpose.[23]

2. Only their belief that God had identified himself with the crucified Jesus, thereby vindicating and confirming him, made it possible for Jesus' followers to receive and understand his death as an "apocalyptic event."[24] Through a specific act of God, that merely human event/defeat was *made* into "the historical locus of 'revelation.'"[25]

3. This act of God came to expression in confessional statements (which Paul took over) about God's having raised Jesus from the dead, which were formulated in this "historical" way as counterparts to the historical statements about Jesus' death. However, the actual "content" of these confessional statements remains God's act of *vindicating* the *crucified* Jesus. Thus (Rom 10:9) the statements about Jesus' resurrection are both interpreted by and themselves interpret the confession that (the crucified) "Jesus is Lord."[26]

4. The conviction that God had vindicated the crucified Jesus was given in the form of a believing, the "essential ingredient" of which was "the certainty that it is not self-generating."[27] Thus the reality confessed "cannot be reduced to or exhausted in the confessing it elicits,"[28] and so far transcends "the contingencies of human believing as to supply warrant for its truth and reliability" and to be "the authenticating signature for 'the truth of the gospel.'"[29]

5. Paul views God's act as having made the crucifixion both "normative" and "the point where human believing and knowing" can find a "coherence to life

22 Ibid., 155.
23 Ibid., 157–158.
24 Ibid., 158.
25 Ibid., 158–159.
26 Ibid., 158–159.
27 Ibid., 157; cf. 158, "the realization that faith is not self-generating."
28 Ibid., 158.
29 Ibid., 157.

and thought" that transcends "the contingent."[30] That is, by God's action the crucifixion has been made "the eternally reliable clue and criterion for discerning God's true nature, presence, and intention."[31]

6. Therefore: in the theologizing present in Paul's letters, one sees how "the fully historical impact of the crucifixion, made the defining event by God's raising Jesus from the dead," has set in motion an ongoing "process of revision" of "traditional language, concepts, convictions and categories . . ." which produces "distinctively *Christian* ways of speaking about God" (and sin, righteousness, etc.).[32] The apostle understands God himself to be present in this process through the preaching of Christ crucified and resurrected, and he associates this divine presence with "the Spirit of Christ" and "Christ in you" (Rom 8:11).[33]

"God's Act" and "Human Believing"

The first of my two concerns is that Meyer's presentation, focused as it is on "God's act" that elicits and confirms faith, takes too little account of the *existential* dimension of the gospel and faith as the apostle understands these. From early on and throughout his discussion, he is intent on making it clear that, for Paul, "the truth of the gospel" is anchored in a reality that elicits "human believing" but is not to be identified with it. There is, indeed, no question about this. For Paul, it is of the essence of faith that it understands itself as "called forth" by a divine act which is "external" to one's own believing; thus, writing about his own call to faith and apostleship he attributes it wholly to "[God's] grace *toward* me" (ἡ χάρις αὐτοῦ ἡ εἰς ἐμέ, 1 Cor 15:10; and in the same verse, "*with* me" [σὺν ἐμοί]). But equally, it is also of the essence of faith, as these same statements about God's grace attest, that it receives the reality of God's acting as decisively significant for the believer's own existence (thus, God's grace "toward *me*," "with *me*"). For Paul, no less than for the tradition he often cites, God's acting in the crucified and resurrected Christ is always understood as ὑπὲρ ἡμῶν ("for us"). To affirm that God has made the death of Jesus an *apocalyptic* event, "the historical locus of 'revelation,'" is indeed to affirm that "the very structure of reality is transformed"—but in a way that includes the believer, apart from whom one cannot properly speak of a *revelatory* event at all.[34]

30 Ibid., 159.

31 Ibid.

32 Ibid., 160. (emphasis original).

33 Ibid.

34 On the general point, see H. Richard Niebuhr's classic study, *The Meaning of Revelation* (New York: Macmillan, 1955); e.g., "When we speak of revelation we mean that something has happened

Let us consider, for example, Meyer's statement that for belief the "content" of God's act in vindicating Jesus by raising him from the dead "is the freshly disclosed status and identity of the previously known historical figure of the Crucified," namely, that he is "Lord" (Rom 10:9).[35] Although this comment is true as far as it goes, it does not go far enough. In *confessing*, κύριος Ἰησοῦς ("Jesus is Lord"), one is simultaneously *accepting* the crucified Jesus as Lord, acknowledging that one is subject to his rule alone (e.g., 1 Cor 7:22–23).[36] Accordingly, we must say that, for Paul, God's act of vindicating the crucified Jesus also discloses one's *own* "status and identity" as *this* Lord's δοῦλος ("slave"), that one has been claimed as well as graced by the saving power of God that Jesus' lordship represents.[37]

Believing therefore involves a new *self*-understanding as well as a new understanding of Jesus. As demonstrated by the example of Abraham, this self-understanding is expressed in one's relying absolutely—staking one's whole future—on the gracious life-giving promise and power of God (Rom 4:16–21). Such trusting is of course far removed from what people usually mean by human "self-realization" or "self-fulfillment." For one thing, Abraham does not exemplify solitary believing but the faith of a believing *community*. From the apostle's standpoint the new self-understanding of faith is not just "personal" but corporate. Moreover, just as true belief always acknowledges that it is not

---

to us in our history which conditions all our thinking and that through this happening we are enabled to apprehend what we are, what we are suffering and doing and what our potentialities are" (138), and "We mean . . . that something has happened which compels our faith and which requires us to seek rationality and unity in the whole of our history" (139). Something like this seems to be recognized by Richard Hays, from whom Meyer ("Pauline Theology," 158) has drawn the quotation about the transformation of "the very structure of reality." See Hays, "Crucified with Christ: A Synthesis of the Theology of 1 and 2 Thessalonians, Philemon, Philippians, and Galatians," *Pauline Theology* I, 227–46, here 239: "Thus, believers living in the eschatological twilight zone at the turn of the ages are called upon to recognize and embody the new creation . . . ."

35 "Pauline Theology," 158.

36 This is already evident from the confessional form itself, which *acclaims* Jesus' lordship as distinguished from stating a belief in it. For remarks on the *homologia* as distinct from the *pistis*-formula in early Christianity, see Werner Kramer, *Christ, Lord, Son of God* (SBT 50; Naperville: Allenson, 1966) 66–67; and for the more general point, Rudolf Bultmann, *Theology of the New Testament*, 1 (New York: Scribner's, 1951) 125.

37 Cf. Schubert M. Ogden's remarks: "Thus, if we take seriously the guidance offered us by Paul, to affirm that Jesus Christ is Lord means both something positive and something negative. It means positively that the human word of promise and demand addressed to us in Jesus Christ is infinitely more than a merely human word and, in fact, has the divine power and authority to claim our ultimate allegiance and thereby also to bring our lives to their authentic fulfillment. And it means negatively that no other promise and demand have this same divine significance" ("What Does It Mean to Affirm, 'Jesus Christ is Lord'?" *The Reality of God and Other Essays* [New York: Harper & Row, 1966] 188–205, here 203).

"self-generating," so the self-understanding that comes with believing always involves, because it is of the very essence of faith, the giving up of all attempts to live out of one's own resources. Therefore, while believing is necessarily human, we would slight Paul's conception to think of it as *merely* "human believing." Precisely because he regards it as both "called forth" and the giving up of every human claim, he writes of faith as always knowing and presenting itself as a response to the *experienced* reality of *God's* saving power in the crucified and resurrected Christ. In this critically important sense all "human believing" is itself an "act of God," and for this reason Paul can think of it as redounding to God's own glory (thus, e.g., Rom 4:20; 15:9; 2 Cor 4:15; cf. Rom 1:21).

"Reality" and "Truth"

My second concern, very closely related to the first, is that Meyer has said less than needs to be said about the "reality" that elicits believing, warrants its reliability, and is "the authenticating signature for 'the truth of the gospel.'" Just what is this "reality"? It does not suffice to answer that it is the reality of God's act in raising Jesus from the dead. Meyer himself has done us the important service of distinguishing between the historically-formulated but nonetheless confessional utterances about Jesus' resurrection and the belief that lies behind those, namely, that God acted to confirm and vindicate the crucified Jesus.[38] And he has done us the further service of pointing out that this belief also finds expression in the acclamation, "Jesus is Lord," which is no less Pauline for its having been taken over from the church's tradition. But with this, of course, we are back to a statement that requires us to take account of the existential character of believing—and also, we must now say, of the existential character of the reality that elicits believing. For Paul, what is the reality that calls forth the kind of absolute trust and total commitment that is expressed in the confession, "Jesus is Lord"?

Perhaps we can make some progress in answering this question by formulating it more generally, and then posing a second question. What is the reality that both warrants believing and authenticates "the truth of the gospel"? And what *is* "the truth" that Paul understands to be definitive of the gospel?

38 "Pauline Theology," 158. I trust that I am not imputing to Meyer more of a distinction than he intends, although he does in certain instances use the word "resurrection"—presumably as shorthand—for God's act of confirming the crucified Jesus as Lord (e.g., "this resurrection makes all the difference in authorizing an understanding of Jesus' death as itself a divine act," ibid.). Strictly speaking, however, the very concept of "resurrection" (even apart from empty tomb stories, and the like) would seem to involve thinking about a contingently historical event.

The answer to the second of these questions helps in answering the first. If my earlier suggestion is correct, that for Paul the gospel is "the actual, eventful working of God's own saving power," then at its core "the truth of the gospel" concerns God's will and power to save (e.g., 1 Cor 1:18–21); or, expressed differently, it concerns the enduring reality of God's justice and faithfulness (e.g., Rom 3:1–7; 15:8). It is the truth, as Paul suggests simply and elegantly in Rom 8:31, that God is "for us" (ὁ θεὸς ὑπὲρ ἡμῶν); or again, and with specific reference to God's self-disclosure in the cross, that God acts in *love* to grace, to claim, and to reconcile (e.g., 2 Cor 5:14–20; Rom 5:6–11; cf. Gal 2:19–21).

If Paul understands "the truth of the gospel" in this way, as the existential reality of God's invincible love for us "in Christ Jesus our Lord" (Rom 8:32–39), then the "authenticating signature" of that truth can only be inscribed existentially. It is inscribed wherever the saving power of God's love comes to expression in the kind of believing that Paul understands the gospel to call forth: believing like Abraham's, who relied unreservedly on the grace and promise of God; and believing like that presupposed in the apostle's summons to place one's self/ body (σῶμα) wholly at God's disposal, as a "living sacrifice" through whom God's love may be concretely embodied and enacted in the world (Rom 12:1–2, 9–21, etc.). Thus for Paul, the reality that confirms "the truth of the gospel"—because it *is* the truth of the gospel—is the reality of the gracious, saving power of God made known in Christ crucified and resurrected. It is nothing else than the reality of God's own being; or better, the reality of God's *being God for us*. The apostle, drawing on the Psalmist's confession, "I believed, and so I spoke," can therefore write to the Corinthians: "We also believe, and so we speak, because we know that the one who raised the Lord Jesus will raise us also with Jesus, and will bring us with you into his presence" (2 Cor 4:13–14).

What I have been suggesting here about the "existential" character of Paul's thought is not, I believe, incompatible with Meyer's own point of view. For example, when he says that Paul regards the crucifixion as "the point where human believing and knowing may genuinely transcend the contingent and find an authentic coherence to life and thought," he seems not to be referring to some *logical* "coherence" of the theological statements and arguments (or "end-products") in Paul's letters, but to an *existential* "coherence" ("to *life* and thought") that is given to faith through God's self-disclosure in the crucified and resurrected Christ. Thus, he says, for Paul the crucifixion "has become the eternally reliable clue and criterion for discerning God's true nature, presence, and intention."[39] This remark, on which Meyer himself does not elaborate, is

39 Ibid., 159.

nevertheless extremely important. I read it as at least implying the very point on which I wish to place special emphasis, that "the truth of the gospel" as Paul understands it is the truth of God's own "nature, presence, and intention"; and more specifically, the truth discerned in Christ that "God is for us."

III

In concluding his essay, Meyer suggests that "Pauline theology" is "what emerged" from the process—from those contingent "persuasion-events"—which the apostle himself referred to as "[taking] every thought captive to obey Christ" (2 Cor 10:5).[40] But what exactly *does* "emerge" as every thought is taken captive to Christ? Meyer thinks of an ongoing "*process of revision*" that leads to ever new and "distinctively *Christian* ways of speaking about God" (etc.).[41] One should add that new ways of speaking about God always reflect new ways of understanding God, and that there is no understanding of God which does not involve, at some level of consciousness and expression, an understanding of human existence (and of oneself) in relation to God.

If this is the character of the theological reflection and argumentation in Paul's letters, then his assertions about "the truth of the gospel," even when they may be identified as theological "conclusions," neither constitute nor lend themselves to the formulation of anything like a theological system. They are not meant to serve the cause of "Christian theology" in the scholastic sense but to contribute to *Christian formation*. Or, to use the apostle's own vocabulary, they are directed toward the "building up" (οἰκοδομεῖν, οἰκοδομή) of the believing community and its members. He can write of his apostolic labors as directed entirely toward this end: "Everything we do . . . is for the sake of building you up" (2 Cor 12:19); and he can urge the same priority upon a congregation, e.g., 1 Cor 14:26: "Let all things be done for building up." Moreover, he identifies love (ἀγάπη) as the energy and therefore content of this οἰκοδομεῖν (1 Cor 8:1); so his appeal that everything be done for building up has a parallel in 1 Cor 16:14: "Let all that you do be done in love [ἐν ἀγάπῃ]." He means the ἀγάπη that inheres in being "known" by God (1 Cor 8:3)—a scriptural expression for being chosen by God and thereby called to live from God's promises and according to God's purposes.[42] Is it not this gracious, saving love of God that we

40 Ibid., 160.

41 Ibid.

42 Cf. Amos 3:2; Exod 33:12, 17 (etc.); for discussions: G. J. Botterweck, *TDOT* 5.468–69; R. Bultmann, *TDNT* 1.709–10.

should identify as the fundamental reality, the *truly* "compelling datum," by which Paul's theological reflection, no less than his apostolic labors, was nourished and indeed required? Must we not say that *this* is the event that gave rise to the proclamation that God had vindicated the crucified Jesus by raising him from the dead? Is not "the word of the cross," and thus "the truth of the gospel" that is affirmed when Christ is preached as raised from the dead, the truth of God's love "for us" (Rom 5:8; 8:31–39, etc.)?

This line of thought leads me to remark, in closing, on a theme to which the apostle's modern interpreters have paid scant attention, even though it would seem an obvious place to begin in approaching his "theology," namely: *the knowledge of God.*[43] Already the fact that this was a major topic of religious and philosophical discourse in the Hellenistic world should make us especially interested in what Paul has said about it. More particularly, a call to acknowledge and serve the *one* "true and living God" had to have been the first and foundational element in his missionary preaching to the Gentiles, and there is no doubt that it was (e.g., 1 Thess 1:9; 4:5; Gal 4:8, 9; cf. 2 Cor 2:14).

Indeed, knowledge of God is the very point at issue when Paul comments about "[taking] every thought captive to obey Christ" (2 Cor 10:5). The military imagery here is prompted by his concern to defend himself against those who charge him with "acting according to human standards" (v. 2). On the contrary, he insists, although his ministry is conducted necessarily in the world (ἐν σαρκὶ . . . περιπατοῦντες), he does not "wage war" for the gospel "by human standards" (οὐ κατὰ σάρκα στρατευόμεθα) but is armed with

43 As far as I have been able to determine, there are only two substantial 20th-century studies devoted specifically to "knowing God" as a theme of Pauline theology, and neither one is very recent. These are Jacques Dupont's 1949 Louvain dissertation, *Gnosis. La connaissance religieuse dans les épîtres des S. Paul* (unfortunately, not available to me) and Heinrich Schlier's essay, "Die Erkenntnis Gottes nach den Briefen des Apostels Paulus," *Gott in Welt: Festgabe für Karl Rahner*, 1 (ed. by Herbert Vorgrimler; Freiburg et al.: Herder, 1964) 515–35. In the first three volumes of the present series, the subject comes up only in my own essay on 1 Corinthians (vol. 2, esp. 67–69, 73–74, 86–87). Usually, if interpreters consider the theme at all they do so either only in passing or else in connection with some particular passage or other issue. Among the more noteworthy of such discussions: Adolf Schlatter, *Der Glaube im Neuen Testament* (5th ed. [repr. of 3d ed., 1905]; Stuttgart: Calwer, 1963) 388–99; Rudolf Bultmann, "γινώσκω κτλ.," *TDNT* 1.689–719, and *Theology of the New Testament*, 1.317–19, 326–27; Kurt Niederwimmer, "Erkennen und Lieben. Gedanken zum Verhältnis von Gnosis und Agape im ersten Korintherbrief," *Kerygma und Dogma* 11 (1965) 75–102; Bertil E. Gärtner, "The Pauline and Johannine Idea of 'To Know God' Against the Hellenistic Background," *NTS* 14 (1968) 209–31; Daniel Marguerat, "2 Corinthiens 10–13: Paul et l'expérience de Dieu," *ETR* 63 (1988) 497–519; John Koenig, "The Knowing of Glory and Its Consequences (2 Corinthians 3–5)," *The Conversation Continues: Studies in Paul & John. In Honor of J. Louis Martyn* (ed. by R. T. Fortna and B. R. Gaventa; Nashville: Abingdon, 1990) 158–69.

weapons which "have divine power [δυνατὰ τῷ θεῷ] to destroy strongholds" (vv. 3–4a). He identifies the battlements that he must tear down in order to accomplish his mission as "arguments and every proud obstacle raised up against the knowledge of God [λογισμοὺς . . . καὶ πᾶν ὕψωμα ἐπαιρόμενον κατὰ τῆς γνώσεως τοῦ θεοῦ]" (vv. 4b–5). The phrase to note here is "the knowledge of God." This is the objective of his entire apostolic campaign, to spread throughout the world "the fragrance of the knowledge of [God]" (2:14, my translation).[44] Why is Paul committed to taking "every thought" (or "mind" [νόημα]) captive to obey Christ? Because in him, through him, by belonging to him (cf. v. 7) one knows God.

The apostle's letters show clearly that his proclamation of one God was inseparable from his preaching of the "one Lord, Jesus Christ" (1 Cor 8:6, etc.), God's "Son" (thus, 1 Thess 1:9–10). According to Paul, specifically through Christ's crucifixion the world is granted the knowledge of God that its own wisdom cannot attain (1 Cor 1:18–21). He also writes of Christ as God's very "image," the one in whose face believers encounter "the light of the knowledge of the glory of God" (2 Cor 4:4, 6). A comment in the same context, that believers themselves "are being transformed . . . from one degree of glory to another" (μεταμορφούμεθα ἀπὸ δόξης εἰς δόξαν, 2 Cor 3:18), brings out the existential character of this "knowledge of the glory of God," and also returns us to the matter of Christian formation. For Paul, beholding "the light of the knowledge of the glory of God in the face of Jesus Christ" involves "that daily inward renewal of one's being (4:16) which occurs where one's life is put at God's disposal" (Rom 12:1–2).[45] Not incidentally, these and similar passages show that it is impossible, without diluting the richness of the apostle's understanding both of God and of Christ, to extract anything like a discrete "Pauline christology" from his letters. In belonging to Christ one belongs also to God, to whom Christ himself belongs (1 Cor 3:23; cf. 11:3); and "to know Christ and the power of his resurrection" (Phil 3:10) will mean, finally, to know the One by whose power we shall be raised from the dead, even as Christ himself was raised from the dead (cf. 1 Cor 6:14; 2 Cor 1:9–11; Rom 8:11, etc.).

From the apostle's point of view, of course, there is no "saving knowledge" of the sort one reads of in various gnostic texts. Faith's knowledge of God derives from *being known by God*, whose electing love both calls faith into being and animates it for obedience in love (1 Cor 8:3; Gal 4:9; 5:6). Hope, too,

44 On the αὐτοῦ ("of him") in 2:14 as a reference to God, see V. P. Furnish, *II Corinthians* (AB 32A; Garden City: Doubleday, 1984) 176, and Margaret E. Thrall, *A Critical and Exegetical Commentary on the Second Epistle to the Corinthians*, 1 (ICC; Edinburgh: Clark, 1994) 199.

45 Furnish, *II Corinthians*, 242.

enters into Paul's thinking about this knowledge of God. Beyond their present life in Christ, in whom they are being transformed already "from one degree of glory to another," believers may look forward to "an eternal weight of glory beyond all measure" (2 Cor 4:17). Then they will "know [God] fully" even as they themselves have always "been fully known" by God (1 Cor 13:12); that is, with the "knowing" of a love that can give itself without condition or reserve, because they have been set free from "bondage to decay" and have been granted "the freedom of the glory of the children of God" (Rom 8:21).

These are but hints of how more attention to Paul's concern for "building up" his congregations in the knowledge of God might be able to enhance our understanding of his theological reflection. At the very least, greater attention to this theme will help to keep us in touch with the specifically religious aspect of the apostle's thought, and with its existential dimensions. Most especially, it will help us to understand why, for Paul, "the truth of the gospel" can never be reduced to a theological doctrine or enshrined within a theological system.

Part IV

Epilogue

10 PAULINE THEOLOGY AFTER PAUL

David M. Hay

ONE OF THE most important methodological decisions of the SBL Pauline Theology Group was to study each of the Undisputed Letters by itself—not presuming knowledge of the other letters as each one was taken up in turn. The same method will prove valuable with the Disputed Letters, even though there are clearly literary relationships between different Disputed Letters and some of their authors certainly had access to some of the Undisputed Letters.[1] Thus, e.g., Colossians seems to have been written by someone who knew Philemon and probably several other Undisputed Letters. The author of Ephesians almost certainly had Colossians on his or her desk. The Pastoral Letters are usually interpreted as a group, but it is important to note that there are differences of ideas and emphasis in each one—they are not simply three statements of the same message. Finally, 2 Thessalonians needs to be examined on its own, even though its author knew 1 Thessalonians. While the present essay emphasizes tendencies shared by several or all the Disputed Letters, it is not at all intended to question the value of studying them theologically one letter at a time.

What do we mean by "theology" when we read these letters? The endeavor to define precisely the kind of quarry being tracked in the Undisputed Letters was the subject of recurrent and creative debate by members of the Pauline Theology Group. Some of the most stimulating discussions in that Group dealt with proposals to define theology as process or activity, as opposed to understanding it in terms of settled ideas or conclusions (focusing on the *how* more

[1] The chief letters now widely classified as Disputed are Colossians, Ephesians, 2 Thessalonians, and the Pastorals (1–2 Timothy, Titus). 2 Thessalonians is discussed in essays by Robert Jewett, Edgar Krentz, and Jouette M. Bassler in *Pauline Theology I: Thessalonians, Philippians, Galatians, Philemon* (ed. Jouette M. Bassler; Minneapolis: Fortress, 1991) 53–85. None of the other Disputed Letters has been considered in this Pauline Theology series.

than on the *what*).[2] This way of seeing things makes plainer the relation between imperatives and indicatives. Both Colossians and Ephesians offer major structural divisions between doctrinal and paraenetic sections (probably following the model of Romans)—but the exhortations in both letters refer so often to God and Christ that readers are forced to see that beliefs and conduct cannot be separated. In the case of the Pastoral Letters, one might say that concerns for morality and church order take center stage while doctrine becomes a kind of side issue or occasional orientation device. Yet this, too, is a way of "doing theology." Because everything in the Disputed Letters is directly or indirectly linked to God's will, nothing in their contents can be ruled "non-theological."

Another significant issue has to do with the impact of individual Pauline letters on later generations of readers, including our own. How is Romans 13 important for people today, or how did it affect readers in the sixth or sixteenth centuries? Such questions were not emphasized in the discussions of the SBL Pauline Theology Group. Yet much important discussion of the Disputed Letters in recent decades has connected them with modern theological debates. The Disputed Letters have sometimes been evaluated in relation to their perceived support for "early Catholicism" or the Protestant principle of "justification by faith apart from good works." Feminist and Liberation theologians have expressed dismay at commands in the Pastoral Letters that women not teach and directives in Colossians and Ephesians that wives submit to their husbands and slaves to their masters. Such instruction seems driven by hierarchical assumptions in obvious tension with Gal 3:28, not to mention the spirit of Jesus' teaching. Another approach to assessing the Disputed Letters is illustrated in the suggestion of Wedderburn that the cosmic theology of the hymn quoted in Colossians 1:15–20 is more meaningful in our ecology-minded age than the theology of the writer of the letter itself.[3] It is difficult to comprehend and delineate the theological content of the Disputed Letters today—even if our primary interest lies in the historical meaning of the Disputed Letters at the time they were written—without taking into account the fact that we read them in the light of modern ideas about faith and responsibility.[4]

2 See Victor P. Furnish's remarks in *Pauline Theology II: 1 & 2 Corinthians* (ed. David M. Hay; Minneapolis: Fortress, 1993) 62 and his essay in the present volume. See also the essays by Jouette M. Bassler, Steven J. Kraftchick, and Calvin J. Roetzel in *Pauline Theology II:* 3–34, 211–33.

3 Lincoln, Andrew T. and Wedderburn, A. J. M. *The Theology of the Later Pauline Letters.* (NT Theology Series; Cambridge: University Press, 1993) 41–42, 66.

4 Cf. Victor P. Furnish, "Paul the Theologian," *The Conversation Continues: Studies In Paul & John* (ed. Robert T. Fortna and Beverly R. Gaventa; Nashville: Abingdon, 1990) 28: genuine interpretation of Paul's letters requires "translating Paul's thought into the conceptual categories that have currency in the interpreter's own cultural setting. This entails no responsibility for making Paul's theology acceptable, only for making it intelligible."

THE QUESTION OF HISTORICAL CONTEXT

One of the most notable features of the Disputed Letters is that they largely lack the particular references to situations and individuals that we often find in the Undisputed Letters. Most notable in this regard is Ephesians, which does not seem especially connected with Ephesus[5] and lacks the kind of references to individual church members that we find in Colossians. Even in Colossians the implied author is addressing a church he has not visited. 2 Thessalonians gives little specific information about the church being addressed. In the Pastoral Letters "Paul" writes co-workers, but he (surely a "he"!) says little about concrete church conditions on Crete or in Ephesus.[6] All the Disputed Letters bear a universalizing tone, as though quietly indicating that the relevance of the apostle's message is not limited by geography or time.[7]

Nevertheless, all writings—even writings that say little or nothing about their historical contexts—are written under specific circumstances, and it is necessary and desirable to try to discern the historical situations in which these letters were produced. Theology is always "earthed," as Frances Young says.[8] The author of each Disputed Letter has a specific agenda, though she or he may labor to conceal it.

What can be deduced about the historical context(s) of the Disputed Letters? Apparently they were all written to communities that knew some things about Paul already and that were disposed to accept his authority without reservation. Scholars have tended to say these letters were written to "Pauline churches," and, more specifically, to churches in Asia Minor and Greece (in accord with the places mentioned in the letters). What exactly were "Pauline churches"? Given the example of Colossians, we need not limit the term to mean "churches founded by Paul." Nor do we have to presuppose that Paul is the only church authority whose ideas are recognized or honored in these churches (al-

5 A recent study by Clinton E. Arnold speaks of Ephesians as "written to a general but concrete situation facing the church(es) at Ephesus and other churches in western Asia Minor"—a situation in which ordinary Christians worried about magic and demonic powers (*Ephesians: Power and Magic: The Concept of Power in Ephesians in Light of its Historical Setting*; SNTSMS 63; Cambridge: University Press, 1989] 165, cf. 123–24, 167–72). Arnold, however, contends that Paul wrote Ephesians (171).

6 Cf. J. Christiaan Beker, *Heirs of Paul: Paul's Legacy in the NT and in the Church Today* (Minneapolis: Fortress, 1991) 46: "the delicate balance in Paul between coherence and contingency is here displaced by a fixed coherent structure that has no direct relation to the contingent crisis situation."

7 Despite their epistolary form, several or all the Disputed Letters themselves may have been written with the idea that they would have lasting and widespread usefulness (Ephesians and the Pastoral Letters in particular have impressed many scholars as more like treatises than letters).

8 Young, *The Theology of the Pastoral Letters* (NT Theology Series; Cambridge: University Press, 1994) 1.

though he is the only apostle named).[9] Nevertheless, it is essential to recognize that in all these letters Paul is assumed to be well-known and authoritative.

What is in dispute, however, is partly what Paul actually said or meant. 2 Thessalonians is preoccupied with misrepresentations and misinterpretations of Paul's eschatology. In recent years several scholars have suggested that the Disputed Letters, and especially the Pastoral Letters, need to be interpreted in relation to apocryphal legends about the apostle, especially those in the Acts of Paul. Dennis R. MacDonald and others have argued that the Pastoral Letters offer a polemic against the ascetic or encratic traditions behind the Acts of Paul.[10] The writers of the Disputed Letters sought to define how Paul and his theological message should be remembered.[11]

The churches addressed in these letters all appear to be securely established. In most of these letters, the addressees seem aware and knowledgeable about Hellenistic Jews and pagans in their neighborhoods. The relationships between Christians and non-Christians appear to be relatively irenic rather than strained or tense, and—at least for the most part[12]—the churches do not appear to be living in fear of persecution. All the letters—particularly Colossians, Ephesians, and the Pastorals—seem to assume that a separation between church and synagogue has taken place, and the authors and addressees appear not to be worried about the condition or destiny of non-Christian Jews. The crisis created by Jewish rejection of the Gospel as Paul describes it, especially in Romans 9–11, seems a thing of the past.[13] Yet the bitterness with which non-Christian Jews

9 Although Raymond Brown contends that in the Pastorals no apostle other than Paul is mentioned or felt to be needed (*The Churches the Apostles Left Behind* [New York: Paulist Press, 1984] 37–38). Cf. the statement of Beker that in the Disputed Letters as a group, "Paul is the *sole* apostle, a person who enjoys indisputable authority and whose gospel is the sole norm of Christian truth" (*Heirs of Paul,* 47; cf. 37–39, 67–68, 71–72, 75). Yet these letters do not flatly claim that Paul is the only normative guide.

10 Dennis R. MacDonald, *The Legend and the Apostle: The Battle for Paul in Story and Canon* (Philadelphia: Westminster Press, 1983) 54–89.

11 E.g., Young, *Theology,* 142–43.

12 2 Thessalonians is the major exception in this regard. Yet even here persecution seems to be considered simply as something "normal" for Christians—it is not something the author has to interpret or argue about (in contrast to the situation in 1 Thessalonians). See R. Jewett, *The Thessalonian Correspondence: Pauline Rhetoric and Millenarian Piety* (Philadelphia: Fortress, 1986) 28. Colossians and Ephesians call on their readers to remember that "Paul" writes from prison, without implying that the readers themselves face persecution. 2 Timothy implies that its intended readers know of Paul's sufferings at the hands of non-Christians and are braced for some kind of suffering (but this suffering may result from internal church conflicts).

13 All of the Disputed Letters seem to imply that salvation is possible only through a relationship with Jesus. There is no suggestion that Jews may be saved apart from such a relationship. On the other hand, these letters seem to offer no direct discussion of the situation of non-Christian Jews per se.

are sometimes mentioned in Matthew, Acts, and John does not have any close parallel in these letters. One may infer that these letters stem from Christian communities whose relation to synagogues was not one of sharp animosity.[14] Likewise the Disputed Letters (apart from 2 Thess 1:9; 2:10–12 and Tit 1: 10–16, 3:10–11) express a generally mild attitude toward false teachers within the churches; hope is held out that they may not be permanently hostile to the Gospel.[15]

For the most part the Disputed Letters imply that the majority of their readers are former pagans. Like the Book of Acts, the Disputed Letters portray Paul as the archetypal "apostle to the Gentiles." The Pastoral Letters may reflect a specific concern to present Christianity as the alternative to the imperial cult.[16] Moral exhortations in these letters often suggest that Christian commitment involves a mastering of passions typically indulged by pagans. At the same time, as we shall see, there are significant respects in which the letters approve and appropriate certain pagan values.[17]

THEOLOGY AS PROCESS

In a previous essay I suggested that theology in 2 Corinthians emerged out of a dynamic interplay of doubts, warrants, and convictions in Paul's mind.[18] Study of the interaction of these three elements in the Disputed Letters may advance our understanding of the processes of theological reflection and rhetorical presentation that lie in or behind these writings. Leaving the category of convictions till later,[19] we may focus for the time being on doubts and warrants.

As regards doubt, one has to say that this is not a major topic on the surface of the Disputed Letters. Otherwise put, the writers of these letters present the implied author, Paul, as essentially a person without doubts or deep worries re-

14 See, e.g., Rudolf Schnackenburg, *Ephesians: A Commentary* (Edinburgh: T&T Clark, 1991) 110, 119, 324–25; Norman A. Beck, *Mature Christianity in the 21st Century: The Recognition and Repudiation of the Anti-Jewish Polemic of the New Testament* (New York: Crossroad, 1994) 117–31.

15 2 Thess 3:15 offers hope for some opponents. Lewis R. Donelson, *Colossians, Ephesians, 1 and 2 Timothy, and Titus* (Westminster Bible Companion; Louisville: Westminster John Knox Press, 1996) 126: the author of 1 Timothy "wants to call the heretical back into the fold of orthodoxy."

16 So Philip H. Towner, *The Goal of Our Instruction: The Structure of Theology and Ethics in the Pastoral Epistles* (JSOTSup 34; Sheffield: JSOT, 1989) 77; Young, *Theology*, 64–65.

17 Investigation of the pagan background can provide historical insights and some basis for an "emancipatory critique" of elements like the *Haustafeln* (H. Räisänen, *Beyond NT Theology: A Story and a Programme.* [London: SCM, 1990] 85 [following G. Petzke]).

18 "The Shaping of Theology in 2 Corinthians: Convictions, Doubts, and Warrants," *Pauline Theology II*:135–55

19 See the next section of this essay.

garding the churches. He writes with unhesitating conviction, and he seems to assume that his readers can be trusted to understand and accept his ideas. These letters show none of the uncertainty that Paul displays in Galatians or 2 Cor 10–13, where his authority and message are under severe attack and where he fears that the churches may finally reject him and his message.

On the other hand, however, some members of the churches addressed in the Disputed Letters seem to be having serious doubts about the adequacy of Pauline Christianity. Those addressed in 2 Thessalonians need to be on their guard against "un-Pauline" teachings about the future and about traditional values like those associated with work. In Colossae there are false teachers[20] who advocate teachings about angels and "elements" which "Paul" regards as a denial of the supremacy of Christ. The Pastoral Letters are written in a situation in which a heresy or heresies are all too appealing, thus bringing into doubt the trustworthiness of the Pauline message.[21]

The types of warrants and the patterns of their functioning in these letters are of special importance. It seems best to define a warrant as anything—an argument, an image, a metaphor, an allusion to or citation of a source assumed to have authority, a reference to a tradition, etc.—that the writers expect to carry weight with their intended readers and move them to embrace the writers' views. A warrant is backing or support for another belief or affirmation.

What are the major kinds of warrants in the Disputed Letters? One category is that of references to the Jewish scriptures. In general OT references are less frequent and appear to have a less formative role in the Disputed Letters than in the Undisputed Letters (to be sure, even within the Undisputed Letters there is great variation in the emphasis given to OT citations and "echoes").[22] OT quo-

20 False, that is, from a Christian viewpoint. One possibility is that the "credible philosophy" creating a problem for the Colossian church was not an early Christian "heresy" but simply a local synagogue apologetic (see J. D. G. Dunn, "The Colossian Philosophy: A Confident Jewish Apologia," *Biblica* 76 [1995] 153–81; cf. Daniel J. Harrington, "Christians and Jews in Colossians," pp. 153–61 in *Diaspora Jews and Judaism: Essays in Honor of, and in Dialogue with, A. Thomas Kraabel* (South Florida Studies in the History of Judaism 41; Atlanta: Scholars Press, 1992).

21 Donelson *Colossians,*119: the Pastorals are written in a situation in which the heretics, not the author and his friends, are "dominant in the church."

22 Cf. Beker, *Heirs,* 93: although the Disputed Letters "would certainly reject Marcion's dismissal of the Old Testament," nonetheless "the nearly complete neglect of the Old Testament by these authors is quite remarkable." Regarding the use of the OT in the Undisputed Letters, see esp. *Pauline Theology I*:131–46 (James D. G. Dunn), 166–76 (J. Louis Martyn), 235–40, 246 (Richard B. Hays); *Pauline Theology II*:151–52 (Hay), 216–17, 226–28 (Calvin J. Roetzel), 239–43 (William S. Campbell); *Pauline Theology III*: 36–62 (N. T. Wright), 135–55 (Andrew T. Lincoln), 169–95 (Frank Thielman), 196–210 (Charles B. Cousar), 223–34 (E. Elizabeth Johnson), 244–49 (Douglas Moo). Of special importance and influence in relation to recent discussions is Richard B. Hays, *Echoes of Scripture in the Letters of Paul* (New Haven: Yale, 1989).

tations and allusions are prominent in Ephesians, but they rarely appear to determine the direction of the author's thought.[23] Colossians to a remarkable degree lacks visible references to the OT, though there are more or less plain allusions in passages like 3:1, 10.[24] There are not many OT references in the Pastoral Letters, and some of these may depend on references in the Undisputed Letters (e.g., 1 Tim 2:14 [cf. 2 Cor 11:3]; 1 Tim 5:18 and 2 Tim 2:6 [cf. 1 Cor 9:7–10]). The theoretical authority of the OT is firmly asserted in these letters, but the writer seems to assume that the addressees are not profoundly familiar with the contents of the Jewish Bible.[25] On the whole, the Disputed Letters do not present the Christian movement as an extension of OT Israel.[26]

Another very important class of warrants in all the Disputed Letters, with the exception of 2 Thessalonians, is that of quotations of or allusions to Christian liturgical materials. It is noteworthy that many of these traditional materials do not seem to be directly dependent on any of the Pauline letters. They constitute another center of authority, apparently comparable in importance to the OT, and one not too closely tied to Paul.[27] Much of the thought in Colossians and Ephesians seems to be a kind of commentary or argument based on traditional materials that are quoted or paraphrased.[28] It can be argued that the liturgical citations in 1 Tim 3:16, 2 Tim 2:11–13, and Tit 3:3–7 likewise shape as well as support the general teaching of those letters. The traditional materials seem to be cited as expressions of normative Christian thinking, foundational expres-

23 See A. T. Lincoln, "The Use of the OT in Ephesians," *JSNT* 14 (1982) 16–57, esp. 48–50.

24 On the general question of the relation of Colossians to the OT, see esp. Markus Barth and Helmut Blanke, *Colossians* (AB 34B; New York: Doubleday, 1994) 64–68, 96, 238–39, 250–51. They recognize the strange absence of direct quotations but argue, with some plausibility, for rather frequent allusions to the OT.

25 One wonders if by "scriptures" the writer of the Pastorals might have in mind not the OT but rather a collection of Paul's letters. But probably the former is intended, and the writer is as keen to affirm Christian "ownership" of the Jewish Bible as he is to warn against "Jewish" speculations and genealogies. The writer and addressees live in the neighborhood of Jews, and recognize essential similarities and boundaries between synagogue and church. George W. Knight III (*The Pastoral Epistles: A Commentary on the Greek Text* [NIGNTC; Grand Rapids: Eerdmans, 1992] 448) argues that the reference to "scripture" in 2 Tim 3:16 may well pertain to both the OT and early Christian writings (including Paul's letters).

26 OT salvation history is basically absent. Cf. the remarks of J. L. Martyn on Galatians (*Pauline Theology* I:172–79).

27 Within the Pastorals, the material quoted or alluded to in Tit 3:3–7 seems particularly close to teaching in the Undisputed Letters. Passages like 1 Tim 3:16 and 6:11–16 are not obviously dependent on distinctively Pauline ideas. Of course the Disputed Letters imply that "Paul" approves of all the traditional materials he uses.

28 Petr Pokorný speaks of traditional materials as "assistants" used by the author of Colossians (*Colossians: A Commentary* [Peabody, MA: Hendrickson, 1991) 29.

sions of belief that writers and readers already accept and can build upon in confronting new challenges.

A third category of warrants consists in references to the previous experiences of church members. For example, in Colossians and Ephesians stress is laid on the readers' experiences of conversion, as a transfer from darkness to light. There are appeals especially in Ephesians to maintain a united church. Readers are urged to remain in something like the Christian "mainstream," a position they are assumed to have already experienced.

A fourth and fundamental category of warrants for the teachings of these letters is that of references to the person of Paul. The mere fact that Paul has said something is assumed to be of fundamental consequence for the churches, and this suggests that Paul's authority is widely recognized by the implied readers. Paul in these letters refers often to himself: as apostle, as exemplary Christian, leader, transmitter of authentic traditions (2 Thess 2:15; 3:6), writer of important letters (cf. 1 Thess 5:27; 2 Thess 2:2, 15; 3:14, 17; Col 4:16), and sufferer for Christ's cause (e.g., Col 1:24; 4:18; Eph 3:1,13; 2 Tim 1:8–14; 3:10–12; 4:6–8). His career can be interpreted as a compelling example of God's mercy for sinners.[29] In all the letters "Paul" writes as one absent in body but present in spirit (Col 2:5)—and his spiritual and literary presence is assumed to have self-evident authority.

Readers who know that Pauline authorship of these letters is widely denied today may find it puzzling or ironic that Paul's authority is so vital a warrant in them. Presumably one major reason why such pseudonymous compositions came to be written was precisely that the apostle's reputation stood high. The psychological, cultural, and moral questions raised by the appearance of pseudonymous writings in early Christianity have been much discussed in recent years, but answers have not been widely agreed upon.[30] Still, Paul's name seems clearly to be a warrant of fundamental importance in all of the Disputed Letters. Under the authority of that name, however, the writers of the Disputed Letters quietly claim the right to extend and redefine the meaning of "Paul" and "Pauline theology," partly on the basis of church traditions, partly on that of

29 Commenting on 1 Tim 1:12–20, Donelson remarks, "In Paul, we see the ever-repeating truths of the Christian life" (*Colossians,* 125). Benjamin Fiore argues persuasively for a skillful use of rhetorical devices in the Pastorals similar to those found in the Socratic letters produced within the Cynic tradition (*The Function of Personal Example in the Socratic and Pastoral Epistles* [AnBib 105; Rome: Biblical Institute Press, 1986], esp. 101–163, 191–236).

30 Two recent studies that arrive at different conclusions about the intention (and value) of the use of Paul's name in the Disputed Letters are Lewis R. Donelson, *Pseudepigraphy and Ethical Argument in the Pastoral Epistles* (Tübingen: Mohr [Siebeck], 1986) and David G. Meade, *Pseudonymity and Canon: An Investigation into the Relationship of Authorship and Authority in Jewish and Earliest Christian Tradition* (Grand Rapids: Eerdmans, 1987).

their own creative intuitions regarding church needs and the meaning of the kerygma.

Despite their use of all these varieties of warrants and considerable rhetorical refinement, the Disputed Letters appear to express theology not so much through extended argumentation as by means of insistent affirmation: this is what Paul teaches, these are reliable traditions, this is what you should believe and do.

Paul Meyer has suggested that Pauline theology is a process in which the apostle only learns what he means as he writes.[31] This approach to interpreting Paul may be especially helpful as we examine a passage like Romans 9–11. Yet such consideration of multiple lines of thought with possible rejection of some in preference to others is *not* obviously present in the Disputed Letters. It is impossible to prove, perhaps, but these letters give the impression that their writers generally had firm ideas where they were heading when they began the writing process.[32] The Disputed Letters do not offer self-corrections on the part of the author(s) or hints of any hesitations about what is to be written. They contain nothing like Paul's troubled confession in Gal 4:20, "I am perplexed about you."

Yet, intentionally or not, the writers of the Disputed Letters produced new types of theology not only in content but also in shape and process. By electing to focus on principles of morality and church offices, for example, the Pastoral Letters imply that these are among the best safeguards of (Pauline) orthodoxy.[33] They imply that in their situation "theology" is best carried on by stressing order and respectable virtues rather than by refining soteriology. In Colossians and Ephesians, on the contrary, theological reflection leads to novel statements about Christ, metaphysics, the cosmos, and the church. The situations of the authors of those letters made such innovations desirable, and these Pauline "authors" had the audacity and creativity to supply them—even though the resulting assertions differed from those in the Undisputed Letters in both language and content.

If a "Pauline School" is responsible for the Disputed Letters,[34] its members did not feel constrained to move in a single direction in extending the apostle's

31 See Meyer's essay in this volume. Cf. Kraftchick's remarks in *Pauline Theology II*: 24.

32 Cf. the remark of G. Bornkamm that Paul "in writing his letters . . . always lets his theological thoughts take shape before his readers and listeners, while Col from the very beginning operates with previously coined and fixed views and concepts" (cited with approval by E. Lohse, *Colossians and Philemon* (Hermeneia; Philadelphia: Fortress, 1971) 178 n. 1.

33 Raymond Brown observes that the Pastorals' recommendation of firm church administrative leadership in response to a crisis "has tended to dominate church history precisely because it worked so well" (*Churches,* 46).

34 See H.-M. Schenke, "Das Weiterwirken des Paulus und die Pflege seines Erbs durch die Paulus-schule," *NTS* 21 (1975): 505–518; Harry Y. Gamble, *The NT Canon: Its Making and Meaning* (Philadelphia: Fortress, 1985) 39–40.

legacy. The author of Colossians certainly moved well beyond the Undisputed Letters regarding Christology, use of philosophical terms, and ethics (especially in the household codes). The writer of Ephesians probably knew Colossians and consciously moved in a different direction, especially regarding ecclesiology. The writer of 2 Thessalonians knew 1 Thessalonians, but was not unduly constrained by it. If the author of the Pastoral Letters knew any of these other Disputed Letters, he did not show it and felt free to go his own way. The "Pauline School" did not maintain a single "party line."[35]

THEOLOGY AS GUIDING CONVICTIONS AND CONCLUSIONS

The fundamental theological convictions expressed in the Disputed Letters may be interpreted as conclusions reached from arguments or trains of thought set forth in these writings or as guiding presuppositions with which the writers began. Some of the most important convictions are apparently taken over, sometimes with modifications, from traditional materials. Ephesians seems designed as a fairly comprehensive statement of Pauline theology. Likewise, 2 Timothy appears to present its ideas as a final "testament" of the apostle. In the other Disputed Letters things seem less conclusively stated, but all present assured teaching on major issues.

God the Father is often portrayed as the ultimate source of salvation, and there is a heightened concern to stress the relationship between creation and redemption: as God created all things and persons through Christ, God now works to save all through Christ. Since the whole world is God's creation, believers must accept it as good and use it responsibly. God as final judge is a prominent theme in the Pastoral Letters and in 2 Thessalonians.[36] Yet the trustworthiness of God and the hope believers have in God's election and saving purpose also are prominent themes in these letters (e.g., Eph 1:4–5; Col 1:12–14; 2 Th 2:13; 3:3–5; 2 Tim 1:12; 2:13; Tit 1:2). No passage in the Bible expresses more clearly the mysterious transcendence of God than some familiar lines in 1 Tim 6:15–16:

> . . . the blessed and only Sovereign, the King of kings and Lord of lords. It is he alone who has immortality and dwells in unapproachable light, whom no one has ever seen or can see; to him be honor and eternal dominion. Amen. (NRSV)

35 Frank W. Hughes suggests that Colossians and Ephesians display the kind of eschatology that troubles the author of 2 Thessalonians (*Early Christian Rhetoric and 2 Thessalonians* [JSNTSup 30; Sheffield: JSOT Press, 1989) 80–86.

36 E. Krentz, "Through a Lens," *Pauline Theology* 1.57–59.

Christology is prominent in all the letters. The concept of Jesus as providing saving knowledge of the invisible God (cf. John 1:18) is strongly suggested in the "icon" assertions of Col 1:15, 3:10–11 as well as by the emphasis on Christ's epiphanies in the Pastorals.[37] 2 Thessalonians shows signs of Christological development beyond Paul by applying to Jesus language reserved for God in the Undisputed Letters,[38] and Tit 2:13 seems to apply the term "God" to Jesus. Colossians and the hymn it cites in 1:15–20 mark a new stage in the use of metaphysical and cosmic categories. Through Christ the entire universe was created and through him all things (not just humans) are reconciled to God. Colossians goes further than any other NT book in developing a cosmic Christology.[39] The ideology and terminology suggest some strong influence from Hellenistic Jewish thinking, especially that of Philo. Christ in Colossians is not only a figure of history but, as in the Johannine prologue, a pre-existent and perhaps eternal being. Likewise Christology is central in Ephesians, though in Ephesians it is explained more extensively in relation to ecclesiology.[40]

Colossians, Ephesians, and the Pastoral Letters move in the direction of affirming the full divinity of Jesus. God the Father is recognized, and Christ does not supplant God the Father. Yet God the Father's saving work is essentially tied to Jesus, with no suggestion that salvation is possible apart from Jesus. "For there is one God, and there is one mediator between God and men, the man Christ Jesus, who gave himself . . . ." (1 Tim 2:5–6). The resurrection and ascension/exaltation of Christ are heavily stressed in Colossians, Ephesians, and 1 Timothy. Yet the death of Jesus is also vital (see, e.g., Col 1:20; 2:14–16, Eph 1:7; 2:14–16; 5:2, 25–27, 1 Tim 2:6; 6.13; 2 Tim 2:11–13; Tit 2:13–14). Like Paul, most of the authors of the Disputed Letters stress both the death and the resurrection of Jesus as core faith assertions, though one may say that the emphasis on exaltation has expanded without any forgetting that Christian redemption occurs through a cross.[41] 2 Thessalonians expresses special interest in Jesus' role as apocalyptic agent, but his past and present roles are not forgotten.[42]

37 On the epiphany Christology of the Pastorals, see now Jouette M. Bassler, *1 Timothy, 2 Timothy, Titus* (Abingdon NT Commentaries; Nashville: Abingdon, 1996) 77, 115

38 See E. Krentz, "Thessalonians, First and Second Epistles to the," *ABD* 6.521.

39 Barth and Blanke, *Colossians,* 45, 244 (against Schweizer's existential interpretation), 246.

40 See, e.g., Arnold, *Ephesians,* 124–66.

41 For Colossians, see esp. Fred O. Frances, "The Christological Argument of Colossians," *God's Christ and His People: FS N. A. Dahl* (ed. J. Jervell and W. A. Meeks; Oslo: Universitetsforlaget, 1977) 201.

42 On this point, see the differing assessments of E. Krentz, "Through a Lens," 56, and Karl P. Donfried in Donfried and I. Howard Marshall, *The Theology of the Shorter Pauline Letters* (NT Theology Series; Cambridge: University Press, 1993) 92.

The "mystical" presence of Jesus Christ in the church is much more clearly affirmed in Colossians and Ephesians than in the Pastoral Letters, though it is probably too much to say that the latter writings conceive of Christ as absent from church and world during the period between incarnation and parousia.[43] The Lord (evidently Jesus Christ) gives understanding to believers now (2 Tim 2:7) as He strengthened Paul in time of persecution (2 Tim 3:11; 4.17). Paul presents a charge to Timothy "in the presence of God and of Christ Jesus, who is to judge the living and the dead, and in view of his appearing and his kingdom" (2 Tim 4:1; cf. 1:12; 1 Tim 5:21)—just as he himself received a commission from Christ (1 Tim 1:12). The teachings of the earthly Jesus are not mentioned (except perhaps in 1 Tim 5:18 and 6:3).

The Holy Spirit is not often spoken of in these letters, apart from Ephesians. Even there the Spirit is referred to in ways that seem anti-charismatic. Rather than saying much about the signs of the presence of the Spirit in the Christian communities, the writers of the Disputed Letters prefer to stress the moral and religious qualities of church leaders and members. Ecclesiology as teaching about the nature and structures of the church is much more prominent than overt pneumatology in the Pastoral Letters. The result in the Pastoral Letters is a sober, practical, and largely anthropocentric approach to describing the church, though the Christian community is fundamentally understood not as a human invention but as "the household of God" (1 Tim 3:15; cf. Eph 2:19).

Salvation is by divine grace, not human merit (Eph 2:8–9; Tit 3:5), though this central Pauline concept is becoming detached from the conflict with Jewish Christians over the relation of Gentile believers to the demands of the Jewish law.[44] Future eschatology is preserved, but only 2 Thessalonians expresses concern about the timetable of the "final events." In the other Disputed Letters there is no hint of "disappointment at the delay of the parousia." Christians are known to live "between the times," and not just in a chronological sense.[45]

The language of faith has undergone interesting shifts from the Undisputed Letters. The verb πιστεύω is never used in Colossians and only twice in Ephesians. The adjective πιστός, relatively uncommon in the Undisputed Letters (a

43 *Pace* Donelson *Colossians,* 148.

44 Notably in Ephesians. See Lincoln and Wedderburn, *The Theology of the Later Pauline Letters,* 131.

45 Cf. R. Bultmann, *Theology of the NT* (New York: Scribners, 1955) 2.185: "The paradox of Christian existence—a new existence within this old world (Tit 2:12)—is here grasped." Cf. his observations on Colossians and Ephesians (p. 175). On the idea—but not the language—of justification by faith in Colossians, see A. Lindemann, *Paulus im ältesten Christentum: Das Bild des Apostles und die Rezeption der paulinischen Theologie in der frühchristlichen Literatur* (BHTh 58; Tübingen: Mohr/Siebeck, 1979) 117–18.

total of nine uses), is employed four times in Colossians, twice in Ephesians, and seventeen times in the Pastoral Letters (five times in the phrase πιστὸς ὁ λόγος). There are five occurrences of the noun πίστις in Colossians, eight in Ephesians, five in 2 Thessalonians, and thirty-three in the Pastoral Letters. The Disputed Letters offer almost no expression susceptible of being interpreted as "the faith belonging to Jesus (Christ),"[46] and very often πίστις seems to designate or imply a fixed body of beliefs.[47]

Perhaps partly to counter elitist interpretations of the Pauline tradition, most of the Disputed Letters articulate universalistic ideas. The Gospel is for all persons, and God desires that all be saved.[48] The universalism of God's saving intention appears to be expressed more directly and frequently in the Disputed Letters than in the Undisputed Letters, though none of the Disputed Letters says flatly that God will finally save everyone.[49]

Ethical exhortation in these letters is marked by world-affirmation. Just as no one outside the church need stay outside, so persons within the Christian community must not neglect responsibilities in the present world. All the Disputed Letters reflect an anti-enthusiastic orientation. Even 2 Thessalonians, though it makes cryptic predictions about the future Anti-Christ and his defeat, probably is best understood as a repudiation of eschatological elitism or fanaticism.[50] The author urges his readers to wait patiently for God's future vindication of their faith and meanwhile to live in the world in an orderly and industrious manner. Colossians and the Pastoral Letters offer a special anti-ascetic emphasis. In Colossians readers are told that their lives in Christ are hidden, but that they should live out their virtues in the ordinary world. Believers should be prepared to answer questions from outsiders with prudence and "saltiness" (Col 4:6), a term suggestive of both friendly openness to non-Christian neighbors and a

46 See the essays on πίστις Χριστοῦ by Dunn, Hays, and Achtemeier in the present volume. The genitival phrases with πίστις in Eph 3:12 and 4:13 could refer to Jesus's own faith. So Markus Barth, *Ephesians* (AB; Garden City: Doubleday, 1974) 34.347, 34A.488–89.

47 The uses of πίστις in Col 1:4, 2:5, 12 indicate faith has Christ, or God's work in Christ, as object. On the Pastoral Letters, see R. F. Collins, *Letters Paul Did Not Write* (Wilmington: Michael Glazier, 1988) 104–105;Young *Theology,* 75, 95.

48 Eph 1:9–10; Col 1:16, 20. On the meaning and motivation for this theme in the Pastorals, see Bassler, *1 Timothy, 2 Timothy, Titus* , 51–55. Luke T. Johnson remarks of 1 Tim 2:1–6, "Nowhere in the NT is there such an inclusive statement of hope concerning all humanity" (*Letters to Paul's Delegates: 1 Timothy, 2 Timothy, Titus* [Valley Forge: Trinity Press International, 1996] 132).

49 Cf. 2 Tim 2:25. In describing the woes of the wicked, it may be significant that the Pastorals tend to emphasize suffering in the present world (e.g., 1 Tim 1:19–20; 6:10; 2 Tim 3:9; Tit 3:11). Future punishment without hope is promised for the wicked in 2 Thess 1:8–9, 2:10.

50 Cf. R. Jewett, *The Thessalonian Correspondence,* 172–78; Donfried, *Theology,* 96–104.

hope for the conversion of at least some of them.[51] In Eph 6:11–18 believers are summoned to battle various temptations and foes, but the foes are not "flesh and blood." In the Pastoral Letters, people are told to accept life in this world[52]—though this is accompanied with a clear message that this world will come to an end and everyone will be judged by Jesus and God the Father. Futuristic eschatology is on the decline in all the Disputed Letters except 2 Thessalonians, yet none of them claims that salvation is completely realized in the church(es) of the present time.

The world-affirming elements, especially the household codes, have been viewed by many modern readers as tokens of domestication, faded idealism, or compromise with paganism (or Judaism) that constitutes a betrayal of the radical Paul of the Undisputed Letters. The virtue and vice lists in these letters often recall Jewish and pagan norms, sometimes suggesting that Christians should manifest the same qualities of character that any good Roman would applaud.[53] Yet all these letters communicate a sense that the Christian lifestyle involves disciplined struggle against the "world" and can lead to suffering. Hence they combine quasi-separation from the world together with acceptance of certain non-Christian moral norms. Ethical teaching is sometimes expressed with absolutist demands reminiscent of the Sermon on the Mount. Still, it is probably fair to speak of some slackening of moral radicalism in the Disputed Letters, especially the Pastorals.

Scholars have often suggested that the general pattern of appropriating moral values and templates of moral discourse from the pagan world was based on a strategy of trying to lessen hostility from outsiders and encourage conversion.[54] One may also suspect a Paul-like willingness to think that certain values of non-believers deserve the respect of believers (cf. Rom 12:17b; 2 Cor 8:21; Phil 4:8).

51 Cf. James D. G. Dunn, *The Epistles to the Colossians and to Philemon* (NIGTC; Grand Rapids: Eerdmans, 1996) 266–68.

52 See, e.g., Martin Dibelius and Hans Conzelmann, *The Pastoral Epistles* (Hermeneia; Philadelphia: Fortress, 1972) 39–41; Carol L. Stockhausen, *Letters in the Pauline Tradition: Ephesians, Colossians, 1 Timothy, II Timothy and Titus* (Wilmington: Michael Glazier, 1989) 190–91. On the sociological conceptuality underlying the Pastorals, incorporating a movement away from a sect-type view to a church-type one, see esp. Margaret Y. MacDonald, *The Pauline Churches: A Socio-Historical Study of Institutionalization in the Pauline and Deutero-Pauline Writings* (SNTSMS 60; Cambridge: University Press, 1988) 160–202.

53 Donelson, *Colossians*, 131–132.

54 Beker, *Heirs*, 46: the writer of the Pastoral Letters "fears that if the heretical opposition, with its emancipatory asocial behavior and deviant thought, prevails, the Roman authorities and society at large will threaten the very survival of the church."

SOME FINAL ISSUES

One question with which we are left is the claim of these letters to be authentic presentations of Pauline theology. Historically it seems clear that these Disputed Letters played a significant role in recommending Paul and the Undisputed Letters to future generations of Christians. *Yet how far can we say the Disputed Letters really present Pauline theology?* Grant that they address different situations and use different terminology. Grant that many scholars today believe that most or all of these letters were written by persons other than Paul. Are there objective criteria on which historians or theologians can agree to decide if these letters re-present "Pauline theology" or not?

In any case, our first or last reactions to the Disputed Letters need not be one of disappointment that they are not "more Pauline." However imperfectly their authors understood the apostle, and however much they relied on traditional materials, they responded to post-Pauline times and challenges not just by repeating old phrases but by redefining the meaning of Paul's legacy. Their authors would have agreed with Albert Schweitzer that "Paul is the patron-saint of thought in Christianity."[55] If their ideas and arguments do not equal or surpass those of the author of Romans, this should not awaken surprise or scorn.

Perhaps there is a still more basic theological question to ask. Although written within some kind of Pauline tradition, and although addressed probably in the first instance to churches that had direct or indirect links with the apostle, the Disputed Letters—like the Undisputed Letters—ultimately seek to present not the theology of Paul but simply Christian theology. No matter how much attention they accord to Paul—as "author," authoritative apostle, model church leader, exemplary or redemptive sufferer—the Disputed Letters center their attention not on Paul but on God's self-disclosure in Jesus. The final critical question must be about the theology of each of these letters as an interpretation of the Christian message, one which has been influential in varied ways in the past and which may still be meaningful today and tomorrow.

55 Schweitzer, *The Mysticism of Paul the Apostle* (London: Black, 1956) 377.

Bibliography

Achtemeier, Paul J. "Finding the Way to Paul's Theology: A Response to J. Christiaan Beker and J. Paul Sampley." In *Pauline Theology, Volume I: Thessalonians, Philippians, Galatians and Philemon*, edited by Jouette M. Bassler, 25–36. Minneapolis: Fortress, 1991.

Arnold, Clinton E. *Ephesians: Power and Magic: The Concept of Power in Ephesians in Light of its Historical Setting*. SNTSMS 63. Cambridge: University Press, 1989.

Barclay, John. *Obeying the Truth: A Study of Paul's Ethics in Galatians*. Edinburgh: T. & T. Clark, 1988.

Barrett, C. K. "The Allegory of Abraham, Sarah, and Hagar in the Argument of Galatians." In *Rechtfertigung: Festschrift für Ernst Käsemann*, edited by J. Friedrich *et al.*, 1–16. Tübingen: Mohr-Siebeck and Göttingen: Vandenhoeck & Ruprecht, 1976.

Barth, Marcus. *Ephesians*. AB 34. New York: Doubleday, 1974.

_______. "The Faith of the Messiah." *Heythrop Journal* 10 (1969) 363–70.

Bassler, Jouette M. *1 Timothy, 2 Timothy, Titus*. Abingdon NT Commentaries. Nashville: Abingdon, 1996.

_______. "Paul's Theology: Whence and Whither?" In *Pauline Theology, Volume II: 1 and 2 Corinthians*, edited by David M. Hay, 3–17. Minneapolis: Fortress, 1993.

_______. "Peace in All Ways: Theology in the Thessalonian Letters." In *Pauline Theology, Volume I: Thessalonians, Philippians, Galatians and Philemon*, edited by Jouette M. Bassler, 71–85. Minneapolis: Fortress, 1991.

Beker, J. Christiaan. *Heirs of Paul: Paul's Legacy in the New Testament and in the Church Today*. Minneapolis: Fortress, 1991.

_______. *Paul the Apostle: The Triumph of God in Life and Thought*. Philadelphia: Fortress, 1980.

_______. "Recasting Pauline Theology: The Coherence-Contingency Scheme as Interpretive Model." In *Pauline Theology, Volume I: Thessalonians, Philippians, Galatians and Philemon*, edited by Jouette M. Bassler, 15–24. Minneapolis: Fortress, 1991.

Betz, Hans Dieter. "Paul." *ABD* 5.192.

Bloom, Harold. *Poetics of Influence*, edited by J. Hollander. New Haven: Henry R. Schwab, 1988.

Boers, Hendrikus. "We Who Are by Inheritance Jews; Not from the Gentiles, Sinners." *JBL* 111 (1992) 273–281.

Bornkamm, Günther. "Faith and Reason in Paul." In *Early Christian Experience*, translated and edited by Paul L. Hammer, 29–46. New York and Evanston: Harper & Row, 1969.

Bruce, F. F. *Commentary on Galatians*. NIGTC. Grand Rapids: Eerdmans, 1982.

Bultmann, Rudolf. "γινώσκω, κτλ." *TDNT* 1.689–719.

_______. "The Primitive Christian Kerygma and the Historical Jesus." In *The Historical Jesus and the Kerygmatic Christ: Essays on the New Quest of the Historical Jesus*, translated and edited by Carl E. Braaten and Roy A. Harrisville, 15–42. New York: Abingdon, 1964.

_______. *Theology of the New Testament*. Translated by K. Grobel. 2 Vols. London: SCM; New York: Scribner, 1951.

Burton, E. D. *Galatians*. ICC. Edinburgh; T. & T. Clark, 1921.

Byrne, Brendan. *Reckoning with Romans*. Wilmington, DE: Glazier, 1986.

Campbell, Douglas. "The Meaning of ΠΙΣΤΙΣ and ΝΟΜΟΣ in Paul: A Linguistic and Structural Perspective." *JBL* 111 (1992) 91–103.

______. *The Rhetoric of Righteousness in Romans 3.21–26*. JSNTSup 65. Sheffield: JSOT Press, 1992.

______."Romans 1:17—A *Crux Interpretum* for the ΠΙΣΤΙΣ ΧΡΙΣΤΟΥ Debate." *JBL* 113 (1994) 265–85.

Campbell, William S. "The Contribution of Traditions to Paul's Theology: A Response to C. J. Roetzel." In *Pauline Theology, Volume II: 1 and 2 Corinthians,* edited by David M. Hay, 234–254. Minneapolis: Fortress, 1993.

Cosgrove, Charles H. *The Cross and the Spirit: A Study in the Argument and Theology of Galatians*. Macon, GA: Mercer University Press, 1988.

______. "Justification in Paul: A Linguistic and Theological Reflection." *JBL* 106 (1987) 653–670.

______."The Justification of the Other: An Interpretation of Rom. 1:18–4:25." In *Society of Biblical Literature 1992 Seminar Papers,* edited by E. H. Lovering, 130–159. Atlanta: Scholars Press, 1992.

Cousar, Charles B. "The Theological Task of 1 Corinthians: A Conversation with Gordon D. Fee and Victor Paul Furnish." In *Pauline Theology, Volume II: 1 and 2 Corinthians,* edited by David M. Hay, 90–102. Minneapolis: Fortress, 1993.

______. *A Theology of the Cross: The Death of Jesus in the Pauline Letters*. Minneapolis: Fortress, 1990.

Cranfield, C. E. B. *A Critical and Exegetical Commentary on the Epistle to the Romans*. 2 Vols. ICC. Edinburgh: Clark, 1979.

Dahl, Nils Alstrup. "The Neglected Factor in New Testament Theology." In *Jesus the Christ: The Historical Origins of Christological Doctrine*, edited by Donald H. Juel, 153–163. Minneapolis: Fortress, 1991

______. "The Particularity of the Pauline Epistles as a Problem in the Ancient Church." In *Neotestamentica et Patristica: Eine Freundesgabe an Herrn Prof. Dr. O. Cullmann zu seinem 60. Geburtstag*, edited by A. N. Wilder, 261–271. NovTSupp 6. Leiden: Brill, 1962.

Davies, G. N. *Faith and Obedience in Romans: A Study of Romans 1–4*. JSNTS 39. Sheffield: JSOT Press, 1990.

Davis, C. A. *The Structure of Paul's Theology*. Lewiston, NY: Mellen, 1995.

de Boer, Martinus C. "Images of Paul in the Post-Apostolic Period." *CBQ* 42 (1980) 359–380.

Dodd, Brian. "Romans 1:17—A *Crux Interpretum* for the ΠΙΣΤΙΣ ΧΡΙΣΤΟΥ Debate?" *JBL* 114 (1994) 470–73.

Donaldson, T. L. "The 'Curse of the Law' and the Inclusion of the Gentiles: Galatians 3.13–14." *NTS* 32 (1986) 94–112.

Donelson, Lewis R. *Pseudepigraphy and Ethical Argument in the Pastoral Epistles*. Tübingen: Mohr-Siebeck, 1986.

Donfried, Karl P. and I. Howard Marshall. *The Theology of the Shorter Pauline Letters*. NT Theology Series. Cambridge: University Press, 1993.

Duncan, G. S. *The Epistle to the Galatians*. Moffatt. London: Hodder, 1934.

Dunn, James D. G. "Christology as an Aspect of Theology." In *The Future of Christology: Essays in Honor of Leander E. Keck*, ed. A. J. Malherbe and W. A. Meeks, 202–212. Minneapolis: Fortress, 1993.

______. *The Epistles to the Colossians and to Philemon*. NIGTC. Grand Rapids: Eerdmans, 1996.

______. "How Controversial was Paul's Christology?" In *From Jesus to Paul: Essays on Jesus and New Testament Christology in Honour of Marinus de Jonge*, edited by Martinus C. de Boer, 148–167. JSNTS 84. Sheffield: Sheffield Academic Press, 1993.

______. "In Search of Common Ground." In *Paul and the Mosaic Law*, edited by J. D. G. Dunn. WUNT 89. Tübingen: Mohr-Siebeck, 1996.

______. "The Justice of God: A Renewed Perspective on Justification by Faith." *JTS* 43 (1992) 1–22.

______. "The New Perspective on Paul." In *Jesus, Paul and the Law*, 183–214. London: SPCK/Louisville: Westminster, 1990.

______. *The Partings of the Ways between Christianity and Judaism and their Significance for the Character of Christianity*. London: SCM/Philadelphia: TPI, 1991.

______. "Prolegomena to a Theology of Paul." *NTS* 40 (1994) 407–32.

______. *Romans*. WBC 38. Dallas: Word, 1988.

______. "The Theology of Galatians: The Issue of Covenantal Nomism." In *Pauline Theology, Volume I: Thessalonians, Philippians, Galatians and Philemon*, edited by Jouette M. Bassler, 125–146. Minneapolis: Fortress, 1991.

______. "Was Paul Against the Law? The Law in Galatians and Romans: A Test-Case of Text in Context." In *Text and Context. Biblical Texts in Their Textual and Situational Contexts: in Honor of Lars Hartman*, edited by T. Fornberg and D. Hellholm, 455–475. Oslo: Scandinavian University Press, 1995.

Ebeling, Gerhard. *Word and Faith*. Philadelphia: Fortress, 1963.

Engberg-Pedersen, Troels. "Proclaiming the Lord's Death: 1 Corinthians 11:17–34 and the Forms of Paul's Theological Argument." In *Pauline Theology, Volume II: 1 and 2 Corinthians*, edited by David M. Hay, 103–132. Minneapolis: Fortress, 1993.

Fee, Gordon D. "Toward a Theology of 1 Corinthians." In *Pauline Theology, Volume II: 1 and 2 Corinthians*, edited by David M. Hay, 37–58. Minneapolis: Fortress, 1993.

Fiore, Benjamin. *The Function of Personal Example in the Socratic and Pastoral Epistles*. AnBib 105. Rome: Biblical Institute Press, 1986.

Fitzmyer, Joseph A. *Paul and His Theology: A Brief Sketch*. Second edition. Englewood Cliffs, NJ: Prentice-Hall, 1989.

______. *Romans*. AB33. New York: Doubleday, 1992.

Francis, Fred O. "The Christological Argument of Colossians." In *God's Christ and His People: Studies in Honour of Nils Alstrup Dahl*, edited by J. Jervell and W. A. Meeks, 192–208. Oslo: Universitetsforlaget, 1977.

Frei, Hans. *Types of Christian Theology*, edited by George Hunsinger and William Placher. New Haven: Yale University Press, 1992.

Fung, R. Y. K. *The Epistle to the Galatians*. NICNT. Grand Rapids: Eerdmans, 1988.

Furnish, Victor P. "On Putting Paul in His Place." *JBL* 113 (1994) 3–17.

______. "Paul the Theologian." In *The Conversation Continues: Studies in Paul and John in Honor of J. Louis Martyn*, edited by Robert T. Fortna and Beverly R. Gaventa, 10–34. Nashville: Abingdon, 1990.

______. *II Corinthians*. AB 32A. Garden City: Doubleday, 1984.

______. "Theology in 1 Corinthians." In *Pauline Theology, Volume II: 1 and 2 Corinthians*, edited by David M. Hay, 59–89. Minneapolis: Fortress, 1993.

Gärtner, Bertil E. "The Pauline and Johannine Idea of 'To Know God' Against the Hellenistic Background." *NTS* 14 (1968) 209–31.

Gaston, Lloyd. *Paul and the Torah*. Vancouver: University of British Columbia Press, 1987.

Gaventa, Beverly R. "Apostle and Church in 2 Corinthians." In *Pauline Theology, Volume II: 1 and 2 Corinthians,* edited by David M. Hay, 182–199. Minneapolis: Fortress, 1993.

_______. "The Singularity of the Gospel: A Reading of Galatians." In *Pauline Theology, Volume I: Thessalonians, Philippians, Galatians, Philemon*, edited by Jouette M. Bassler, 147–159. Minneapolis: Fortress, 1991.

Hansen, G. Walter. *Abraham in Galatians*. JSNTSup 29. Sheffield: JSOT Press, 1989.

Harrisville, Roy A. III. *The Figure of Abraham in the Epistles of St. Paul.* Lewiston, NY: Mellen Press, 1992.

_______."ΠΙΣΤΙΣ ΧΡΙΣΤΟΥ: Witness of the Fathers." *NovT* 36 (1994) 233–41.

Haussleiter, J. "Der Glaube Jesu Christi und der christliche Glaube." *NKZ* 2 (1891) 109–145, 205–130.

Hawthorne, Gerald F. *Philippians*. WBC 43. Waco, TX: Word, 1983.

Hay, David M. "*Pistis* as 'Ground for Faith' in Hellenized Judaism and Paul." *JBL* 108 (1989) 461–76.

_______. "The Shaping of Theology in 2 Corinthians: Convictions, Doubts, and Warrants." In *Pauline Theology, Volume II: 1 and 2 Corinthians,* edited by David M. Hay, 135–155. Minneapolis: Fortress, 1993.

Hays, Richard B. "Christology and Ethics in Galatians: The Law of Christ." *CBQ* 49 (1987) 268–90.

_______. "Crucified with Christ: A Synthesis of the Theology of 1 and 2 Thessalonians, Philemon, Philippians, and Galatians." In *Pauline Theology, Volume I: Thessalonians, Philippians, Galatians, Philemon*, edited by Jouette M. Bassler, 227–246. Minneapolis: Fortress, 1991.

______. *Echoes of Scripture in the Letters of Paul.* New Haven: Yale University Press, 1989.

______. *The Faith of Jesus Christ: An Investigation of the Narrative Substructure of Galatians 3:1–4:11*. SBLDS 56. Chico: Scholars Press, 1983.

_______. "'Have we found Abraham to be our forefather according to the flesh?' A Reconsideration of Rom. 4.1." *NovT* 27 (1985) 76–98.

______. "Justification." *ABD* 3.1129–1133.

______. *The Moral Vision of the New Testament: Community, Cross, New Creation*. San Francisco: HarperSanFrancisco, 1996.

______. "Psalm 143 and the Logic of Romans 3." *JBL* 99 (1980) 107–115.

______. "'The Righteous One' as Eschatological Deliverer: A Case Study in Paul's Apocalyptic Hermeneutics." In *Apocalyptic and the New Testament: Essays in Honor of J. Louis Martyn*, edited by Joel Marcus and Marion L. Soards, 191–215. JSNTSup 24. Sheffield: JSOT Press, 1988.

Hebert, A. G. "'Faithfulness' and 'Faith'." *Theology* 58 (1955) 373–379.

Hengel, Martin. *Crucifixion*. Philadelphia: Fortress, 1977.

Hodgson, Peter C. *Winds of the Spirit: A Constructive Christian Theology*. Louisville: Westminster John Knox, 1994.

Hooker, Morna D. "ΠΙΣΤΙΣ ΧΡΙΣΤΟΥ." *NTS* 35 (1989) 321–42.

Howard, George. "Faith of Christ." *ABD* 2.758–60.

______. *Paul: Crisis in Galatia*. Second edition. SNTSMS 35. Cambridge: Cambridge University Press, 1990.

______. "On the 'Faith of Christ'." *HTR* 60 (1967) 459–465.

______. "The Faith of Christ." *ExpT* 85 (1974) 212–215.

Hultgren, Arland. "The *Pistis Christou* Formulations in Paul." *NovT* 22 (1980) 248–263.

Hurtado, Larry W. *One God. One Lord. Early Christian Devotion and Ancient Jewish Monotheism*. Philadelphia: Fortress/London: SCM, 1988.

Jewett, Robert. "Ecumenical Theology for the Sake of Mission: Romans 1:1–17 + 15:14–16:24." In *Pauline Theology, Volume III: Romans,* edited by David M. Hay and E. Elizabeth Johnson, 89–108. Minneapolis: Fortress, 1995.

______. "A Matrix of Grace: The Theology of 2 Thessalonians as a Pauline Letter." In *Pauline Theology, Volume I: Thessalonians, Philippians, Galatians and Philemon*, edited by Jouette M. Bassler, 63–70. Minneapolis: Fortress, 1991.

______. *The Thessalonian Correspondence: Pauline Rhetoric and Millenarian Piety*. Philadelphia: Fortress, 1986.

Johnson, E. Elizabeth. "Romans 9–11: The Faithfulness and Impartiality of God." In *Pauline Theology, Volume III: Romans,* edited by David M. Hay and E. Elizabeth Johnson, 211–239. Minneapolis: Fortress, 1995.

Johnson, Luke Timothy. "Romans 3:21–26 and the Faith of Jesus." *CBQ* 44 (1982) 77–90.

Johnson, W. "The Paradigm of Abraham in Galatians 3:6–9." *TrinJ* 8 NS (1987) 179–99.

Kaufman, Gordon D. *In Face of Mystery: A Constructive Theology*. Cambridge: Harvard University Press, 1993.

Keck, Leander E. "'Jesus' in Romans." *JBL* 108 (1989) 443–60.

______. "Paul as Thinker." *Int* 47 (1993) 27–38.

______. "Toward the Renewal of New Testament Christology." *NTS* 32 (1986) 362–377.

______. "What Makes Romans Tick?" In *Pauline Theology, Volume III: Romans,* edited by David M. Hay and E. Elizabeth Johnson, 3–29. Minneapolis: Fortress, 1995.

Kertelge, K. *"Rechtfertigung" bei Paulus*. NtA 3. Münster: Aschendorff, 1967.

Koch, Dietrich-Alex. "Der Text von Hab 2.4b in der Septuaginta und im Neuen Testament." *ZNW* 76 (1985) 68–85.

Koenig, John T. "The Knowing of Glory and Its Consequences (2 Corinthians 3–5)." In *The Conversation Continues: Studies in Paul & John. In Honor of J. Louis Martyn*, edited by Robert T. Fortna and Beverly R. Gaventa, 158–169. Nashville: Abingdon, 1990.

Koperski, V. "The Meaning of *Pistis Christou* in Philippians 3:9." *LS* 18 (1993) 198–216.

Kraftchick, Steven J. "Death in Us, Life in You: The Apostolic Medium." In *Pauline Theology, Volume II: 1 and 2 Corinthians*, edited by David M. Hay, 156–181. Minneapolis: Fortress, 1993.

_______. "A Necessary Detour: Paul's Metaphorical Understanding of the Philippian Hymn." *HBT* 15/1 (1993) 1–37.

_______. "Seeking a More Fluid Model." In *Pauline Theology, Volume II: 1 and 2 Corinthians*, edited by David M. Hay, 18–34. Minneapolis: Fortress, 1993.

Kramer, Werner. *Christ, Lord, Son of God*. Translated by Brian Hardy. SBT 50. Naperville: Allenson, 1966.

Krentz, Edgar. "Through a Lens: Theology and Fidelity in 2 Thessalonians." In *Pauline Theology, Volume I: Thessalonians, Philippians, Galatians and Philemon*, edited by Jouette M. Bassler, 53–62. Minneapolis: Fortress, 1991.

Lampe, Peter. "Theological Wisdom and the 'Word About the Cross.'" *Int* 44 (1990) 117–31.

Levenson, Jon. "Historical Criticism and the Fate of the Enlightenment Project." In *The Hebrew Bible, the Old Testament, and Historical Criticism*, 106–126. Louisville: Westminster/John Knox, 1993.

Lincoln, Andrew T. "From Wrath to Justification: Tradition, Gospel and Audience in the Theology of Romans 1:18–4:25." In *Pauline Theology, Volume III: Romans*, edited by David M. Hay and E. Elizabeth Johnson, 130–159. Minneapolis: Fortress, 1995.

_______ and A. J. M. Wedderburn. *The Theology of the Later Pauline Letters*. NT Theology Series. Cambridge: University Press, 1993.

Lindemann, Andreas. *Paulus im ältesten Christentum: Das Bild des Apostels und die Rezeption der paulinischen Theologie in der frühchristlichen Literatur*. BHTh 58. Tübingen: Mohr-Siebeck, 1979.

Longenecker, Bruce W. "ΠΙΣΤΙΣ in Romans 3.25: Neglected Evidence for the 'Faithfulness of Christ'?" *NTS* 39 (1993) 478–80.

Longenecker, Richard N. *Galatians*. WBC41. Dallas: Word, 1990.

______. "The Obedience of Christ in the Theology of the Early Church." In *Reconciliation and Hope* , edited by R. Banks, 142–152. Grand Rapids: Eerdmans, 1974.

______. *Paul: Apostle of Liberty*. New York: Harper & Row, 1964.

Lull, David J. "Salvation History: Theology in I Thessalonians, Philemon, Philippians, and Galatians: A Response to N. T. Wright, R. B. Hays, and B. Scroggs." In *Pauline Theology, Volume I: Thessalonians, Philippians, Galatians and Philemon*, edited by Jouette M. Bassler, 247–265. Minneapolis: Fortress, 1991.

MacDonald, Dennis R. *The Legend and the Apostle: The Battle for Paul in Story and Canon*. Philadelphia: Westminster, 1983.

MacDonald, Margaret Y. *The Pauline Churches: A Socio-Historical Study of Institutionalization in the Pauline and Deutero-Pauline Writings*. SNTSMS 60. Cambridge: University Press, 1988.

Marguerat, Daniel. "2 Corinthiens 10–13: Paul et l'expérience de Dieu." *ETR* 63 (1988) 497–519.

Martin, B. L. *Christ and the Law in Paul*. NovTSupp 62. Leiden: Brill, 1989.

Martyn, J. Louis. "Apocalyptic Antinomies in Paul's Letter to the Galatians." *NTS* 31 (1985) 410–424.

_______. "Events in Galatia: Modified Covenantal Nomism versus God's Invasion of the Cosmos in the Singular Gospel: Response to Dunn and Gaventa." In *Pauline Theology, Volume I: Thessalonians, Philippians, Galatians, Philemon*, edited by Jouette M. Bassler, 160–179. Minneapolis: Fortress, 1991.

______. "A Law-Observant Mission to Gentiles: The Background of Galatians." *SJT* 38 (1985) 307–24.

Matera, Frank J. *Galatians*. Sacra Pagina 9. Collegeville, MN: Liturgical Press, 1992.

Meade, David G. *Pseudonymity and Canon: An Investigation into the Relationship of Authorship and Authority in Jewish and Earliest Christian Tradition*. Grand Rapids: Eerdmans, 1987.

Morgan, Robert. *Romans*. Sheffield: Sheffield Academic Press, 1995.

Moule, C. F. D. "The Biblical Conception of 'Faith'." *ExpT* 68 (1956–57) 68.

Niebuhr, H. Richard. *The Meaning of Revelation*. New York: Macmillan, 1955.

Niederwimmer, Kurt. "Erkennen und Lieben. Gedanken zum Verhältnis von Gnosis und Agape im ersten Korintherbrief." *KD* 11 (1965) 75–102.

O'Brien, P. T. *The Epistle to the Philippians*. NIGTC. Grand Rapids: Eerdmans, 1991.

Ogden, Schubert M. "What Does It Mean to Affirm, 'Jesus Christ is Lord'?" In *The Reality of God and Other Essays*, 188–205. New York: Harper & Row, 1966.

Patte, Daniel. *Paul's Faith and the Power of the Gospel. A Structural Introduction to the Pauline Letters*. Philadelphia: Fortress, 1983.

Perkins, Pheme. *Resurrection: New Testament Witness and Contemporary Reflection*. Garden City: Doubleday, 1984.

Pokorný, Petr. *Colossians: A Commentary*. Peabody, MA: Hendrickson, 1991.

Räisänen, Heikki. *Paul and the Law*. Tübingen: Mohr, 1983.

Richard, Earl. "Early Pauline Thought: An Analysis of 1 Thessalonians." In *Pauline Theology, Volume I: Thessalonians, Philippians, Galatians and Philemon*, edited by Jouette M. Bassler, 39–52. Minneapolis: Fortress, 1991.

Robinson, D. W. B. "'Faith of Jesus Christ' — A New Testament Debate." *Reformed Theological Review* 29 (1970) 71–81.

Roetzel, Calvin J. "The Grammar of Election in Four Pauline Letters." In *Pauline Theology, Volume II: 1 and 2 Corinthians,* edited by David M. Hay, 211–233. Minneapolis: Fortress, 1993.

Sampley, J. Paul. "From Text to Thought World: The Route to Paul's Ways." In *Pauline Theology, Volume I: Thessalonians, Philippians, Galatians and Philemon*, edited by Jouette M. Bassler, 3–14. Minneapolis: Fortress, 1991.

Sanders, E. P. *Paul, the Law, and the Jewish People*. Philadelphia: Fortress, 1983.

_______. *Paul and Palestinian Judaism*. Philadelphia: Fortress, 1977.

Sandmel, Samuel. *The Genius of Paul: A Study in History*. Philadelphia: Fortress, 1958.

Schenk, Wolfgang. "Die Gerechtigkeit Gottes und der Glaube Christi." *TLZ* 97 (1972) 161–74.

Schenke, H.-M. "Das Weiterwirken des Paulus und die Pflege seines Erbs durch die Paulus-Schule." *NTS* 21 (1975).

Schlatter, Adolf. *Der Glaube im Neuen Testament*. Fifth edition (reprint of third edition, 1905). Stuttgart: Calwer, 1963.

Schlier, Heinrich. *Der Brief an die Galater*. KEK. Göttingen: Vandenhoeck & Ruprecht, 1965.

_______. "Die Erkenntnis Gottes nach den Briefen des Apostels Paulus." In *Gott in Welt: Festgabe für Karl Rahner*, edited by Herbert Vorgrimler, 1.515–35. Freiburg, *et al.*: Herder, 1964.

Schmidt, H. W. *Der Brief des Paulus an die Römer*. THKNT 6. Berlin: Evangelische, 1963.

Schreiner, R. *The Law and its Fulfillment: A Pauline Theology of Law*. Grand Rapids: Baker, 1993.

Schweitzer, Albert. *The Mysticism of the Apostle Paul*. New York: Holt, 1931.

Scroggs, Robin. "Salvation History: The Theological Structure of Paul's Thought (1 Thessalonians, Philippians, and Galatians)." In *Pauline Theology, Volume I: Thessalonians, Philippians, Galatians and Philemon*, edited by Jouette M. Bassler, 212–226. Minneapolis: Fortress, 1991.

Segal, Alan F. *Paul the Convert: The Apostolate and Apostasy of Saul the Pharisee*. New Haven: Yale University Press, 1990.

Silva, Moises. *Philippians*. Wycliffe Exegetical Commentary. Chicago: Moody, 1988.

Stendahl, Krister. *Paul Among Jews and Gentiles*. Philadelphia: Fortress/London: SCM, 1977.

Stout, Jeffrey. "The Relativity of Interpretation." *The Monist* 69 (1986) 111–112.

Stowers, Stanley K. "᾿Εκ πίστεως and διὰ πίστεως" in Romans 3:30." *JBL* 108 (1989) 665–74.

_______. "Friends and Enemies in the Politics of Heaven: Reading Theology in Philippians." In *Pauline Theology, Volume I: Thessalonians, Philippians, Galatians and Philemon*, edited by Jouette M. Bassler, 105–122. Minneapolis: Fortress, 1991.

_______. *A Rereading of Romans: Justice, Jews, & Gentiles*. New Haven: Yale University Press, 1994.

Strobel, August. *Untersuchungen zum eschatologischen Verzögerungsproblem auf Grund der spätjudisch-urchristlichen Geschichte von Habakuk 2,2ff.* NovTSup 2. Leiden: Brill, 1961.

Taylor, G. "The Function of ΠΙΣΤΙΣ ΧΡΙΣΤΟΥ in Galatians." *JBL* 85 (1966) 58–76.

Thielman, Frank. *Paul and the Law: A Contextual Approach*. Downers Grove, Ill.: Intervarsity, 1994.

_______. "The Story of Israel and the Theology of Romans 5–8." In *Pauline Theology, Volume III: Romans,* edited by David M. Hay and E. Elizabeth Johnson, 169–195. Minneapolis: Fortress, 1995.

Thrall, Margaret E. *A Critical and Exegetical Commentary on the Second Epistle to the Corinthians*. 2 Vols. ICC. Edinburgh: T & T Clark, 1994.

Torrance, T. F. "One Aspect of the Biblical Conception of Faith." *ExpT* 68 (1956–57) 111–114, 221–222.

Towner, Philip H. *The Goal of Our Instruction: The Structure of Theology and Ethics in the Pastoral Epistles*. JSOTSup 34. Sheffield: JSOT, 1989.

Wallis, Ian G. *The Faith of Jesus Christ in Early Christian Traditions*. SNTSMS 84. Cambridge: Cambridge University Press, 1995.

Walter, Nikolaus. "Zur Interpretation von Römer 9–11." *ZTK* 81 (1984) 172–195.

Wedderburn, A. J. M. *The Reasons for Romans*. Edinburgh: T. & T. Clark, 1988.

Westerholm, Stephen. *Israel's Law and the Church's Faith: Paul and his Recent Interpreters.* Grand Rapids: Eerdmans, 1988.

Wilckens, Ulrich. *Resurrection. Biblical Testimony to the Resurrection: An Historical Examination and Explanation*. Louisville: John Knox, 1978.

Williams, Sam K. "Again *Pistis Christou*." *CBQ* 49 (1987) 431–47.

_______. "The Hearing of Faith: ΑΚΟΗ ΠΙΣΤΕΩΣ in Galatians 3." *NTS* 35 (1989) 82–93.

_______. *Jesus' Death as Saving Event.* HDR 2. Missoula: Scholars Press, 1975.

_______. "Justification and the Spirit in Galatians." *JSNT* 29 (1987) 91–100.

_______. "*Promise* in Galatians: A Reading of Paul's Reading of Scripture." *JBL* 107 (1988) 709–720.

_______. "The 'Righteousness of God' in Romans." *JBL* 99 (1980) 241–290.

Witherington, Ben, III. "The Influence of Galatians on Hebrews." *NTS* 37 (1991) 146–52.

_______. *Paul's Narrative Thought World.* Louisville: Westminster/John Knox, 1994.

Wrede, Wilhelm. *Paul.* London: Philip Green, 1907.

Wright, N. T. *The Climax of the Covenant*. Edinburgh: T. & T. Clark, 1991.

______. "Putting Paul Together Again: Toward a Synthesis of *Pauline Theology* (1 and 2 Thessalonians, Philippians, and Philemon)." In *Pauline Theology, Volume I: Thessalonians, Philippians, Galatians and Philemon*, edited by Jouette M. Bassler, 183–211. Minneapolis: Fortress, 1991.

______. "Romans and the Theology of Paul." In *Pauline Theology, Volume III: Romans*, edited by David M. Hay and E. Elizabeth Johnson, 30–67. Minneapolis: Fortress, 1995.

Young, Frances. *The Theology of the Pastoral Letters*. NT Theology Series. Cambridge: Cambridge University Press, 1994.

Index of Ancient Sources

OLD TESTAMENT

NEW TESTAMENT

APOCRYPHA

OTHER JEWISH WRITINGS

GRECO-ROMAN AUTHORS

Index of Modern Authors